PROGRAMMING WITH LATINO CHILDREN'S MATERIALS

A How-To-Do-It Manual for Librarians

Tim Wadham

HOW-TO-DO-IT MANUALS FOR LIBRARIANS

NUMBER 89

NEAL-SCHUMAN PUBLISHERS, INC.
New York, London

Published by Neal-Schuman Publishers, Inc.
100 Varick Street
New York, NY 10013

Printed and bound in the United States of America.

Library of Congress Cataloging-in-Publication Data

Wadham, Tim.
    Programming with Latino children's materials : a how-to-do-it manual for librarians / by Tim Wadham.
      p. cm.—(How-to-do-it manuals for librarians ; no. 89)
    Includes bibliographical references and index.
    ISBN 1–55570–352–8
      1. Children's libraries—Activity programs—United States.
    2. Children's libraries—Services to Hispanic Americans.   3. Latin America—Civilization—Study and teaching—United States.
    4. Children's literature, Latin American—Bibliography.   I. Title.
II. Series: How-to-do-it manuals for libraries ; no. 89.
2718.2.U6W34   1999
027.62'5—dc21
                                     98–52056
                                       CIP

CONTENTS

PREFACE

Latinos are the fastest-growing ethnic group in the United States. This group's rich heritage includes a tapestry woven from the culture of every country where Spanish is spoken as well as the Latino-American (or Chicano) culture. Despite this rich cultural heritage and the fact that many Latino children are bilingual, they score consistently lower on language-skills tests than their counterparts who speak only English. As a children's librarian who has worked directly with Latino children for almost 12 years, I have seen firsthand the tremendous difference that librarians, teachers, and caregivers can make in educating Latino children when they effectively model language and reinforce cultural heritage. It is also advantageous for all children, regardless of their background, to gain a sense of the beauty and richness of the Spanish language and Latino culture.

When I began my career with the Dallas Public Library, I was working as a children's librarian in a neighborhood heavily populated with Latinos. Even though I spoke fluent Spanish, I quickly discovered that I was stymied in my programming because there were few resources to help me find Spanish language materials to use in storytimes and other programs. I especially wanted to use materials that were indigenous to Latin American countries instead of just using translations of material originally presented in English. Much to my dismay, I found that appropriate materials were virtually unavailable in the United States. While I began to gather rhymes, finger plays, and stories from disparate sources, I often wished for a comprehensive guide that gathered these resources in a systematic fashion. You are holding the book that I wished I could have found when I was starting out.

SCOPE

Programming with Latino Children's Materials is both a reference tool and a resource guide. It is a reference tool for locating high-quality Latino children's literature—rhymes, fingerplays, poetry, stories, plays, and books—available in the United States; it is a resource guide full of successful ideas for using this wonderful literature with children of all cultures. This book is for anyone who works with Latino children or who desires to share the Spanish language and cultures with any group of children. This book is for the person who speaks Spanish fluently, as well as the person who speaks no Spanish, but is willing to learn just enough to properly pronounce a Spanish word or two in a story.

This guide's primary focus is on working in the U.S. Latino community. The diversity of this community means that there must be a diversity of materials considered. Particular emphasis is placed on books by Latino authors, whether in English or Spanish or both, and on books originally published in Spanish by Latin American authors. These last are not given very much attention in this country, and many of them deserve more. It is from these materials that you can develop a feeling in your programs for the richness of the Latino cultural heritage.

The material in this book was developed over twelve years of planning and implementing programs for kids and teens in Latino neighborhoods. I've also had the opportunity to work with community groups such as the Concilio of Hispanic Service Organizations. During community outreach visits, I've had the opportunity to consult many Latino parent groups. All of these experiences have influenced my selection of material for inclusion in this manual.

ORGANIZATION

Part I, Planning and Program How-To, features five chapters that introduce Latino culture and present program ideas using poetry, stories, and plays.

- Chapter 1, The Latino Child, examines Latino children, the culture they represent, and how that culture is manifested in language.
- Chapter 2, Latino Children's Literature, explores the history of Latino literature both in Latin America and the United States and spotlights the most important authors.
- Chapter 3, Latino Folklore and Folk Rhymes, provides a cornerstone for programming with the best known Latino folktales. It also features the texts for nursery rhymes in both English and Spanish. Other programming ideas include scripts for English, Spanish, and bilingual puppet shows.
- Chapter 4, Beyond Folklore: Other Types of Latino Children's Literature and Art, offers a brief sampling of nonfiction that relates to Latino concerns, children's theater, and music by Latino artists.

- Chapter 5, School and Library Programs, is a collection of sample programs for all ages, including inter-generational programs, using materials I culled over the past 12 years, including special programs for all major Latino holidays.

Part II: Planning and Programming Resources, includes sources of materials, book lists, a Spanish primer for children's librarians, and an annotated bibliography.

- Chapter 6, Collection Development Issues, offers help in assessing the quality of translations. It also provides tips on working with distributors, finding Internet resources, developing policies, and recommends sources for book reviews.
- Chapter 7, Finding Latino Materials, is a directory of online resources, organizations, vendors, distributors, and publishers.
- Chapter 8, Awards and Prizes, lists the recipients of the major Latin American children's book awards: the Lazarillo Award, the Americas Award, and the Pura Belpré Award.
- Chapter 9, A Spanish Primer Just for Children's Librarians, features a pronunciation guide and vocabulary needed in library services. It includes the Dewey Decimal Classification in Spanish and useful phrases for the circulation desk.
- Chapter 10, An Annotated Bibliography of Latino Children's Literature, includes professional books, as well as the best Latino children's titles in all formats.

HOW TO USE THIS BOOK

In order to make *Programming with Latino Children's Materials* accessible to those with no knowledge of Spanish, the English translation of Spanish titles follows in parentheses. Where there is a dual-language edition or both Spanish and English editions are available, both titles appear in italics.

The play scripts and promotional pieces are copy-ready. You can use them to put on programs that are extremely simple or very elaborate. They will work for anything from using a script in readers' theater style to a polished production with costumes and props. Likewise, puppet shows can be simple or extravagant. Tailor the program to your community, your time schedule, and your budget. The important point is to share the riches of Latino culture with children and young adults.

My hope is that readers will come away with a new enthusiasm for the richness and breadth of Latino literature, a deeper appreciation for working with Latino children, and a sense of respect for the culture these children represent. If I have been successful, *Programming with Latino Children's Materials* will spark new ideas in the minds of teachers and librarians as well as a contagious enthusiasm for sharing Latino literature with children from all cultures.

ACKNOWLEDGMENTS

For their help in the preparation of this manual, I wish to acknowledge Theresa Mlawer of Lectorum Publications Inc. and Isabel Schon of the Center for the Study of Children's Books In Spanish. Both of them helped immensely in finding information about award books, and in giving advice about which awards should be included. Oralia Garza de Cortés gave helpful suggestions, and is the author of several articles that I found invaluable in preparing this book. Most especially, I wish to acknowledge my wife, Penny, who is my editor-in-chief and my daughter, Hannah, who will hear these rhymes and stories.

PART I:
PLANNING AND
PROGRAMMING HOW-TO

1 LATINO CHILDREN AND THEIR CULTURE

Accepting the first Pura Belpré Award for fiction, Judith Ortiz Cofer said that people of different cultures represent "a universe of little islands connected by visions and dreams." That metaphor is especially appropriate when you realize that one of the primary ways that these culturally disparate islands can be connected is through literature, which represents the visions and dreams of our respective communities. Unfortunately, there are still too many boundaries, both national/political and mental/spiritual between cultures. One of the tasks facing the professional working with Latino children is to construct bridges between these "little islands."

The poet Naomi Shihab Nye (1995) has said "We have no borders when we read" (7). Literature can be the key to forging connections between teachers/librarians and children of different national origins, and between the children themselves. To make these connections, the professional must have what D. Bryan Stansfield (1988) calls "ethnic competence," which is a concept " . . . that includes knowledge and skills with cultural heritage's and their values" (550). I would add to this that, besides developing an empathy for a culture that is not your own, ethnic competence means an ability to go beyond an "us versus them" mentality and to appreciate the universal qualities of humanity that transcend national origin. I realize that many readers of this book are already working in Latino neighborhoods and are well aware of the cultural issues surrounding the children they serve. There are also many Latino teachers and librarians who have firsthand cultural competence. My desire is to convey, from the point of view of someone who has spent a great deal of time with Latino children, some cultural observations which others might find helpful. This chapter relates cultural information that provides professionals with a foundation from which to develop a philosophy of service to Latino children, and demonstrates that one does not have to be of a particular culture to become a part of it.

LATINO POPULATION IN THE UNITED STATES

It has been frequently noted that Latinos are the fastest growing ethnic group in the United States, increasing 39% since 1980, with a population expected to exceed "30 million by the year 2010" (Schick and Schick, 1991: 2). It is widely expected that Latinos will become the largest minority group by about the same time. Two factors that contribute to this are the immigration rate and a birth rate higher than the rest of the population. While the Latino population continues to be centered in California, Texas, and New York, there is an increasing dispersion throughout the United States.

Yolanda J. Cuesta (1990) writes about what this means for teachers and librarians: "Many states not known previously for significant concentrations of Hispanics, including Alaska, Hawaii, Idaho, Maine, Massachusetts, Nevada, New Hampshire, Oregon, Rhode Island, South Carolina, Vermont and Washington, showed population growth exceeding 100 percent. This dispersion has serious implications for librarians. We can no longer view services to the Spanish-speaking population as a concern of libraries only within specific geographic areas" (26). Latinos now make up 5 percent of the population of Charlotte, North Carolina. An estimated 35,000 have moved there in the last five years (Brumley, 1996: 1A). The number of Latinos has tripled in Alaska since 1980, and they now comprise 4.2 percent of the population (Rangel, 1996: 10A).

As the Latino population grows, so does the need for culturally sensitive library services to Latino children. In the past, the term Hispanic has been used to refer to Spanish-speaking people. Lately, the term Latino has come into favor as more accurately describing this community and will be used throughout this manual, with the exception of quotations in which the term "Hispanic" was used.

WHO IS THE LATINO CHILD?

The key word in attempting to understand the Latino child is diversity. There are cultural differences as well as differences in language. As you look over a group of children in storytime you might see children who have recently arrived from any number of countries with little or no knowledge of the English language. Next to them may be a family who speaks English better than Spanish—perhaps the grandparents immigrated here, but the parents grew up in an English-language environment, and the child may speak no Spanish at all. Behind them could be a family who immigrated a few years ago. The parents speak no English, but the children have learned English in the public schools and are fully bilingual. Each of these children has a different socio-economic status and brings with them a particular set of cultural values from their native lands, or in the case of the children born here, the Latino-American culture.

For the professional to begin forming bridges between themselves and these children, and to facilitate bridges being built between the children themselves, it is important to understand their cultures, and the differences and similarities between those cultures. The differences are manifested primarily through language variations and issues relating to national origin.

LANGUAGE VARIATIONS

Latino peoples are linked and separated by the Spanish language. Spanish is now one of the world's major languages, spoken by over 400 million people, yet there is constant disagreement on what constitutes "bona fide" Spanish (Preston, 1997: 12A). The differences in spoken and written Spanish from country to country and within regions can be compared to the differences between the English spoken and written in England and from country to country (e.g., Canada, Australia, etc.) and within regions. All Spanish traces its roots to Castilian, which originated in the Provence of Castilia in northern Spain.

Since many of the colonists, conquistadors, and sailors who settled in Latin America during the sixteenth and seventeenth centuries came from the southern part of Spain, they brought with them the grammar and pronunciation spoken in that region of Spain during that time period. Over time hundreds of Indian words such as *chocolate* and *chile* entered the Spanish vocabulary, especially in countries with large Indian populations such as Bolivia, Ecuador, Peru, Bolivia, Guatemala, and Mexico. It is important to note that the existence of separate and distinct Indian languages accounts for wide variations in word meanings in different parts of Latin America. Latinos have learned to celebrate these language differences and generally have little trouble understanding each other. The common thread, as noted in an article about Spanish personal names by Roberto Cabello-Argandoña (1983), is that "Virtually all Hispanic Americans (81 percent) believe that Spanish language is the aspect of their tradition that is most important to preserve" (3). Many cultural differences are reflected in the use of language, and maintaining the language in a new country helps maintain a sense of identity.

To understand how language differences translate into cultural differences, we need to understand how language reflects culture. Mexican culture, for example, has a laid back attitude as far as the concept of time is concerned. The Spanish word *ahora* is translated as "now." In the American culture which is ruled by the clock, we would understand it to mean this exact moment in time. In Mexican culture, the concept more loosely means "today." Their scope of time is much more broad. In order to specify this exact moment in time, you would say *ahora mismo* or "right now."

Another example found in Mexican culture is a certain fatalism as reflected in a common response to requests for commitments. If I'm asking someone if they will be able to make it to a particular program, the response might very well be "*Si Dios quiere.*" or "If God wills it." This reflects a heightened awareness in the culture of the uncertainty of life and the inevitability of death. In Tómas Rivera's novel (1996) . . . *y no se lo trago la tierra* (And the earth did not part) he comments that "*Sólo la muerte nos trae el descanso a nosotros,*" or "Only death brings us rest" (46).

Cultural attitudes toward public libraries manifest themselves through language as well. Since there is no strong tradition of free public library service in many Latin American countries, a Latino patron will likely refer to the public library as a *librería,* which refers to a bookstore, instead of *biblioteca,* which refers to a library. This is often an obstacle to be overcome in serving these patrons. In some cases it will be necessary for you to make them aware of your services and that most public library services are of no cost to the patrons. Other cultural attitudes that may create barriers include a notion that the public library is designed solely for the use of children, or that it is an " . . . artificial service structure designed for someone else" (Stansfield, 1998: 550). These barriers can be overcome through outreach into the Latino community by dedicated and enthusiastic librarians who can articulate what the library is and how it is relevant to them.

After you have been among Spanish-speakers for a period of time it is possible to pick up on differences in speech between nationalities. Latinos themselves are aware of these differences and each national group insists in a spirit of friendly rivalry that theirs is the correct way of speaking. Regionalism does not have to become a barrier in building bridges. Alma Flor Ada has said, "The children can learn regionalisms from the different Latin American countries and they should have the opportunity to get exposed to a multitude of cultures that constitute their *patria grande*" (Aguirre, n.d. 287). For the librarian, this raises the issues of the type of Spanish language used in books and the quality of translations. These issues are addressed in Chapter 6 on collection development.

NATIONAL ORIGIN

It is important to separate ourselves immediately from negative stereotypes when discussing issues of national origin. One of the most common preconceptions, is the generalization that all people of Latino origin are from Mexico, or that "Mexican" refers to all Latinos. This could not be farther from the truth. Recognizing the diversity represented in national origin is extremely important when working with Latino children. There are, in fact, some major differences in Latino cultures.

A common thread to the history of Mexico, and Central and Latin America is the story of native peoples conquered by the Spanish, who are then assimilated. This has led to populations of mixed origin living alongside those native peoples who managed to maintain their identity. Countries such as Argentina and Uruguay exhibit a great deal of European influence, whereas countries such as Guatemala, Bolivia, and Peru are shaped more by Indian influences. The native cultures continue to thrive in these countries. Mexican culture is a mixture of Spanish and Indian (Stansfield, 1998: 549). I focus primarily on the three most prominent Latino cultures in the United States: Mexican, Puerto Rican, and Cuban.

Mexican Culture

Naomi Shihab Nye (1995) said that Mexico " . . . has always been a country of spirit, a country where magic feels close and possible, a country of passionate color and deep ties" (7). You can probably trace the genesis of much of Mexican culture to its roots in the Spanish culture brought to the new world by the conquistadors. Whatever you may think of the morality of this conquest, the results cannot be changed, and they have indelibly stamped the culture. This conquest left Mexico as a racially mixed country, with native European Spaniards, Mexican-born Spaniards, people with Indian and Spanish blood, and the Indians. This racial mixture created societal classes that remain in Mexico to this day and are a continuing source of tension. The native Indian peoples still exist on the lowest tier of society. This is also a fusion of cultures that creates what Isabel Schon called a "marvelous richness" of heritage (1978: 92).

Politics is yet another source of tension. The continuing effects of the Mexican Revolution are still felt. The Mexican Revolution was a call for social justice, it was about the toppling of dictatorial regimes and bringing democracy to the country. The Institutional Revolutionary Party, or PRI, came about as a group embodying the revolution's call for social justice. As the PRI became the governing party to the exclusion of any opposition, the specter of what caused the revolution in the first place has always been present. The continuing calls for social justice in Mexico are made in the name of the revolution.

As we realize how the trajectory of Mexican history is primarily a reaction to the conquistadors, it is important to remember that the conquistadors were, in fact, involved in a primarily religious crusade. The Catholic religion that they brought with them has been and continues to be an abiding influence on the culture of the Mexican people. Given a new religion that they were commanded by the Spanish invaders to accept, the Indian people of Mexico managed to synchronize it with their native religion, creating a unique blend of Catholic faith and Indian practice.

The more recent history of Mexico continues to reflect the struggle between classes and, particularly, the extreme poverty of the indigenous Indian peoples. It is this very poverty that has been the primary motivating factor encouraging emigration, both legal and illegal, to the U.S. Much of this immigration has been young males trying to find work in order to send money back to their families. They move often—to follow the flow of seasonal work or to stay ahead of immigration officials. The fact that they are willing to do manual labor, such as agricultural work, for low wages, has made it difficult for the tide of immigration to be halted. Many companies whose bottom line would be severely affected without the cheap labor afforded by these workers tacitly make it possible for illegal immigration to continue.

The issues of Indian heritage and immigration continue to resonate in literature created by Latinos. A children's book that beautifully demonstrates the mixture of religion and culture is *Spirit Child: An Aztec Nativity*, translated by John Bierhorst (1984) from a manuscript written by Aztec poets. In reading this lovely story you can feel the rhythms and poetry of Aztec speech. Barbara Cooney has illustrated the story completely within a native Aztec frame of reference, demonstrating visually how the Christian story and the Aztec culture become mixed together. While the story follows closely the biblical account, it adds details that are clearly brought from Aztec culture. The place where the devil takes people who follow him is referred to as the "Dead Land" where "there is nothing but hunger and arguments all the time, and sickness, and hard work." Barbara Cooney's accompanying illustration shows a scene of dancing skeletons straight out of a Day of the Dead celebration.

In Victor Martinez's autobiographical National Book Award-winning novel, *Parrot in the Oven: Mi vida* (1996), he speaks of the sense of heritage that had been instilled in him as a child of migrant farm workers in Fresno, California, and the pride that can be derived from that heritage: "We were descendants of Indians blessed with a color that was as necessary as dirt to the earth, as important as the sun to all the trees. We had treasures buried deep inside our blood, hidden treasures we hardly knew existed" (119). The autobiographical character that Martinez creates, Manuel Hernandez, gets this sense of heritage and culturally defining stories from people like his grandfather, an immigrant whose only memory at the end of his life was " . . . of the desert he crossed to plant his foot in this country" (81).

Cuban, Puerto Rican, and other Latino Cultures

Much of the story of Cuba and Puerto Rico is similar to that of Mexico—a story of domination by and subsequent revolution against the Spanish government. Both these countries were conquered and colonized by Spain, beginning with the discovery of Puerto Rico, then called *Boriquén* by Christopher Columbus. (*Boriqua* is still a name that Puerto Ricans use to refer to each other, as well as to the island itself.) In both countries there were several revolts against the Spanish regime during the 1800s. The Puerto Rican revolution began in 1868 when Dr. Ramón Emeterio Betances organized a rebellion against the Spaniards, which was put down. In the case of Cuba, a rebellion began the same year, and the rebels were harder to defeat. A series of revolts continued until 1898 when Spain's heavy-handed attempts to quell the unrest led to the sinking of the U.S.S. Maine, which in turn led to the four-month Spanish-American War. This conflict ended with a treaty that made Cuba and Puerto Rico, among others, territories of the United States.

Puerto Rico has, in the ensuing years, gained a great deal of independence, though it is still in many ways under the control of the United States government. Cuba, on the other hand, after becoming independent from American control in 1933, experienced a series of dictators and revolutions that ended with the takeover of the government by Fidel Castro in 1959. Castro's communist government and the economic conditions, as well as the political repression it created, has been the motivating factor for the large numbers of Cuban immigrants to the United States who have settled primarily in the Miami area, as well as New York and New Jersey. Miami is the main base for Cuban political exiles actively seeking the end of Castro's rule, with an area known as Little Havana. While the immigration from Cuba is primarily because of the political climate, immigration from Puerto Rico has been a result of economic conditions on the island, along with its ties to the United States which make immigration easy.

Beyond Cuban and Puerto Rican, the cultures a librarian or teacher working with Latino children is most likely to encounter are those from Central America, which were part of Mexico until the 1800s. Because of this, the cultural traditions are similar. These countries, particularly Guatemala and El Salvador, have been rife with political strife and difficult economic conditions. Different ideological factions battle for control of the governments and bring innocent citizens, particularly children, into the crossfire. Because of their geographical proximity to Mexico, people from Honduras, El Salvador, and Guatemala can easily cross their own borders to escape this turbulence and get on the path that leads to this country. Generally, immigration has occurred when either political or economic conditions have made it necessary for people to seek a new situation.

For example, there was a surge of immigration from El Salvador during the early 1980s, as a result of the civil war in that country. These were primarily young men trying to escape forced conscription into the army. The terror of this political oppression is well portrayed in Frances Temple's book *Grab Hands and Run* (1993), in which a young boy, Felipe, has nightmares about the soldiers coming to his village, calling everyone out of their homes, and forcing them to put their hands over their heads (14). Death is an everyday occurrence, just something taken for granted. As Felipe is driving with his brother and sister down a dirt road they see something that first appears to be a log, but upon closer inspection it turns out to be the body of a woman. Their driver explains in a matter-of-fact tone that "The military, the *escuadrones*, throw people they've killed in the road to make it look like a traffic accident . . . .You'll see more" (43). Children who grow up in these situations obviously have a maturity of experience that has to be taken into account as we plan programs and share literature with them.

Chicano and North American Latino Culture

All of this turbulent history has filled the U.S. with deep-rooted Latino influences. Many city and place names, particularly in the border states of California, New Mexico, Arizona, and Texas, as well as in Florida and New York, reflect Latino origin. At least 400 Spanish words such as "rodeo," "patio," and "plaza" have entered the English vocabulary (De Varona, 1996: xvii). Latin culture has always been a part of the United States. California, Nevada, Utah, Arizona, New Mexico, Texas, and parts of Colorado, Kansas, and Oklahoma were once part of Mexico. There have been Spanish-speaking residents in the United States since the 1500s. Spanish settlements, whose remnants can be seen in the remaining missions, dot areas like San Antonio and the Pacific coast. Latino culture is an essential part of the heritage of all Americans.

Beyond history, the presence of Latinos in this country has given rise to cultures that have come, not from a blending of Spanish and Indian culture, but from a combination of Latino and North American cultures. Many groups identify themselves through names that reflect their national heritage. *Tejano* refers to Mexican Texans. Puerto Ricans born in New York might refer to themselves as *Nuyoricans*. *Chicano* is someone of Mexican descent, born in America. The term Chicano carries with it overtones of radicalism and activism associated with the Chicano movement that was born in the ferment of the

1960s. This movement gave rise to some wonderful literature and theater by authors such as Rudolfo Anaya and Rolando Hinojosa.

Holidays and Traditions

One of the most important expressions of a country's culture is its holidays and traditions. The most well-known Latino holidays in the United States are of Mexican origin. They betray all of the influences we have talked about before—Spanish, Indian, and Catholic.

Cinco de Mayo. May 5th is a celebration of the battle of Puebla in 1862. The forces of Napoleon III had advanced on this small Mexican town on their way to Mexico City to backup a French effort to support a monarchy in Mexico. They did not recognize the government of Benito Juarez. The French forces believed they would have an easy march from the port city of Veracruz to Mexico City. In this decisive conflict, the outnumbered Mexican Army heroically defeated the French army force led by veteran General Charles Ferdinand Latrille de Lorencz.

The victory halted the French advance and provided a rallying point for the Mexican people to continue fighting for their freedom. Cinco de Mayo is now celebrated as an official holiday in Mexico with festivals, military parades, and official gatherings of social and political leaders. In the United States it is commemorated less formally. Most communities with a large Latino population have celebrations that include community parades, mariachi bands, or folkloric dancers. Schools in the U.S. generally use this opportunity for units on Mexico. This is the most popular Latino holiday, even if there are many who would be hard pressed to tell you exactly what it commemorates. Regardless, it provides Latinos with the opportunity to touch base with their cultural heritage.

Día de Independencia. Mexicans celebrate September 16th as the day they began to gain their independence from the Spaniards. This is the day that Father Miguel Hidalgo y Castillo rang the bell of his little church in Dolores, Mexico, and spoke to his congregation, asking if they would be free of Spanish rule. He decried the oppressive government of the Spaniards, and appealed to their sense of pride in what was indigenously Mexican. "¡Viva la Virgen de Guadelupe!" he cried, "*¡Viva México!*" This "*grito de Dolores*" or "cry from Dolores" was the beginning of Mexico's war to win its independence. It is celebrated similarly to *Cinco de mayo,* with patriotic orations, parades, and picnics. The importance of this date has led to September 15th through the 15th of October being celebrated as Hispanic Heritage Month in the United States. These two celebrations, the 16th of September along with *Cinco de mayo,* which are both related to political events, underscore the huge impact that the revolution against Spanish rule had on Mexican culture.

Día de los Muertos. The Day of the Dead is actually a two-day celebration, November 1 and 2, that incorporates All Saints Day along with a particularly Mexican sensibility about death. Over this period, altars are created in homes with pictures and favorite effects of departed loved ones. Food is a part of the altar and also a part of the offering that is taken to the cemeteries. Food and other items are placed on the tombs of the departed so that their spirits can partake. The decoration of graves is a primary part of this celebration.

The Mexican Day of the Dead is marked with unique artistic and culinary creations. The major motif is the skeleton. Edible skulls are created from sugar. These are not viewed as morbid—a little girl preparing to do a Day of the Dead art project in a library program asked if she could draw her grandfather's skeleton. During the same program, a mother expressed her lament that the day was no longer celebrated as it had once been in Mexico. Mexicans in the United States who no longer have access to their family cemeteries in Mexico often express dissatisfaction and disappointment in the holiday and its less spiritual U.S. transformation. The good news is that this holiday seems to be growing in popularity in the United States as the influence of Latino culture grows. San Antonio is now noted for its observances, and there are other major celebrations in Chicago and Los Angeles (Schwiesow, 1996).

Las Posadas. The Christmas season is marked by nightly processions from December 16 to December 24. These processions re-enact the journey of Mary and Joseph into Bethlehem. Groups go from house to house carrying candles, asking if there is room for lodging. As they go from place to place they sing the traditional songs of las posadas. At each house they will be told that there is no room. This pattern continues until they are welcomed into a house where a party is held. The party traditionally includes breaking a piñata, although the use of a piñata is not limited to Christmas time. Tamales are a chore to make so they are often reserved for special occasions. They are usually made for Christmas Eve. They might be accompanied by *buñuelos,* fried flour tortillas sprinkled with cinnamon. Midnight on Christmas Eve is the magic hour when presents are opened. An excellent recounting of this traditional celebration can be found in Marie Hall Ets' Caldecott-winner, *12 Days before Christmas.*

Pastorelas. In Mexico, the Christmas season is also celebrated with *pastorelas*, plays that describe the journeys of pilgrims or shepherds to pay homage to the Christ child. These journeys are almost always delayed or made difficult by devils and other hindrances. In a story about the *pastorelas* done for National Public Radio, reporter David Welna noted that at the beginning of the production that he saw, the narrator pointed out that this play was a celebration of Indian and Spanish cultures, highlighting again how this bicultural sense is at the heart of the Mexican soul.

Día de los Reyes. In Latin cultures, Christmas Day is traditionally celebrated as a religious holiday. The day for presents, however, in many Latino cultures, particularly those of the Caribbean and Puerto Rico is January 6, Day of the Kings. In Christian tradition, this is the day that the three kings arrived at the stable. Instead of Santa, it is the three kings who bring presents to the children. Children often put their shoes out to be filled with treats. In Mexico, families might prepare a special bread filled with almonds, coins, or a doll representing the baby Jesus. Cubans might eat roast pig, black beans, and rice.

Día de los Niños: There is currently a movement to celebrate April 30 as *Día de los Niños: Día de los Libros* (Day of the Child: Day of Books) throughout the U.S. and Puerto Rico. April 30 is traditionally celebrated as Día de los Niños in Mexico, and creating this tradition in the United States would tie in with National Library week. Pat Mora, poet and children's book author, is the prime moving force to declare April 30th such a literary event in the U.S. Some Latin countries, such as El Salvador, celebrate this event on October 1 instead of April 30, but the intent is the same: to celebrate children and childhood.

In the meantime, those who work with Latino children and their families can celebrate "*Día de los Niños: Día de los Libros*" and promote programs and activities that support children, books, and literacy. Some excellent suggestions for celebrating this day, along with a letter from and poem by Pat Mora, can be be found on the Texas State Library Web site at www.tsl.state.tx.us/LD/publications/ninos/title.htm.

Quinceñera. Perhaps the most important day in the life of a Mexican girl is her 15th birthday. This is the day that she becomes a woman and traditionally can start to date. The day is generally marked by attendance at mass and a huge party with dancing and plenty of food. This is a once-in-a-lifetime event and often no expense is spared by the parents. The girl celebrating her *quinceñera* is most often accompanied by fourteen *madrinas* (attendants) and their escorts. The madrinas all have matching dresses, and the celebrant wears a white dress and a crown.

These holidays and traditions have deep roots in the political and religious history of the countries and say much about the souls of the

Latin people. Understanding the significance of these days can open up a window into understanding their hopes and dreams.

GENERAL CULTURAL TRAITS

I have observed that there are also some general cultural traits that bridge national and language barriers. Generally, Latino people exhibit a courteousness and graciousness from which other cultures could learn. They will feed you, even at times giving up their own food to be gracious. The warm hospitality of the Latino people is extremely notable.

If you visit someone's home, you might be told "*Esta es su casa*," (This is your house), or "*Mi casa es su casa*" (My home is your home). In general, as Suzanne Romaine has observed, it can be said that "Spanish statements are personalized while English reflects more distance" (1989: 150). This cultural conditioning is likely to make a Latino child more shy and reserved. While this is not a universal generalization, in many cases both Latino adults and children are more passive in terms of accepting whatever vicissitudes they may face. This same trait gives them a tendency toward not being confrontational and to humbly accept criticism.

Compadrismo: The Extended Family

The concept of extended family is extremely important to understanding Latino culture. There is general agreement that "The extended Mexican and Mexican-American family is a constant source of support and encouragement to all its members" (Schon, 1978: 48). In working within Latino communities, programs that involve the entire family are the most successful. Most Latino parents need a program to which they can bring siblings of different ages. Single caregiver/ single child programs are rarely successful as they are not an option for Latino parents with larger families. The adults/parents overriding concern is always for their children and their children's education. Practical programming ideas that involve families are discussed in Chapter 5.

BILINGUALISM AND THE AMERICAN CHICANO CULTURE

I have made the point that culture cannot be understood except as expressed through language. In North America, the language spoken by much of the Latino population has become a mixture of Spanish and English, and within the Latino population there is a great difference in the level of competence with one or the other language. Bilingualism has become a hot button at the heart of controversies such as "English-only" or "English as the official language of the United States" as opposed to those who favor bilingual education and believe "that developing literacy in the first language can make a substantial contribution to literacy development in the second language" (Schon, 1978: 393). There has been a great deal of argument and discussion in the professional literature, regarding the relative merit of bilingual education in the schools. It is difficult to keep the political issues separate from the purely linguistic issues. While it is not within the scope of this manual to provide a complete overview of these arguments, a few comments seem necessary.

Even within the debate over bilingualism, there is disagreement as to the goals of bilingual education. Sonia Nieto (n.d.) has stated that "The commonly accepted objectives of bilingual education in the United States are fairly straightforward: to develop skills in English *while at the same time* learning content through the native language" (5). Cabello-Argandoña (1983) notes that if content is not taught at the same time as the new language, children "find themselves far behind their classmates and unable to catch up. Gradually, a slow-learner group develops in most schools in Hispanic neighborhoods teaching Spanish-speaking children, followed by social stigma and poor ethnic identity. Knowledge of Spanish, the mother-tongue, is not seen as an asset but rather as a liability for those children" (8). On one side is the idea that bilingual education should be truly bilingual. That is, both languages should be used throughout a student's education. This is known as the "maintenance" approach (Nieto, n.d.: 6). The other point of view is that bilingual education is temporary, that it should only be used until a student is fluent in English. This, Nieto says, is the "transitional" method (6). Transitional programs try to assimilate students into a situation where English is spoken exclusively. This second view of bilingual education is described, interestingly enough, using the same bridge metaphor as author Judith Ortiz Cofer uses. As Nieto says, "In effect, it is much like using their language as a bridge—and then burning the bridge" (6). Bilingualism, however, can be used to build bridges to another language and culture, without burning the bridge behind you. Nieto speaks of classrooms where English and Spanish are used interchangeably, and where students, regardless of cultural background, learn cultural sensitivity, and where Latino students feel less isolated (6). Lori Carlson has put it eloquently: "Speaking more than one language, I have found, enriches life, broadens perspective, extends horizons of opportunity, and makes us more sensitive to nuance, difference, contrast" (xiv).

What bilingualism creates is a new language that goes back and forth between Spanish and English, or that creates new words which are a mixture of both languages. In Texas for example, it's called Tex-Mex. Sometimes it is manifest in the Latinization of an English word such as a truck being referred to as a *troque* instead of the standard Spanish *camion*. The bilingual person might *parquear* (park) instead of *estacionar* his *troque*. As explained by Suzanne Romaine (1989), this is a classic example of borrowing verbs from one language and making them fit another. She says "Borrowed verbs are often slotted into the most common verb class of the language. Spanish, for example, puts loan words into the class of verbs ending in *-ear* (e.g., *checkear*—'to check')" (64). This bilingualism can also be made manifest in sentences spoken in English with a few Spanish words thrown in, or the other way around. Listen to the radio in a place like San Antonio, and you might hear something like "*La Fabulosa*, the station with the most *tejano* music, *para ustedes*!"

Nieto says that " . . . because of the interrelationship of language and culture, students' cultural heritage is an equally important aspect of bilingual education" (5). When bilingualism is encouraged rather than discouraged, a much richer culture develops through a *mezcla* or mixture of cultures. The author Alma Flor Ada, born in Cuba, has devoted much time to her concern that Spanish not disappear from the "everyday life" of Latino children (Aguirre, n.d.: 287). Ada speaks of how, after coming to this country, she tried to speak to Latino children in Spanish. They refused to speak to her in that language and denied they even knew it (287). I have seen a similar attitude in young library patrons who can speak Spanish fluently, but prefer to speak English. Sometimes it seems that Spanish becomes something that is only part of their insular family life and not a part of their larger social interaction outside of the family. A bilingual child can "switch codes," or go back and forth between languages, and " . . . step out of one language system and . . . view it in the perspective of the other" (Romaine, 1989: 205). Some of the issues a bilingual child faces are very clearly expressed in the book *Pepita Talks Twice* by Ofelia Dumas Lachtman (1995), a daughter of Mexican immigrants. In the story, Pepita gets tired of being the one who has to translate because she is bilingual. She feels like she has to say everything twice, and so she refuses to speak Spanish. She even begins calling her dog, *Lobo*, by the English equivalent, Wolf. It is only when Lobo doesn't respond to his English name in a perilous situation that Pepita realizes the important part that the Spanish language plays in her identity. It is interesting how much language and names play a role in the personal identity of Latino children.

The identity of a Latin American speaking English as the primary language is much easier to develop if the child is born in this country. Ada speaks eloquently to the loss of cultural identity in her story *My Name is María Isabel* (1993). In this short novella, she writes of a young girl from Puerto Rico. On her first day of school in the United States María Isabel is told that since there are already two Marías in her class, that she will be called Mary Lopez. María Isabel doesn't recognize herself in this "strange new name" (12). She has always loved her name because she was named for her father's mother and for her Puerto Rican grandmother. María's desire to regain her identity is poignantly expressed in a paragraph she writes for her teacher on the theme "My Greatest Wish."

> " . . . I think my greatest wish is to be called María Isabel Salazar López. When that was my name, I felt proud of being named María like my papás mother, and Isabel like my Grandmother Chabela. She is saving money so that I can study and not have to spend my whole life in a kitchen like her. I was Salazar like my papá and my Grandpa Antonio, and López, like my Grandfather Manuel. I never knew him but he could really tell stories. I know because my mother told me. If I was called María Isabel Salazar López, I could listen better in class because it's easier to hear than Mary López" (49–51).

WHAT DOES THIS MEAN FOR THE PRACTICING PROFESSIONAL?

The primary goal of bilingual programming can be found in this statement by Elaine Goley (1985): "Bilingual storytimes and puppet shows for children of various ages improve their mastery of their own languages as well as ties to their culture through the use of folklore, song, and rhyme. The children will eventually learn English in school bilingual education programs and from their peers, but the function of library programming and collections is to help children become integrated into American society while enabling them to maintain cultural ties with their ethnic group" (94). So often the information needs of the Latino community focus on immediate survival issues such as finding food, shelter, jobs, and learning to speak English, that it is difficult to get Latino parents to support bilingual storytimes or other programs that focus on literature and art, which are not perceived as essential to survival. The challenge in schools and libraries is to provide opportunities to reinforce the cultural heritage of children; to instill a love and familiarity with literature, which is sometimes difficult to achieve for a bilingual child struggling to read and communicate in two languages; and to bring families closer together in the process.

I hope that the information presented here will give the professional more empathy for the Latino child, and give them the cultural background necessary to locate appropriate materials for whatever group they are working with, as well as planning programs that mesh with the culture and lifestyle of the community being served.

SAMPLE FLYERS

Pages 19–22 are some sample flyers that deal with issues discussed in this introduction. The first is a flyer that describes the difference between a bookstore and a library. This flyer is courtesy of the Commerce, California Public Library. The second is a flyer that helps parents encourage their children to read.

BOOKSTORE OR LIBRARY?

They may seem alike but there's a **BIG** difference.

BOOKSTORES **SELL** you books, magazines,
videos, and cassettes.
LIBRARIES **LEND** you books, magazines,
videos, cassettes, CDs, and much more for **FREE**.

Libraries offer free services and programs including:

- Library cards.

- Books and magazines in Spanish.

- Books about all subjects.

- Public access computers.

- Public typewriters.

- Videos that inform and entertain.

- Classes and materials to improve your English.

- Programs for children and families.

COME VISIT US!

Copy and paste your library logo,

addresses, phone numbers,

and operating hours in this space.

¿LIBRERIA O BIBLIOTECA?

Se parecen pero hay una <u>GRAN</u> diferencia.

LAS LIBRERIAS les **<u>VENDEN</u>** libros, revistas, periódicos, cassettes y a veces hasta café.
LAS BIBLIOTECAS les **<u>PRESTAN GRATIS</u>** libros, revistas, videos cassettes, CDs y mucho más.

Las Bibliotecas proveen servicios y programas gratuitos como:

- Tarjetas para la biblioteca.

- Libros y revistas en español.

- Libros sobre cualquier tema.

- Computadoras públicas.

- Máquinas de escribir.

- Videos en español.

- Clases y materiales para mejorar su inglés.

- Programas para niños y familias.

¡VENGAN A VISITARNOS!

Copy and paste your library logo,

addresses, phone numbers,

and operating hours in this space.

How to Help Your Child Become a Reader

BEFORE YOUR CHILD CAN READ

- Read books, newspapers, and magazines yourself. Children learn by example. If they see parents reading on a regular basis, they will view reading as being worthwhile. They will learn to respect books, and they will find pleasure in reading.
- Read out loud to your child. Continue this practice even after a child learns to read.
- Select reading material appropriate to your children's ages. Toddlers and babies enjoy nursery rhymes. For this age, choose books such as board books that a child won't destroy. For children ages 3 to 7, use picture books and longer stories. Introduce older children to chapter books, but they will still enjoy picture books as well.
- Make reading time special. Schedule a time when you can read to your children <u>every</u> day. Good times are after dinner or before bedtime, but do it whenever it works for your family and be consistent.
- Both parents should take turns reading. Children need to see and hear their father read, so they see that reading is a habit for men as well as women.

AFTER YOUR CHILD CAN READ

- Carefully select reading material for beginning readers. Books that are too hard cause frustration and children quit trying. Books that are too easy can bore them.
- Older children can, little by little, learn to read to their siblings. Listen to them attentively and allow them to practice reading.
- Continue reading to your children.
- Encourage children to read when they are bored. Reading is a pleasure, not an obligation.
- Books stimulate children's creativity. Develop this by encouraging not only reading, but also activities such as drawing, writing, and acting out stories with puppets, etc.

BE CAREFUL!

- It is very obnoxious for a child to be continually corrected when reading out loud. This can make children dislike reading.
- Reading should be a reward. Books can be given as gifts for birthdays and other special days. Never use books or reading to discipline children.
- During the first stage, do not get discouraged if the child does not appear to be listening. It takes time to develop a reading habit and depends fundamentally on your patience and perseverance.
- Be careful about distracting your children when they are reading. Reading time is valuable to a child's development. Whenever possible, don't disrupt that time.
- Learning to read well takes time. Don't set up a spirit of competition between siblings. Never make fun of mistakes.
- Never force your children to read. Respect the reading tastes of your children. Don't insist they read something that they dislike.

THE HOME LIBRARY

- Teach children to care for books. Help them learn simple rules such as: don't eat while reading, read with clean hands, use bookmarks to save your place instead of folding pages, treat books carefully so they don't get damaged, and always put books back where they belong.
- Give each child a special place, such as part of a shelf, for their personal library. Help them build their library. Garage sales, thrift stores, library book sales, and second hand book stores are all good places to find inexpensive books. Let relatives and friends know that books are always welcome gifts.
- Designate a place in your home to put books checked out from the public library. This way, they can be enjoyed, and when it is time to return them, you know where they are.

Qué hacer para que sus hijos lean

ANTES DE QUE SU HIJO PUEDA LEER

- Lea libros, periódicos, y revistas usted. Los niños aprenden por medio del ejemplo. Si ven a los padres leer habitualmente, verán a la lectura como si sea algo que vale la pena. Comenzarán a respetar a los libros y hallarán placer en el hábito de la lectura.
- Lea a sus hijos en voz alta. Sigue con este actividad después de que aprenden a leer.
- Seleccione lecturas de acuerdo a la edad de sus hijos: A los niños pequeños les gustan rimas de la cuña. Escoge libros para niños de este edad que ellos no se pueden destruir. Use libros con dibujos y cuentos más largos para los niños de 3 a 7 años de edad. Introduce los niños más grandes a los libros con capítulos, pero a ellos todavía les gustarán a los libros con dibujos también.
- Tenga un tiempo cuando puede leerles a sus hijos <u>cada</u> día. Tiempos buenos son después de la comida o antes de la hora de acostarse, pero hágalo cuando quiera mientras sea consistente.
- Ambos padres deben leer a los niños. Los hijos necesitan ver y escuchar a su padre lee, y así comprenderán que la lectura es un hábito de los varones tanto como las mujeres.

DESPUÉS DE QUE SUS HIJOS PUEDAN LEER

- Cuidadosamente seleccione material de lectura para los lectores principiantes. Libros demasiado duros causan la frustración, y los niños dejan de seguir tratando. Libros que son demasiado fáciles puedan aburrirles.
- Los niños mas viejos puedan aprender a leerles a sus hermanos. Escuche a ellos atentamente y dejan que practiquen la lectura.
- Continúa lectura a sus hijos.
- Animan a los niños leer cuando están aburridos. Leer no es obligación, es placer.
- Los libros estimulan la creatividad de los niños. Desarrolle esto impulso proponiendo no solamente la lectura, pero también actividades tal como dibujar, escribir, la realización de los cuentos por medio de títeres, etc.

¡SEA CUIDADOSO!

- Es muy molesto para niños que se los corrige continuamente mientras que están leyendo. Esto puede hacerlos rechazar la lectura.
- La lectura debe ser un premio. Los libros puedan ser regalos para los cumpleaños o otros días especiales. Nunca use libros o la lectura para disciplinar a los niños.
- Durante la primera etapa no se desaliente si el niño parece que no escucha. El hábito de la lectura lleva su tiempo y depende fudamentalmente de su paciencia y perseverancia.
- Sea cuidadoso de distraer a sus niños cuando leen. El tiempo de la lectura, es muy valioso al desarrollo de un niño. Cuando sea posible, no rompe este tiempo.
- Leer bien toma su tiempo. No lo haga un espíritu de competición entre los hermanos. Nunca se burle de los equivocaciones.
- Nunca fuerza sus niños leer. Respete los gustos en la lectura de sus hijos. No insista que leen algo que les detesta.

LA BIBLIOTECA DEL HOGAR

- Enseña a los niños como cuidar por los libros. Ayuda que aprenden reglas sencillas tal como: no coma mientras que estén leyendo, lea con manos limpios, usa un marcador de libros para marcar su lugar en ves de doblar la pagina, trata a los libros cuidadosamente par que no se ponen daño, y siempre regrésalos donde pertenecen.
- Le da un lugar especial a cada niño, tal como un parte de un estante, por su biblioteca personal. Ayúdalos aumentar libros a su biblioteca. Ventas del garaje, tientas, ventas bibliotecarios de libros y tiendas de libros de mano segundo son todos buenos lugares para hallar libros baratos. Permite que los parientes y amigos saben que los libros siempre son bienvenidas para regalos.
- Designa un lugar en su hogar para poner los libros prestados de la biblioteca pública. En esta manera, se puedan disfrutar de ellos, y cuando es hora de volverles, sabrá donde están.

WORKS CITED

Ada, Alma Flor. *My Name is María Isabel*. Trans. Ana M. Cero. New York: Atheneum, 1993.

Aguirre, Rosainés. "The Dragons Came on a Hot Summer Day: A Word with Alma Flor Ada." *Lector*. 3 no. 6: (n.d.) 287.

Bierhorst, John. *Spirit Child: A Story of the Nativity*. Illus. Barbara Cooney. New York: William Morrow, 1984.

Brumley, Al. "Beyond Border States: Booming Economy in Carolinas Luring Hispanic Immigrants." *Dallas Morning News*. November 11, 1996: 1A, 10A.

Cabello-Argandoña, Roberto, and Roberto Peter Haro. "General Considerations of Spanish Personal Names." California Spanish Language Data Base, 1983. Mimeographed.

Cuesta, Yolanda J. "From Survival to Sophistication: Hispanic Needs=Library Needs." *Library Journal*. 115, no. 9 (May 15, 1990): 26–28.

De Varona, Frank. *Latino Literacy: The Complete Guide to Our Hispanic History and Culture*. New York: Holt, 1996.

Golen, Elaine P. "Developing Library Collections to Serve New Immigrants." *School Library Journal*. 32, no. 2 (October 1985): 93–97.

Lachtman, Doris. *Pepita Talks Twice*. Illus. Alex Prado de Lange. Houston: Piñata (Arte Público), 1995.

Martinez, Victor. *Parrot in the Oven: Mi vida*. New York: HarperCollins, 1996.

Nieto, Sonia. "Equity in Education: The Case for Bilingual Education." *Interracial Books for Children Bulletin N*. 17 (n.d.): 4–8.

Nye, Naomi Shihab. *The Tree Is Older Than You Are: A Bilingual Gathering of Poems and Stories from Mexico with Paintings by Mexican Artists*. New York: Simon and Schuster, 1995.

Preston, Julia. "Spain Losing Command of the King's Spanish." *Dallas Morning News*. April 20, 1997: 1A, 12A.

Rangel, Enrique. "Immigrants Being Lured to Alaska by Tales of Riches." *Dallas Morning News*. November 11, 1996: 10A

Rivera, Tómas. . . . *y no se lo tragó la tierra* (. . . and the Earth did not Part). Houston: Piñata (Arte Público), 1996.

Romaine, Suzanne. *Bilingualism*. New York: Basil Blackwell, 1989.

Schick, Frank L. and Renee Schick. *Statistical Handbook on U.S. Hispanics*. Phoenix, Ariz.: Oryx, 1991.

Schon, Isabel. *A Bicultural Heritage: Themes for the Exploration of Mexican and Mexican-American Culture in Books for Children and Adolescents*. Metuchen, N. J.: Scarecrow, 1978.

———. "Latino Children's Books." Silvey, Anita ed. *Children's Books and Their Creators*. Boston: Houghton Mifflin, 1995.

Schwiesow, Deirdre R. "A Growing Respect for the Day of the Dead." *USA Today*. November 1, 1996: 11D.

Stansfield, D. Bryan. "Serving Hispanic Persons: The Cross-Cultural Border Experience at Fabens." *RQ*. 27 no. 4. (Summer 1988): 547–561.

Temple, Frances. *Grab Hands and Run*. New York: HarperCollins, 1993.

Welna, David. "Christmas Celebrations in Mexico." *Morning Edition Saturday*. National Public Radio. 21 Dec 1996.

FURTHER READING

Carlson, Lori ed. *Cool Salsa: Bilingual Poems on Growing Up Latino in the United States*. New York: Holt, 1994.

Cockroft, James D. *Latinos in the Making of the United States*. The Hispanic Experience in the Americas Series. New York: Watts, 1995.

Culturegrams: The Nations Around Us. Volume 1: The Americas and Europe. Provo, Utah: David M. Kennedy Center for International Studies, Brigham Young University, 1996.

De Varona, Frank. *Latino Literacy: The Complete Guide to Our Hispanic History and Culture*. New York: Holt, 1996.

Meltzer, Milton. *The Hispanic Americans*. New York: Crowell, 1982.

2 LATINO CHILDREN'S LITERATURE

Latino children's literature is as diverse in character and theme as Latino children are themselves. There is a world of books to explore that form literary bridges to the "islands" of new and different cultural outlooks. Children's literature reflects a certain shared humanity, regardless of the culture from which it comes. Latin American children's books provide a panorama that is every bit as colorful as the sights and sounds of the countries themselves. This section provides a brief overview of the history of children's literature in Spain, Central America, Mexico, and the United States. In each case, the most important authors from these countries will be highlighted.

In one sense, the history of Latino children's literature is the history of attitudes toward children in the various countries from which it originates. In the United States, it is also the history of the changing attitudes toward Latino culture and people. This history will give you a context from which to understand the Latino literature you will be using with children in schools and libraries.

A WORD ABOUT PRIZES

A sign that children's Spanish-language books and books about Latino culture have gained attention and promoters is the existence of awards specifically for these books. Although none of these awards has the status of the Newbery or Caldecott awards, they are becoming increasingly better known.

The establishment of the Premio Lazarillo in Spain in 1958 has given increased visibility to children's literature in the Spanish language. This prize honors both authors and illustrators. It is probably the premier prize given for Spanish-language children's literature, and the closest in intent to the Newbery and Caldecott awards. Information about this award and a list of the winners are in Chapter 7, along with the recipients of other prestigious awards.

The now-defunct "Antoniorobles" prize was named after an important figure in Mexican children's literature. It was administered by the Asociación Mexicana Para el Fomento del Libro Infantil, the Mexican section of the International Board on Books for Young People (IBBY), and discontinued because of lack of funding. It honored the outstanding children's books of Mexico. This organization now publishes an annual list of recommended books.

The first biennial Pura Belpré Awards for text and illustration were presented in August 1996. Named after the first Latina storyteller at the New York Public Library and spearheaded by Oralia Garza de Cortéz, then of the San Antonio Public Library, these awards fill a longtime need similar to the Coretta Scott King awards for African-American authors and illustrators in the U.S. Books must exhibit cultural content, in other words, they must be about something relevant to Latino culture. The establishment of this prize has now given Latino children's literature in the U.S. a credibility and impetus that it has never before experienced.

CHILDREN'S LITERATURE IN SPAIN

The history of children's literature in Spain is a history that has been duplicated in other Spanish-speaking countries. Up until the twentieth century, there was no concern for literature written specifically for young people. However, Spain is rich in traditional stories and folklore, which have always been a part of the lives of Spanish children. While not necessarily written or published for children, these stories have been told to children and been embraced by them. In addition to indigenous folklore, youngsters in Spain have grown up with translations of the world's folklore—the Grimms, Joseph Jacobs, Andersen, and Perrault. In this century, a large portion of the literature for children published in Spain has been European and American classics in Spanish translation. The development of a purely Spanish children's literature by Spaniards is fairly recent, only in the latter half of this century. Even then, some of this literature is extremely didactic, written for purely educational purposes rather than as art. This comes from a belief that children's books are primarily of educational rather than recreational value. There are, however, treasures to be found.

Over the years a couple of works have stood out as being children's classics. Cervantes' *Don Quixote de la Mancha* is the touchstone of Spanish literature. Much of it is accessible to children, and there are illustrated, abridged editions available both in Spanish and English. Don Quixote is actually part of a tradition that began with *Lazarillo de Tormes*, which is the first of the Spanish picaresque tales that would influence so much Spanish literature and folklore. This work by an unknown author, first published in 1553, portrays Lazarillo as a rogue. His adventures with a series of employers forms the bare thread of what can hardly be called a plot. Lazarillo cheats some of his employers in his endless search for food and money. For example, the priest thinks rats have gotten into his larder when it is simply Lazarillo gnawing holes in the bread to make it appear that rats had found it.

Another important Spanish author whose works are enjoyed by both children and adults is Juan Ramón Jimenez, whose fame rests on *Platero y yo* (Platero and I), a series of prose poems about an unnamed narrator and his relationship with a silver-gray donkey named Platero. These idyllic little pieces are without much plot, but rich in language. The narrator, rather than taking his donkey to kindergarten, where there are no chairs big enough for him, takes his animal's education to the fields, where they can learn about flowers and stars. This book has been embraced by Spanish children and is certainly accessible to all children. An English translation, published for children, is available that includes some of the more memorable episodes.

Two authors who are exemplary of the state of Spanish writing at the middle of the twentieth century are Elena Fortún and Miguel Buñuel. Fortún is the author of the immensely popular Celia books. Celia is based on a child whom Fortún actually knew. Celia is a very original creation, ingenious, and alive. She is also somewhat of a liar, except that she sincerely believes that what she is saying is true. She has a strong fantasy life. Because of this, she is always getting into trouble with grownups, even though her apparent mischief is always full of the best intentions. The books follow Celia as she grows up and gets married.

Buñuel won the Lazarillo prize for a remarkable novel *El niño, la golondrina y el gato* (The child, the swallow, and the cat). This is a poetic fantasy about an unnamed boy who is accompanied by a swallow and a cat on adventures through earth, sea, and sky. They are assisted by forest animals, stars, and constellations, which is what they eventually become. Sample chapters of this beautifully written book can be found in Carmen Bravo-Villasante's *Antología de la literatura infantil española* (Anthology of Spanish children's literature) volume 2. A bibliography of her more important works is on pages 28–30.

Among the notable contemporary authors living and writing in Spain is Juan Farias. Farias was born in Galicia, Spain. He has lived a nomadic life, spending time as a crew member on a ship. He won the National Award for Children's Literature in Spain for his book *Algunos niños, tres perros y mas cosas* (A few children, three dogs, and more things). This collection of short stories uses the device of a blue ribbon to tie together the events that take place in Farias' fantasy world. Farias adapted one of these stories for separate publication—*40 niños y un perro* (40 children and a dog), which has been enormously popular. Farias has also written hard-hitting stories about war. His book *Crónicas de media tarde* (Afternoon chronicles) includes "Años difíciles" (Difficult years), a story that explores with tragic realism the effect of the Spanish Civil War on a village, even though the battles are far away. Food becomes scarce, then expensive. Cigarettes are no longer available for the protagonist's dad. The young men flee to the mountains to hide out, or are recruited by force for one side or the other. Some are shot for draft evasion or desertion.

Another name to remember is Concha López Narváez. Born in Seville and having grown up in a vineyard surrounded by olive trees, she was a teacher for a number of years and now devotes herself to full-time writing. She has been active in the promotion of children's literature, through involvement in IBBY and as a former president of the Spanish Association of the Friends of Books for Young Children and Teens. Representative of her books is *La tejedora de la muerte* (The death weaver), a suspense tale about a woman followed by a shadow. She won the Premio Lazarillo for *El amigo oculto y los espiritus de la tarde*. (The hidden friend and the spirits of the afternoon). This is another suspense novel about a boy left alone in an abandoned village after his grandfather dies. He soon begins to think that he may, in fact, have company.

While actually born in Uruguay, Ricardo Alcántara is a citizen of Spain and writes from a Spanish sensibility. He is a winner of the Premio Lazarillo and many other honors for his writing, which has put him in the top echelon of Latino children's authors. A psychologist as well as a children's author, Alcántara writes stories of everyday family life as well as books that capture the dream worlds in which children can live.

Some of his work has political themes, such as *La ronda de cada dia* (Each day's patrol), which uses animal characters to allegorically retell the story of the mothers of central plaza in Argentina whose sons disappeared under a harsh political regime. One of his most representative books is *Uña y carne*. An English translation should still be available under the title *Two of a Kind*, illustrated by Jackie Snider and translated by Laura M. Perez and Kathryn Corbett. It is published by American Printing House for the Blind, 1994.

A popular figure in contemporary Spanish children's literature is Barcelona native Jordi Sierra i Fabra. He is a journalist and editorial director of one of Spain's most influential rock music magazines. He is also a radio program director. In addition to his books on the history of rock and biographies of rock stars, he finds time to write children's books. His stories demonstrate a real understanding for the concerns of contemporary children. He is known especially for a series of books about a character named Victor and his friend Patricia (Cía). He has a wry sense of humor, and can even poke fun at himself—in one of his Victor and Cía books, *El Rockero* (The rock star), he has Victor reading a biography of John Lennon by the "extraordinary and sensitive Jordi Sierra i Fabra."

Other authors familiar to children are Fernando Alonso, Asun Balzoa, Montserrat del Amo, Pilar Molina Llorente, Pilar Mateos, Ana María Matute, and Juana Auorora Mayoral. In addition to authors, Spain boasts illustrators who are every bit as sophisticated as any on the international scene. Carmé Sole Vendrell has done outstanding work in books such as the delightful *Cepillo* (Brush). Vivi Escrivá is an illustrator and puppet designer. Her career began with an illustrated Bible. She won the Premio Lazarillo, and has illustrated books by Alma Flor Ada, among others.

SPOTLIGHT ON CARMEN BRAVO-VILLASANTE

Of all contemporary Spaniards working in children's books, the person who has had perhaps the most influence is Carmen Bravo-Villasante. Carmen Bravo-Villasante's contributions to Latino children's literature are inestimable. Born in Madrid, but a resident of Barcelona, she was first and foremost a folklorist, and spent her life collecting traditional rhymes, games, songs, and stories. Besides having published many collections of these folk rhymes and stories, she edited and compiled histories and anthologies of Spanish and Latin American children's literature. She was also a professor of Spanish literature at Smith College in the U.S. and the *Instituto de Cultura Hispanica* (Institute of Hispanic Culture) in Spain. While some are out of print and difficult to find, these books are full of gems and are worth the effort of seeking them out. They are standard works and the premier sources from which to understand the full breadth of children's literature from Spain and Latin America. Carmen Bravo-Villasante was very active in the IBBY. Through her work, many people throughout the Latin American world were inspired to set up national sections of IBBY in their countries. Sadly, she passed away in 1994. The following is a list of her most important collections and anthologies.

Adivina adivinanza. (Guess the Riddle). Madrid: Ediciones Didascolia, 1978.
  A collection of riddles for children to guess and try out on others.

Antología de la literatura infantil en lengua española (Anthology of Children's literature in the Spanish language). vol. I, II. Madrid: Editorial Doncel, 1973.
  As Bravo-Villasante states in her introduction, this anthology goes beyond her anthology of children's literature from Spain to embrace that of all Hispanic countries. It is is arranged chronologically, and includes biographical information about the authors. Here you can find a wealth of all kinds of literature including riddles, stories, songs, poems, and plays.

Antología de la literatura infantil española (Anthology of Spanish children's literature) vol. I, II. Madrid: Editorial Doncel, 1962; 9th ed., 1989.
  The standard anthology of children's literature from Spain. It is organized historically.

China, china, capuchina, en esta mano esta la china (Nonsense rhyme). Illus. Carmen Andrada. Valladolid: Editorial Miñón, 1981.
  Riddles, rhymes, and games with appealing illustrations.

Colorín colorete (Nonsense rhyme). Madrid: Ediciones Didascolia, 1983.
  A book of riddles, rhymes, tongue twisters, lullabies, carols, and prayers.

La hermosura del mundo y otros cuentos españoles (The Beauty of the world and other Spanish stories). Barcelona: Editorial Noguer, 1984, c. 1980.
A collection of retellings of popular Spanish stories. Includes versions of "The Rooster Who Went to His Uncle's Wedding" (El Gallo), and "Martina the Cockroach" (*La cucarachita y el ratoncito*).

Historia de la literatura infantil española (History of Spanish children's literature). Madrid: Editorial Doncel, 1983.
Chronicles the story of the children's literature of Spain from medieval times up through the present day. Helpful features include a list of histories and other studies of children's literature as well as a catalog of Spanish children's books. It is indexed by author and title.

Historia y antología de la literatura infantil iberoamericana (History and anthology of Latin American children's literature) vol. I, II. Madrid: Editorial Doncel, 1965. 3rd ed. 1988.
These books supply a history of children's literature in each Latin American country. They include folklore and samples of the works of the most important authors from each country as well as a brief description of their careers.

El libro de las fabulas (The book of fables). Illus. Carmen Andrada. Valladolid: Editorial Miñón, 1982.
Fables in verse by Spanish as well as Latin American authors.

Una, dola, tela, catola: el libro del folklore infantil (The book of children's folklore). Valladolid: Editorial Miñón, 1976.
A collection of Children's folklore: rhymes, riddles, and games.

CHILDREN'S LITERATURE IN MEXICO, CENTRAL, AND SOUTH AMERICA

As with Spain, the history of children's literature in Mexico and Central and South America begins with traditional tales. Some of these tales reflect the Spanish heritage of the *conquistadores*, or are wonder tales populated by princesses, castles, and dragons, which betray European influences. Children are also familiar with the western classics translated into Spanish. In addition to stories, the rich traditional literature of Latin America includes riddles, play rhymes, tongue twisters, and songs that all sing with the beauty of the Spanish language. These are discussed in more detail in the next chapter.

In Mexico and Central and South America those who have concerned themselves with this literature have looked at it primarily from the standpoint of educators, and have encouraged a literature written with didactic, rather than artistic intent. Almost unfailingly, these countries have primarily produced textbooks and didactic materials for their children to the extent that many people have grown up reading no children's books at all. The reasons for this are many. Much of it has to do with the politics, economics, and the social order in these countries that creates a great deal of inequality (Robleto, 1984: 30). Reading may not necessarily be associated with the pleasure of art, but rather with school and education. The level of literacy is very low in some cases. There has been a vicious circle of very little publishing activity for children which, in turn, gives artists little incentive to make writing a career. Children's publishing has been financially risky for Latin American publishers because demand has been small and uncertain. Print runs are not large, thus there is little chance of making money. Artists have been forced to finance their own publishing at times. The governments of many Latin American countries have historically shown little interest in helping to provide an environment in which artists can make a living at their art (Santa, 1984: 12). Systems of book distribution are limited, though in recent years this has been changing with the appearance of mail order book clubs, such as the *Círculo Infantil de Lectores* (Young Reader's Club), and more book vendors. In Latin America you are more likely to see books being sold by street vendors than in bookstores. Price has also been a barrier.

Libraries, too, are problematic. There is no strong tradition of public library service in Latin America. Where children's libraries do exist they are seen as serving the schools and education, not as support for recreational reading.

Another barrier to children's literature in Latin America is competition from imported books, which are of higher quality than what is published in the countries themselves. Additional competition comes from the really popular reading material—comic books, *foto novelas*, and magazines. Many children have grown up with comics and children's magazines rather than books. This is not to say that all children's magazines are of poor quality. In Argentina the children have an excellent magazine called *Billiken*, which began publication in 1919. It is now available on the Internet.

The more recent history of Latin American children's literature is much more promising because many of these barriers are being overcome. Since the 1970s, a more favorable climate for literature has arisen, as evidenced by the numerous children's book prizes that have been popping up. These provide additional encouragement for artists to create. Organizations dedicated to the support of and dissemination of information about children's books such as the Banco del Libro in Venezuela have begun too. Banco del Libro created a publishing arm, Ediciones Ekaré, in 1977. Ediciones Ekaré has published illustrated versions of folk songs and rhymes that rival picture books produced in the United States. Printing technologies have improved as well.

All of this means that there will be much more Spanish-language literature written by Latino authors available to the children of this and future generations. The downside is, that while scores of American books are being translated into Spanish, there are very few Spanish-language titles being translated into English. The next breakthrough will be when publishers can make the discovery that there are some excellent books that transcend cultural boundaries and could delight children of any culture. For the time being, translations aren't considered to be, for the most part, commercially viable. One reason for this is that differences in culture are considered to be too great to survive translation, or to be of interest to American children. For the teacher and librarian who does not speak Spanish, this presents an understandable limitation.

I have had to provide my own translations from Spanish to English or vice versa, to make these books accessible to children. Perhaps you know someone who is fluent and who might assist you. This can be most successful with folktales and rhymes, but longer chapter books should be made available as well. I hope that as the Latino population in the United States grows, it will become more viable for publishers to market translations of works originally published in Spanish.

Each of the Latin American countries do claim their classic children's works, ones that are known by most children growing up. The following is a brief overview of some of the names and books that stand out. This list is not all inclusive either in the books mentioned or in the nations mentioned, but is rather a sampling of some of the most notable works. The countries listed are those in which the tradition of children's literature is now most strongly established.

ARGENTINA

Most Argentine children will have heard of the stories of the Argentine cowboy *Martín Fierro*, as told in the epic poem by José Hernandez. Argentine children have also grown up with the magazine *Billiken*. It is remembered fondly by those who are now adults, and it is enjoyed by today's children as well. The magazine was started by Constancio C. Vigil. The significance of *Billiken* is that it brought children's literature to a wide audience. It also introduced popular anthropomorphized animal characters such as Juan Pirincho, the magpie. Germán Berdiales is known for poetry, stories, and dramas that continue to be published in new editions. Among contemporary Argentines, María Elena Walsh has not only made a name for herself in writing poetry for children, but also as a composer and musical performer who has done television as well as albums of music for children. She wrote her first book at age 17. Her songs are known and sung by millions of Argentine children, and her nonsense verse is reminiscent of Edward Lear. An excellent representative book is *El reino del revés* (The backwards kingdom). *Zoo loco* contains the Spanish equivalent of limericks. Walsh's short novel *Dailan Kifki* is full of humor and hyperbole. It hinges on unbelievable but true situations and misunderstandings, all within the framework of a realistic story. The protagonist is a little girl who tells the story about the day an elephant arrived at the door of her house as if it is the most normal event in the world. Information about María Elena Walsh, as well as a couple of her poems are available on the World Wide Web at opium.q1.fcen.uba.ar/MEWalsh/MEWalsh.html.

CHILE

The classic of Chilean children's literature is the Papelucho series by Marcela Paz. Papelucho is a typical middle class Chilean child, and the books are presented as his diaries. Paz was inspired when her husband-to-be gave her a calendar-diary. The Papelucho books are distinguished by a great sense of humor and by Paz's ability to assume a very natural voice for Papelucho. While the first Papelucho book was published in 1947, these books are not dated and continue to be enjoyed by generations of Chilean children. As with Argentina, a magazine was the primary vehicle for disseminating children's literature to young people. *El peneca*, which began publication in 1908 was full of fables, stories, poems, narrations of Latin American folklore, and classic European stories. Lucila Godoy Alcayaga, who wrote under the pseudonym of Gabriela Mistral, won the Nobel Prize, and wrote some lovely poems for children. Her fable *Crickets and Frogs* tells the delightful story of a musical battle between the crickets and the frogs to see which can sing the loudest. Also deserving of mention is Jacqueline Balcells. She began her writing career in France, but subsequently moved to Chile. Some of her poetic fantasies can be found in the book *The Enchanted Raisin*. Another notable Chilean author is Victor Carvajal. He writes in a more realistic mode, conscious of social problems.

COLOMBIA

An important Colombian figure is Rafael Pombo. His outstanding books are *Cuentos pintados* (Colorful stories), *Cuentos morales para niños* (Moral tales for children), *La hora de las tinieblas* (The hour of the shadows), and *Fabulas y verdades* (Fables and truths). This last title is full of riches and was chosen by the Circulo de Lectores book club as a "jewel" of Colombian literature. Most children will know Pombo's poem *"El renacuajo paseador"* (The strolling tadpole). *Cuentos morales para niños* is considered one of the first children's books in all of Latin America. The most recognized author/illustrator in contemporary Colombian children's literature is Ivar da Coll. He has created a significant body of work and has achieved a personal voice where everyday things are seen with new eyes (Reyes, 1996: 13). Many of his books, such as *Tengo miedo* (I'm scared), which Colombian children have made a classic, deal with the real concerns of very young children. From the moment Eusebio goes to bed he is scared—scared of all different kinds of monsters. In the story, these imaginary monsters become humanized and are no longer scary. Gloria Cecelia Díaz has made a name for herself with her novels *El valle de los Cocuyos* (The valley of the fireflies) and *El sol de los venados* (The deer's sun). Although she now lives out of the country and is published by Spanish publishing houses, her books are clearly Colombian. Jana, the protagonist of *El sol de los venados* is a child who reflects the experience of many Colombian children.

Lyll Becerra de Jenkins's novel, *Celebrating the Hero* (Lodestar, 1993), gives some current insight into conditions in this country. This story about teenager Camilla Draper, who travels from Connecticut to her mother's hometown for a ceremony honoring her grandfather and discovers the ugly truth about his life, gives a portrait of Colombian village life.

COSTA RICA

Among the classic books of Costa Rica is *Cuentos de mi tía Panchita* (Stories of my Aunt Panchita) by María Isabel Carvajal, who used the pseudonym Carmen Lyra. Published in 1920, this collection of stories includes indigenous tales of Tío Conejo as well as retellings of the Grimms' fairy tales. Lyra's influence was such that the national prize for Costa Rican literature was named after her. *Cuentos Viejos* (Old stories, 1923) by María Leal de Noguera is a book of stories about personified animals told in a regional dialect. *Mulita Mayor* (Mulita the older) by Carlos Luis Sáenz is a popular work that is often mentioned.

Among the popular contemporary books are *Almófar, hidalgo y aventurero* (Almófar, the noble adventurer) by Lilia Ramos. This is the story of a small elf who works in the mines but goes above ground and interacts with both the forest animals and the witch Cinzolín. Two winners of the national Carmen Lyra prizes are a play by Juan Andrés Solano called *Viudita Laurel* (Widow Laurel) and *Pedro y su teatrino maravilloso*, (Pedro and his marvelous theater) a short story collection by Carlos Rubio and stunningly illustrated by Vicky Ramos.

CUBA

Now available only as a book, *La Edad de Oro* (The age of gold) by the Cuban author José Martí was actually a magazine and is now a classic of Latino children's literature. Only four issues of this magazine were published during the time that Martí was exiled in New York. Martí's desire was the same as those reading this book who work with Latino children: that the children not lose their precious cultural heritage. *La Edad de Oro* is notable for Martí's ability to talk to children on their level, and not to talk down to them. Much of the material in these four issues was informational, but Martí certainly knew how to make it interesting. His "The History of Mankind as Told through His Houses" is a classic of its type.

GUATEMALA

One of the most important Guatemalan authors is Daniel Armas. His two books, which are considered classics of Guatemalan literature, are *Barbuchín* and *Pepe y Polita*.

Omar S. Casteñeda, who died tragically in a car accident in January 1997, was a Guatemalan native transported to the United States. He was one of only a few Latino authors writing books with significant cultural content published in English. His book *Among the Volcanoes* (Lodestar, 1991) tells the story of a Mayan Indian girl, Isabel Pacay, who is struggling to reconcile her ancient beliefs and culture with the values of modern society, particularly the differing views of women's roles. She finds difficulty when she tries to get western-style medical help for her mother. They have to live in the shadow of the mysterious disappearances of men from their village—victims of political instability. A sequel, *Imagining Isabel* (Lodestar, 1994), shows Isabel marrying and becoming a teacher, which was her dream. Both books contains many details of Mayan culture and of politics and life in Guatemala.

MEXICO

The lack of Mexican children's literature by Mexicans is saddening. There are a few authors worthy of note, however. In 1816 José Joaquín Fernández Liardi wrote *El periquillo sarniento*, which is considered to be the first Latino American novel. José Rosas Moreno is said to be the first Mexican to write exclusively for children. He wrote books such as *Lecciones de moral en verso* (Moral lessons in verse) and *Libro de la infancia* (Book of childhood) which is described as a treatise on Christian virtues (Schon, 1977: 9). One of the most influential figures in Mexican children's literature was Antonio Robles. The national prize for children's literature in Mexico was named after him. Even so, he favored a didactic approach to the retelling of traditional fairy tales for children, modifying those portions he felt "encouraged murderers and evil-doers" (Schon, 1978: 126). His work has also been criticized for containing " . . . long, dull narrations and descriptions" (Schon, 1978: 128).

Notable among contemporary Mexican authors and illustrators is Laura Fernandez, who was born in Mexico City and studied graphic design there but has devoted herself to children's book illustration since 1982. She has worked on various children's magazines such as *Chispa*. Laura Fernández has won the Antoniorobles Prize twice for text and illustration. Her first book, *Pájaros en la cabeza* (Birds in the head) has been described as "the" book of Mexican children's literature. It was one of the first to break away from the didactic mold and to tell a fresh story. The idea was taken from a friend in primary school who had long hair down to her knees. She wore her hair all different ways, but Laura's favorite was the "nest" look (Cerda, 1996: 35). Another book she both wrote and illustrated, *Luis y su genio* (Luis and his genie) is also an absolute delight. Luis wakes up to find a genie in his room one morning, a boy his same age. Unlike the genies we're used to, this one wants to grant wishes only for himself.

Carlos Pellecier López has written and illustrated two outstanding picture books, *Juan y sus zapatos* (Juan and his shoes) and *Julieta y su caja de colores* (Julieta and her box of crayons). Both of these books show the power of a child's imagination. Another outstanding illustrator is Felipe Dávalos. He is known for his ability to create realistic drawings, for his manipulation of color, his technical skill, and the way he combines graphic elements in his illustrations. He won the Ezra Jack Keats prize for his illustrations for *Las tortugas del mar* (The sea turtles) and his work has been highly influential. Carlos Ocampo's book *Si ves pasar un condor* (If you see a condor pass by) also treats Mexican animal life in telling the history of the relationship between an old man and the animals in the Chapultepec Zoo in Mexico City. This book poetically evokes the ambiance of the park and its animals. Francisco Hinojosa mined the previously unexplored territory of Mexico's revolutionary history in his book *A golpe de calcetín* (By means of a sock) a story about a young boy who sells newspapers during the Mexican Revolution.

SPOTLIGHT ON EDUARDO ROBLES BOZA (TÍO PATOTA)

Perhaps the most well-known figure of contemporary Mexican children's literature is Eduardo Robles Boza, who is known to Mexican children as *Tío Patota* or Uncle Bigfoot. This unusual moniker, which he gave himself, makes him something of a Mexican Dr. Seuss. He was born in Mexico City and, besides writing children's books, is a magazine writer and editor. His career began when he approached a children's librarian at the American Children's Library in Mexico City, offering to tell stories. His writing grew out of his storytelling. He was a founding member of the Mexican section of IBBY, and was heavily involved in the annual selection of the now-defunct Antoniorobles Prize. His book *Los cuentos de Tío Patota* (The stories of Uncle Bigfoot) received national and international prizes, and was cited by IBBY International as being an original example of literature of international importance. While some of his work may be a tad didactic for some, it is always full of good will and a lot of fun. The following is an annotated bibliography of some of his books.

Abuela del juicio (Wise grandmother). Mexico D.F.: Editorial Trillas, 1984.
A group of children get to know an old woman and find out she's not half bad.

Barranco el rebelde. (Barranco the rebel). León, Spain: Editorial Everest, 1985.
"Una escoba es una escoba y se pone a barrer, pero hay escobas differentes . . . ¡No me van a creer!" (A broom is a broom and they are used for sweeping. But there are different sorts of brooms . . . You won't believe me!)
A story about an unusual broom that moves on its own and causes complications until it is discovered that it is actually a horse. A broom can also be a horse in the imagination of a child.

Cajon de los tiliches (The box of junk). León, Spain: Editorial Everest, 1985.
"Lo que no sirve o estroba lo metemos a un cajón. A eso le llaman tiliches y viven en un rincón." (Whatever is of no use any more we put in a box. We call them junk and they live in a corner.)
A story about a special box, like all houses have. One day a boy opened it and marbles, a string, and an electric plug came out among other miscellaneous objects. These objects talk to the boy, and one of them, a top, helps him when they stop talking.

Carlota es una pelota (Carlota is a ball). León, Spain: Editorial Everest, 1985.
"Carlota es una pelota de teni de campeonato y desertó, ¡vaya broma! a causa de un raquetazo." (Carlota is a championship tennis ball, who left, what a joke, all because of a racquet.)
A story about a super ball that broke things and caused problems. It follows the storyteller, and gets caught up in a game of tennis, which it doesn't like. It spends the rest of its days on the storyteller's shelf with his books.

Chispa de luz (A spark of light). Illus. Gloria Calderas Lim. Mexico, D.F.: Editorial Trillas, 1984.
A spark of light leaves its lightbulb in its desire to be free. It finds its place sparkling in a child's eyes.

La Computadora K-J (K-J the computer). Mexico, D.F.: Editorial Trillas, 1984.
Santiago helps a computer packing box realize its dreams and become a computer itself.

La Cosquilla (The tickle). Mexico, D.F.: Editorial Trillas, 1985.
Erika tries to find out where tickles come from.

Cuatro letras se escaparon (Four letters escaped). Illus. Rebeca Cerda. Mexico, D.F.: Editorial Trillas, 1986.
Four letters escape from a page and try to form a word.

Los cuentos de Tío Patota (The stories of Uncle Bigfoot). Patria, 1980.
Six stories illustrated by children.

En la maleta vivia un poeta (In the suitcase lived a poet). León, Spain: Editorial Everest, 1985.
"Un lápiz desconchinflado que tiene muchos problemas, pero vive illusionado." (A pencil who has a lot of problems, but who is a dreamer.)
A letter from Tío Patota. He describes his cabin in the mountains. One day he found a briefcase there that contained things from his childhood. Among them is a pencil that wants to be a poet.

Ha nacido un libro (*A book has been born*). León, Spain: Editorial Everest, 1985.
The story of how a book comes from the imagination of an author.

Las increíbles peripecias de una hoja de papel (The Incredible viccissitudes of a piece of paper). León, Spain: Editorial Everest, 1985.
A piece of paper gets thrown away, then goes on a journey, being blown by the wind, carried by a stream, and finally found by a little girl who draws a heart on it.

Las letras de mi maquina de escribir (The Letters on my typewriter). Leon, Spain: León, Editorial Everest, 1985.
An author talks with the letters on his typewriter.

Mi amigo dice mentiras (My friend lies). Illus. Roberto López. Mexico D.F.: Editorial Grijalbo, 1989.
Series: Los problemas de me amigo (My friend's problems). Didactic story about lying.

Mi amigo tiene miedo (My friend is afraid). Mexico D.F.: Editorial Grijalbo, 1989.
Series: Los problemas de mi amigo (My friend's problems). Kind of like a Spanish version of *There's A Nightmare in My Closet*, only more didactic.

Rollito. Mexico D.F.: Editorial Trillas, 1985.
Rollito is a caterpillar who eats alot. The little girl Xóchitl, who takes him to school, doesn't realize he'll turn into a butterfly.

Una noche en la escuela (One night in school). León, Spain: Editorial Everest, 1985.
Two friends spend the night in their school, where the school supplies appear to have come to life.

Vida secreta de una maceta (The secret life of a flowerpot). Spain: Editorial Everest, 1985.
The secret life of a flowerpot that helps a tree grow until it is time to be transplanted.

URUGUAY

Although he lived in Argentina after 1901, Horacio Quiroga is a stellar figure claimed by his home country, and his book *Cuentos de la selva* (Stories of the jungle) is a touchstone work. Quiroga loved the jungle and his stories demonstrate his knowledge of its animal inhabitants. His stories are full of deep emotion and celebrate the relationships between man and animal. In "La tortuga gigante" (The giant turtle), for example, a turtle saves the life of a man who saved the turtle's own. Quiroga creates a mythical world for children, never losing touch with what is real.

VENEZUELA

Venezuela is one of the countries where children's literature is the strongest. As with other Latin American countries, Venezuelan children's literature began with retold fairy tales and didactic stories. An important early book is *El libro de la infancia por un amigo de los niños* (The book of infancy written by a friend to children), written by Amenodoro Urdaneta and published in 1856. This book contained fables after the European model, but with it's philosophizing monkeys and pigs in love, it showed the beginnings of children's literature with a particularly Venezuelan sensitivity. Another important early figure is Aquiles Nazoa. Venezuelan children have grown up through the twentieth century with magazines such as *El amigo de los niños* (The children's friend), *Onza, tigre y león* (Tiger and lion), and *Tricolor*.

Rafael Rivero Oramas brought new life to the tales from the oral tradition calling himself El tío Nicolas, or Uncle Nicholas. Through this storytelling persona he brought new life to such folklore figures as Tío Conejo (Uncle Rabbit). Pilar Almoina has also retold these stories to acclaim in her books *El camino de Tío Conejo* (The path of Uncle Rabbit) and *Habia una vez . . . veinteiséis cuentos y Once cuentos maravillosos* (Once upon a time: 26 stories and 11 fantastic stories).

Two contemporary Venezuelan picture books that have received international acclaim and broken the translation barriers are Orlando Araujo's *Miguel Vicente, pata caliente* (Miguel Vicente, hotfoot) and Kurusa's (pseudonym of Carmen Diana Dearden) *La calle es libre* (The streets are free). Miguel Vicente is a shoeshine boy who loves to talk with anyone he meets. His desire is to travel and to see the world. This desire is fulfilled in the sequel *Los viajes de Miguel Vicente, pata caliente* (The travels of Miguel Vicente, hotfoot), where Miguel retains his dreams, imagination, and a hopeful attitude through difficult circumstances. *La calle es libre* tells the story of children who break through bureaucracy and manage to have a vacant lot full of trash turned into a playground. The book has been an international success, translated into eight languages.

In illustration, Monika Dopert, the art director at Ediciones Ekaré in Caracas, Venezuela, has done excellent work, especially with *La calle es libre*, as has fellow Venezuelan Vicky Sempere.

LATINO CHILDREN'S LITERATURE IN THE UNITED STATES

Up until the 1970s, the majority of children's books (with some notable exceptions) that included Latino characters and settings, if they were included at all, were created by non-Latinos who attempted to articulate the Latino experience to young children. The problem was that these books reflected the attitudes of an Anglo culture looking in on the Latino world. They promoted the separatism of cultures with the notion that somehow Anglos had to come in and rescue Latinos from their poverty, and generalizing that poverty was the state of all Latinos in the United States.

In a perceptive article called "Paternalism and Assimilation in Books about Hispanics," Opal Moor and Donnarae MacCann point out how most of these books reflect what they call "classic 'liberal' attitudes of the 1950s variety: that privileged whites have a moral obligation to uplift and improve the world's unfortunate" (1987, part 1: 99–100). These books propose " . . . condescending liberalism as a virtue" (100). The authors suggest, with some insight, that perhaps these attitudes, especially towards Latinos as reflected in children's literature, arise from the whole American experience of United States intervention in Latin America (Moore and MacCann, 1987, part 2: 157). America has intervened in the affairs of Latin American countries throughout this century, taking on what Moor and MacCann call a "managerial" role. Some of the books they mention that fall into this category are: *Viva Chicano* (Dutton, 1970) by Frank Bonham; *The Street of the Flower Boxes* (Coward McCann, 1966) by Peggy Mann; *Maria Luisa* (Lippincott, n.d.) by Winifred Madison; and *A Shadow Like a Leopard* (Harper, 1981) by Myron Levoy.

The primary problem is that these books present Latino culture as inferior and quaint, and Latino people as fine at heart but needing to adopt superior Anglo ways. They sometimes present stereotypes as the norm. Especially when a book has a Latin American setting during this period, stereotyping can present a problem. A book like *The Story of Pancho and the Bull with the Crooked Tail* (Macmillan, 1942) by Berta and Elmer Hader shows a sombrero and tortilla view of Mexican village life. The story itself is delightful and shows a child succeeding where adults cannot. Hader drew from her personal experience living in Mexico, but the stereotyping mars an otherwise delightful story.

In the sixties, as cultural attitudes changed, awareness of the Latino community became more heightened. Cesar Chávez was fighting for the rights of migrant workers, and the Chicano movement was visible. During this same period there was an emerging awareness of Latino culture in literature, even if many of the well-intentioned books that reflected this concern actually marginalized it. There were some books, however, that managed to transcend the prevalent social attitudes.

Four Newbery award-winning books were also published between 1953 and 1966 that reflected and respected Latino life. Interestingly enough, these books received the award in pairs, and they are all coming-of-age stories of young men. Ann Nolan Clark's *Secret of the Andes* in 1953 was followed the succeeding year by . . . *And Now Miguel* by Joseph Krumgold. Maia Wojciechowska won the Newbery medal in 1965 for *Shadow of a Bull*. The year following the award went to *I, Juan de Pareja* by Elizabeth Borton de Treviño. While none of these authors were Latino, they do show a respect for Latino life and culture that rose above condescension. *Secret of the Andes* portrays the tension so prevalent in Latin American life between indigenous Indian peoples and the mixed-race Mestizos. The boy, Cusi, lives with the ancient llama-herder, Chuto, in a valley hidden amidst the grandeur of the Andes mountains. He knows nothing of his parentage or of why he stays with Chuto. It is only after making a journey into the city of Cusco and learning of discrimination and then returning to his valley that he is given the secret of which he is to be the guardian for the rest of his life. . . . *And Now Miguel* is set in New Mexico and chronicles Miguel's desire to be considered a man and to be able to go with the other men into the mountains with the sheep. *Shadow of a Bull* is a story set in Spain about a young man who by birthright is expected to be a great bull fighter, but who ends up following his own path. *I, Juan de Pareja* is a story set in seventeenth century Spain about the slave of the court painter Velázquez. Each of these books paved the trail for the changing of attitudes by presenting children dealing with universal concerns.

While the majority of books dealing with Latino culture during the 1950s, 1960s, and 1970s were being written by Anglos, there are three Latina authors who stood out during this period, and who are the founders of a Latino-American literature written by Latinos.

SPOTLIGHT ON PURA BELPRÉ

Pura Belpré is one of the pioneering figures both in Latino children's librarianship as well as in children's literature. Born in Puerto Rico, she moved to the United States and became involved in a storytelling program at the New York Public Library. She gradually added puppets to her storytelling repertoire. She also discovered folklore while at NYPL. Her classic retelling of the romance of Perez and Martina grew out of an assignment in a storytelling class in library school. Here are her most important books:

Firefly Summer. Houston: Piñata Books (Arte Público), 1996.
> This book was the first in Arte Público's Recovering the U.S. Hispanic Literary Heritage Series. It is the story of young Teresa's return to the Puerto Rican countryside set at the turn of the century.

Juan Bobo and the Queen's Necklace: A Puerto Rican Folktale. Illus. Christine Price. New York: Warne, 1962.
> When the Queen's pearl necklace is stolen, Juan Bobo tells his mother that he wants to get the reward. He is accepted at the palace even though he is a Bobo because no one else has been able to find the necklace. While staying in one of the rooms of the palace he is waited on by three maids who believe that he has discovered that they stole the necklace because of a nonsense song he sings to nightingales

flying by as he looks out the window. They confess to him, and he saves their skins by making it appear that the necklace was eaten by a goose that is cooked for dinner.

Oté: A Puerto Rican Folktale. Illus. Paul Galdone. New York: Pantheon, 1969.
One day when Oté is off in the forest in search of food for his impoverished family he meets the nearsighted devil. Being hungry, he tries to steal the devil's food, but is caught in the attempt. The devil hops on Oté's back and is carried home. Before each meal, the devil causes the members of the family to fall down as if they are dead and eats all their food. Oté goes to the wise woman in search of a solution. She gives him magic words to say which will only work if he eats nothing on the way home. But the temptation of lovely green fruit is too much. Oté forgets the magic words and his family is even hungrier than usual. The next day their littlest boy, Chiquitín, follows Oté to the wise woman. He remembers the words and becomes a hero finally eradicating the devil.

Perez and Martina. New York: Viking, 1960, 1991.
Spanish translation, *Perez y Martina*, published by Warne, 1966. The beautiful cockroach, Martina, chooses Ratoncito Perez above all her other suitors. Tragedy ensues when the small but gallant mouse falls in the soup Martina is cooking for dinner and dies. (In other versions of the story he is magically resurrected).

Santiago. Illus. Symeon Shimin. New York: Warne, 1969. Spanish translation 1971.
Santiago lives in two worlds at once: Puerto Rico and New York. His grandmother Seline has sent him a stereoscope with pictures of Puerto Rico. He wants to take it to school, but he ends up bringing his class home to look at it.

The Tiger and the Rabbit and Other Tales. Illus. Tomie DePaola. New York: Lipincott, 1965.
This selection of folk tales from Puerto Rico includes "The Tiger and the Rabbit," which is a "Tío Conejo" story. There is also a "Juan Bobo" tale. These are the stories that Belpré heard while growing up in her family.

SPOTLIGHT ON NICHOLASA MOHR

Nicolasa Mohr was born in New York to Puerto Rican parents. Her books have mainly concerned the Puerto Rican experience in New York. Along with Pura Belpré, she is one of the first Latinas to publish children's books in this country. As such she is spoken of reverentially by those who have followed. Happily she is writing again after a dry spell.

El Bronx Remembered. New York: HarperTrophy, 1993.
These twelve short stories about life in the Bronx are often sad, but they tell the truth of the constant struggle for life in the barrio.

Felita. New York: Dial, 1979.
Felita loves her neighborhood, the Puerto Rican barrio in New York. She knows everyone and plays street games with her friends. When her parents want to move to a better neighborhood, she can't understand it.

Going Home. Houston: Arte Público, 1988.
In this sequel to Felita, our heroine turns twelve and finally gets her dream of spending two months in Puerto Rico. But when the time comes to go, Felita realizes how difficult it is to leave her friends in New York. And in Puerto Rico, she becomes homesick and is not accepted by some of the girls her age.

In Nueva York. Houston: Arte Público, 1988.
These seven connected short stories set in tenements in a Puerto Rican barrio focus on individual lives.

The Magic Shell. Illus. Rudy Gutierrez. Scholastic, 1995.
Spanish translation: El regalo mágico. Jamie Ramos has to leave the Dominican Republic when his dad gets a good job in New York City. He doesn't like the cold, and he can't speak English. He has a shell that takes him back to his island in his imagination.

Nilda. New York: Harper, 1973. Houston: Arte Público, 1986.
Set during World War II, this novel tells the story of a young Puerto Rican girl growing up in New York's Spanish Harlem amidst racial prejudice and poverty.

Old Letivia and the Mountain of Sorrows. Viking, 1996. Spanish translation *La vieja Letivia y el monte de los pesares*.
Old Letivia is a *curandera* (healer) who goes on a quest with her whistling turtle Cervantes and a tiny boy named Simon whom she has found floating in a river. Together they save a village that is besieged by a terrible wind. After undergoing many adventures, the group finds the wind and learns that it is stuck in the mountain by mistake and wants to be free. They assist the wind, and Old Letivia gets four wishes in return.

The Song of El Coqui and Other Tales of Puerto Rico. Viking, 1995. This is a collection of three animal stories from Puerto Rican folklore. One story is about a mule who comes from Spain to an awful work camp. He escapes with a slave to the mountains.

SPOTLIGHT ON HILDA PERERA

Hilda Perera was born in Cuba but immigrated to the United States in 1964 and currently resides in Miami, Florida. She won the Premio Lazarillo in 1975 and 1978, and also won the Hispanic Heritage Award in 1994. She loved writing as she was growing up and won awards for her essays. One of her books, *Kike,* (pronounced kee-kay) universalizes the experiences she and so many others had leaving Cuba to escape the communist regime of Fidel Castro. Like many other books by Latino authors who relocated to this country, this book describes the difficulty of adjusting to a new culture and living between two cultures. Unfortunately, this is the only book by this outstanding author that has been translated into English. More about Hilda Perera can be found in the book *Famous People of Hispanic Heritage* vol. 6 by Barbara J. Marvis and Theresa Swanson Scott (1996).

THE 1990s AND BEYOND: THE BOOM

In the 1990s the number of bilingual and Spanish-language children's books published in the United States has skyrocketed. The explosion of Latino authors, such as Colombian Gabriel García Marquez, onto the worldwide literary scene in the seventies was known as the "boom." This would also be an apt term to apply to what has been happening in Latino children's literature in the United States since 1990. This new "boom" is a result of several factors.

Since publishing is driven by economics, one of the primary factors has been that with the increasing Latino population in the United States, publishers now see that it makes economic sense to publish for this market. The demand for books that reflect our multicultural society has grown exponentially. As Isabel Schon notes in her article on "Latino Children's Books" in Anita Silvey's *Children's Books and Their Creators* (1995):

The statistics are difficult to ignore: The U.S. Hispanic-origin population is approaching 25 million—an almost 60% increase from the 1980 census. The U.S. Department of Education estimates that Hispanic children make up 73 percent of the two million children in the United States who have limited proficiency in English. In addition, it is important to note that Spanish is now the second language in the Western world. . . . These numbers, coupled with the fact that the field of children's literature in many Spanish-speaking countries is barely developing, may be the catalyst for the constantly improving selection in the quality and quantity of books for and about Latino children (392–3).

The United States is now "the fifth-largest Spanish-language market in the world, after Spain, Mexico, Argentina, and Colombia" (Taylor, 1996: S3). Publishing for Latino children has grown in leaps and bounds. Starting in the early 1970s independents such as Harriet Rohmer of Children's Book Press began to fill a need that they saw for bilingual and multicultural books, which at that time was not being met by the mainstream publishers. Children's Book Press began in 1975 and focuses on bilingual traditional and contemporary stories. Reflecting this growth, in the past six years many of the major United States publishing houses, such as HarperCollins; Farrar Straus and Giroux; Penguin; and Scholastic have begun Spanish-language imprints.

The Houston-based Arte Público Press has established a children's imprint, Piñata Books, and has become a major force in publishing English-language and bilingual fiction and picture books by Latino authors. They are engaged in a publishing project, Recovering the U.S. Hispanic Literary Heritage, which is bringing back into print some previously unknown classics by Latino writers. While these imprints have primarily been outlets for Spanish translations of books on their lists, the number of books by Latino authors being published has grown as well. Scholastic, Inc., recently acquired the distributor Lectorum Publications, which will provide wider distribution and awareness for titles by Latino authors, especially those from outside the United States. Publishers in Latin American countries are thinking in terms of all Spanish-language markets. For instance, by publishing books in a generic Spanish that can be understood everywhere, when they bring out children's books there should be an increasing presence of these books in the United States (Taylor, 1996: S3). Latin American publishers, of course, are also acquiring rights to publish American books in Spanish, such as the *Goosebumps* series. Disney books are also extremely popular. For the librarian and the teacher this means that there will be an increasing number of American children's books available in Spanish translations.

Increased awareness of the need for children to see their own cultures in their literature has been another driving force behind the increasing numbers of U.S. Latino authors now publishing books for children. This is not to say that there aren't still problems. There could be much more Latino children's literature than there is now. Even with the current boom, the proportion of Latino writers to that of other groups is still low. Too many books celebrating Latino cultural heritage focus on the exotic celebrations and native costume, perpetuating the stereotypes that have always plagued Latinos. The following are the most notable United States Latino authors.

SPOTLIGHT ON ALMA FLOR ADA

Alma Flor Ada is known as an author, natural born storyteller, and translator. Besides her work with schools and children, she also teaches at the University of San Francisco. Her desire has been to provide school children with materials that are not boring or didactic. She was born in Cuba and studied in Peru. She has been a major force in promoting bilingualism in this country as well as writing original stories and retelling delightful versions of folktales, some of which she heard as a child and now wants to share with other children. Her daughter, Rosalma Zubizaretta, has translated many of her books. Her philosophy is well-expressed in this statement: "Nothing can surpass the inherent musicality of the [Spanish] language, the deep cultural values incorporated in it" (*Something about the Author*, 7).

The Lizard and the Sun: An Old Mexican Folk-Tale. Illus. Felipe Dávalos. Trans. Rosalma Zubizarreta. New York: Doubleday, 1997.
   When the sun disappeared from the sky all the animals gave up in their search for it except for the lizard. The lizard discovered the sun sleeping beneath a glowing rock. But neither he nor anyone else could make the sun wake up. The emperor then organized a tremendous feast to wake the sun so it would never fall asleep. And to this day, lizards like to laze in the light of the sun.

MedioPollito/Half-Chicken. Illus. Kim Howard. Trans. Rosalma Zubizarreta. New York: Doubleday, 1995.
   A bilingual folktale that explains the origins of weathercocks. Half-Chicken is just that, and he hops along on one foot on a journey to Mexico City helping the stream, the fire and the wind on the way. When he's about to be turned into chicken soup for the viceroy, they help him escape.

My Name is María Isabel. New York: Atheneum, 1993.
   María Isabel Salazar Lopez moves, and there are already two Marías in her class, so the teacher calls her Mary Lopez. She doesn't readily recognize this new name, and feels that it takes her identity away from her. Latino names encapsulate the entire family genealogy, and there is the additional special connection María feels for relatives after whom she was named.

The Rooster Who Went to His Uncle's Wedding: A Latin-American Folktale. Illus. Kathleen Kuchera. New York: Whitebird (Putnam), 1993.
   Rooster dirties his beak on his way to his uncle's wedding. He tries to get the grass to clean it, but it won't. He tries to get the goat to

eat the grass so the grass will clean his beak, but the goat won't. So it continues until Rooster's friend the sun comes to his rescue.

SPOTLIGHT ON GEORGE ANCONA

George Ancona is a photographer and author who creates "photo essays." While much of his work does not reflect his own Latino heritage—his parents were from Mexico; he was born in New York and raised in an Italian neighborhood—he has begun to explore his heritage more and more. Besides creating children's books, he has worked for television, radio, and in film.

Fiesta U.S.A. New York: Dutton, 1995.
> This book provides an introduction to four Latino holidays celebrated here in the United States: The Day of the Dead, *las posadas*, the dance of *los matachines*, and the Day of the Three Kings. Ancona shows celebrations in four different communities, which emphasizes the diversity of the Latino population.

Pablo Remembers: The Fiesta of the Day of the Dead. New York: Lothrop, 1993.
> Spanish translation: *Pablo recuerda el día de los muertos.*
> Ancona's photos show 12-year-old Pablo Montano Ruiz participating in Day of the Dead rituals near Oaxaca, Mexico. Ancona shows how this holiday is a mixture of Christian belief and Aztec and Mayan cosmology. The holiday is portrayed as a time when a family lovingly remembers those loved ones who have departed.

The Piñata Maker/El piñatero. San Diego, Calif.: Harcourt, 1994.
> Tío Rico is an old man who makes piñatas, puppets, and masks for the people of his village. Ancona's photos bring the story to life.

Ricardo's Day/El día de Ricardo. New York: Scholastic, 1994.
> Ricardo goes to nursery school.

SPOTLIGHT ON PAT MORA

Pat Mora is an award-winning poet, essayist, and lecturer who is currently based in New Mexico. She has held teaching positions at both the secondary and college levels, but she now writes full time. She was born in El Paso, Texas, and much of her writing reflects not only the Latino culture, but also the landscape of the southwest. This sense of place is one of the defining qualities of her writing. In her poetry she celebrates the little everyday things that are at the heart of Latino cultural identity. She has written poetry for adults along with her children's books, and is generally considered a voice for Latinas.

Mora, Pat, and Charles Ramírez Berg. *The Gift of the Poinsettia/El regalo de la flor de nochebuena*. Illus. Daniel Lechón. Houston: Piñata (Arte Público), 1995.
This story takes place in the Mexican town of San Bernando. Carlos worries about what gifts he'll have for *las posadas*. He has songs. He gives a plant he finds by a favorite rock—it turns into a poinsettia. Use with Tomie De Paola's *The Legend of the Poinsettia*.

A Birthday Basket for Tía. Illus. Cecily Lang. New York: Macmillan, 1992.
Cecelia searches for the perfect present for her great aunt's ninetieth birthday. She ends up putting together a memory basket, objects that represent their favorite activities together.

Confetti. New York: Lee & Low, 1996.
These poems mix English and Spanish and touch on familiar things in Latino life. Mora's best book to date.

Delicious Hullabaloo/Pachanga deliciosa. Illus. Francisco X. Mora. Trans. Alba Nora Martínez and Pat Mora. Houston: Piñata (Arte Público), 1998.
Birds, armadillos, and an assortment of other creatures cavort at night in a kitchen to the music of a lizard mariachi band. They are all very hungry and will eat anything.

The Desert Is My Mother/El desierto es mi madre. Illus. Daniel Lechon. Houston: Piñata (Arte Público), 1994.
A girl with long, dark hair narrates this simple text and evokes the power of the desert.

Listen to the Desert/Oye al desierto. New York: Clarion, 1994.
A bilingual chant that describes the sounds of the desert.

Pablo's Tree. New York: Macmillan, 1994.
Every year on his birthday, Pablo goes to his grandfather Lito's house. Lito decorates a special tree in Pablo's honor that was planted when he was adopted. Each year Lito uses something different to decorate—chimes, balloons, paper lanterns, and tiny birdcages.

The Race of Toad and Deer. Illus. Maya Itzna Brooks. New York: Orchard, 1995.
This Guatemalan folktale is a version of the tortoise and the hare. In this case it's Tío Sapo, or Uncle Toad, whose friends trick Venado, the deer, into running himself out before the end of the race.

Tomás and the Library Lady. Illus. Raul Colón. New York: Knopf, 1997.
Spanish Translation: *Tomás y la señora de la biblioteca*. This is based on the true story of Tomás Rivera, who grew up to be the first chancellor of the University of California system. Tomás hears stories from his grandfather, who then takes him to the library for more. The "Library Lady" becomes an important influence in his life.

Uno, dos, tres: One, Two, Three. New York: Clarion, 1996.
A bilingual rhyme that is about girls going to the market to buy birthday presents for their mother.

SPOTLIGHT ON GARY SOTO

Gary Soto has risen quickly to be perhaps the most outstanding American Latino writing for children and young adults. First known for his poetry, he has now written many middle-grade and young adult novels that show a deep respect for the Latino experience. This respect comes from Soto's own upbringing in the barrio of Fresno, California. His work is full of the imagery of the barrio where he grew up, such as the raisin factory he could see in the distance (Schon, 1995: 614), but his books are accessible to all children. Though written in English, they are also filled with Spanish words and phrases, which occur as a natural part of the storytelling. He generally includes glossaries to help readers. Soto is a second generation American, both his parents were born here, but his sense of heritage is strong, as clearly evidenced in his writing. Although coming from an illiterate family, he discovered poetry at Fresno City College. He obtained a master's degree in creative writing from the University of California at Irvine and has taught at the University of California at Berkeley.

The move to writing for young people came naturally as Soto found himself writing autobiographical stories about his childhood. His first book marketed specifically for young adults was *Baseball in April*. Since then he has continued to write excellent books for young adults as well as for a younger audience. He has also produced films based on his stories, one of which, *The Pool Party*, won the Carnegie Medal for excellence in children's video.

Baseball in April and Other Stories. San Diego, Calif.: Harcourt Brace, 1990.
This collection won the Pura Belpré honor award for writing in 1996. It includes "No-Guitar Blues," upon which a film was based.

Boys at Work. New York: Delacorte, 1995.
Rudy and Alex, characters from the novel *Pool Party*, have to raise

money when one of them breaks the local neighborhood thug's portable CD player.

Buried Onions. New York: Harcourt, 1997.
Eddie's friends pressure him to seek revenge for the murder of his cousin. A slice-of-life about teenagers living in Fresno, California, Soto's own stomping grounds.

Canto Familiar (Familiar song). Illus. Annika Nelson: San Diego, Calif.: Harcourt, 1995.
Canto Familiar, a companion to *Neighborhood Odes*, contains 25 poems about the daily life of Mexican-American children.

The Cat's Meow. Illus. Joe Cepeda. New York: Scholastic, 1995.
Graciela's cat starts speaking to her in Spanish.

Chato's Kitchen. Illus. Susan Guevara. New York: Putnam, 1995.
Guevara received the Pura Belpré Award for Illustration in 1996 for this book. Chato, a cool, low-riding cat invites the mice who've moved in next door over for dinner. Chato and his friend Novio Boy prepare a feast of tortillas and guacamole to lure the mice, but the mice also bring a surprise with them.

Crazy Weekend. New York: Scholastic, 1994.
Hector and Mando and Hector's Uncle Julio are the only witnesses to a robbery.

A Fire in My Hands: A Book of Poems. Illus. James M. Cardillo, New York: Scholastic, 1991.
In addition to the poems, Soto gives advice to young poets, and provides anecdotes about the poems. Soto's poetry beautifully celebrates the ordinary and commonplace things in life.

Jesse. New York: Harcourt, 1994.
Jesse leaves home to escape his alcoholic father. Set during the Vietnam war, this story details Jesse's difficulties as he moves in with his brother, takes classes at Fresno City College, becomes involved with César Chavez's farm workers movement, and struggles to communicate with girls and against racial prejudice.

Living Up the Street. San Francisco, Calif.: Strawberry Hill Press, 1985.
Narrative recollections describe growing up in Fresno.

Local News, San Diego, Calif.: Harcourt, 1993.
In this follow-up to *Baseball in April* Soto tells more neighborhood

yarns. In "Blackmail" Javier threatens to take a picture he took of Angel in the shower to all the girls at school. "First Job" is a nightmare for Alex when he sets fire to his neighbor's fence. In another story a girl takes what she thinks is her good-natured kitten to school to protect it from another feline back home, only to find it killing a mouse on the playground. Full of humor, the appeal of these stories extends beyond ethnic boundaries.

Neighborhood Odes. Illus. David Díaz. San Diego, Calif.: Harcourt, 1992.
Twenty-one poems that celebrate *el barrio.*

No Guitar Blues. New York: Phoenix/BFA, 1991. 27 min.
A video of a story taken from *Baseball in April.* Fausto is ridden with guilt over the dishonest way he obtains money to buy the guitar he wants. Later he receives a present of a bass *guitarrón* that has been in the family.

Novio Boy: A Play. San Diego, Calif.: Harcourt, 1997.
Rudy doesn't believe it when an older girl (11th grade) accepts a date with him. Now he needs to know what to say, how to behave, and he needs money. And then, everyone shows up at the restaurant during the date itself. This could be presented fully staged or as a reading.

Off and Running. New York: Delacorte, 1996.
This story involves characters from previous Soto books—Miata from *The Skirt,* and Rudy and Alex from *Boys at Work.* They run against each other for class president.

The Old Man and His Door. Illus. Joe Cepeda. New York: Putnam, 1996.
This wise-fool story is about a man who doesn't listen to his wife's instructions, and instead of taking a pig (*puerco*) to a barbecue party, he sets off with a door (*puerta*) on his back. Everything comes out right, however.

Pacific Crossing. San Diego, Calif.: Harcourt, 1992.
Lincoln Mendoza goes to Japan on a summer exchange program. This takes a new look a culture clashes.

The Pool Party. Illus. Robert Casilla. New York: Delacorte, 1993.
Rudy Herrera gets invited to Tiffany Perez's pool party. Tiffany is one of the richest kids in school. Rudy's family tries to help him get ready and select a gift.

The Skirt. Illus. Eric Velasquez. New York: Delacorte, 1992.
Miata has been preparing to perform with her folklorico dance group. A small crisis is precipitated when she leaves her decorative skirt on the school bus. She and her girlfriend have to retrieve it, a process not without complications. This is a very short early reader.

Snapshots from the Wedding. Illus. Stephanie García. New York: Putnam, 1997.
Unique three-dimensional illustrations tell the story of a typical Latino wedding.

A Summer Life. Hanover, N.H.: University Press of New England, 1990.
In this collection of 39 essays and short stories, Soto vividly conveys Latino life through a child's eyes.

Summer on Wheels. New York: Scholastic, 1995.
This is a sequel to *Crazy Weekend*. Hector and Mando make an eight-day bike ride from L.A. to Santa Monica. They stay with family all along the way.

Taking Sides. San Diego, Calif.: Harcourt, 1991.
Lincoln Mendoza deals with prejudice as he moves from the barrio into a mostly white neighborhood. Soto shows the kind of stress that racial prejudice puts on children.

Too Many Tamales. Illus. Ed Martinez. New York: Putnam, 1993.
Spanish translation: *¡Qué montón de tamales!* Illus. Ed Martinez. Trans. Alma Flor Ada and F. Isabel Campos.
This delightful story centers around an important cultural tradition—making tamales on Christmas Eve. Since tamales take so much effort to make, homemade tamales are a special event. María tries on the ring her mother has taken off while making the tamales. It slips off her finger and into the *masa*. Horrified when she makes the discovery, María and her cousins secretly eat all the tamales trying to find the missing ring. This is Soto's first picture book, and one of the first picture books to provide an authentic cultural experience.

ADDITIONAL AUTHORS OF IMPORTANCE

Rudolfo Anaya is the acknowledged dean of Chicano writers. While he has written only two children's picture books, *The Farolitos of Christmas* and *Maya's Children*, many of his novels are accessible to Latino young adults. Anaya's novel *Bless Me, Ultima* is generally celebrated as the classic of Chicano literature and is uniquely interesting to teens. It tells the story of six-year-old Antonio, who becomes friend and apprentice to the *curandera*, or healer, named Ultima. Antonio's life is full of questions and doubts. Each chapter includes a dream sequence in which his worst fears are given a voice. When it was published in 1972, it was one of the very first books written from a Latino perspective to gain visibility on the national scene.

Carmen Lomas Garza is an artist born in Kingsville, Texas. She now makes her home in San Francisco. She has made a name for herself through two picture books of reminiscences illustrated with her folk-art style paintings. Two books, *Family Pictures/Cuadros de familia*, and *In My Family/En mi familia* were milestones in the presentation of Latino family life as it was and is and were Pura Belpé Honor Books. Her vignettes are lovingly remembered real moments in time. They give Latino children a mirror through which to view their own lives, and provide an inspiration to honor family traditions.

Born in Puerto Rico, **Lulu Delacre** is another outstanding artist who has illustrated important collections of Latino folklore as well as songs. She decided to pursue a career in children's books after seeing an exhibit of Maurice Sendak's work while she was studying in Paris.

The first book to receive the newly established National Book Award for Young People's Literature was *Parrot in the Oven: Mi Vida* by Victor Martinez. Martinez comes out of the same milieu as Gary Soto, from Fresno, California. His book is a sometimes harsh but sympathetic look at barrio life through the eyes of the 14-year-old protagonist, Manny Hernandez. Manny deals with violence, an absent father, and a sister who gets pregnant out of wedlock but then loses the baby. Like Soto, his life changed when he took creative writing at the University of California at Fresno, was encouraged by a professor, and fell in love with poetry. It is certain that we can look forward to more good work to come from him.

WORKS CITED

"Ada, Alma Flor." *Something about the Author*. Vol. 84. Ed. Kevin S. Hile. Detroit, Mich.: Gale, 1996: 1–7.

Moore, Opal, and Donnarae MacCann. "Paternalism and Assimilation in Books about Hispanics: Part One of a Two-Part Essay." *Children's Literature Association Quarterly*. 12, no. 2 (Summer, 1987): 99–102, 110.

———. "Paternalism and Assimilation in Books about Hispanics: Part Two of a Two-Part Essay." *Children's Literature Association Quarterly*. 12, no. 3 (Fall, 1987): 154–157.

Reyes, Yolanda. "¿Literatura infantil Columbiana?" (Columbian children's literature?) *Revista latinoamericana de literatura infantil y juvenil*. No. 3. (January-June, 1996): 12–15.

Robleto, Vidaluz Meneses. "Nicaragua." *Phaedrus: An International Annual of Children's Literature Research*. Vol. 10. New York: Columbia University, 1984: 30–32.

Santa, Irene Piedra. "Guatemala." *Phaedrus: An International Annual of Children's Literature Research*. Vol. 10. New York: Columbia University, 1984: 11–16.

Schon, Isabel. *A Bicultural Heritage: Themes for the Exploration of Mexican and Mexican-American Culture in Books for Children and Adolescents*. Metuchen, N.J.: Scarecrow, 1978.

———. "Latino Children's Books." Silvey, Anita ed. *Children's Books and Their Creators*. Boston: Houghton Mifflin, 1995.

———. *Mexico and Its Literature for Children and Adolescents*. Special Study—Arizona State University, Center for Latin American Studies; no. 15. Tempe, Ariz.: Arizona State University Center for Latin American Studies, 1977.

Taylor, Sally. "Big Changes South of the Border." *Publisher's Weekly*. September 23, 1996: S3–S20.

FURTHER READING

The following articles and books articulate the history of Latino children's literature in greater detail for those who want to learn more.

Castelo, Hernán Rodríguez. "El destacado papel de Argentina en la literatura infantil de este America nuestra." (The Leading role of Argentina in children's literature in this our America). *Revista latinoamericana de literatura infantil y juvenil*. No. 3. (January-June, 1996): 16–25.

Castrillon, Sylvia. "Aislamiento: el problema mas serio." (Isolation: The most serious problem). *Revista latinoamericana de literatura infantil y juvenil*. No. 3. (January-June, 1996): 3–5.

Cerda, Rebeca. "Ayer y hoy: notas sobre libros infantiles en Mexico." (Yesterday and today: Notes on children's books in Mexico). *Revista latinoamericana de literatura infantil y juvenil*. No. 4. (July-December, 1996): 28–37.

Echeverria de Sauter, Marilyn. "Literatura infantil Cosarricense" (Costa Rican children's literature). *Revista latinoamericana de literatura infantil y juvenil*. No. 2. (July-December, 1995): 24–27.

"Hoja de vida: Ivar Da Coll." (A Page out of life: Ivar Da Coll). *Revista latinoamericana de literatura infantil y juvenil*. No. 3. (January-June, 1996): 34–35.

Maggi, María Elena. "Literatura infantil en Venezuela: géneros, autores y tendencias." (Children's literature in Venezuela: Genres, authors and tendencies). *Revista latinoamericana de literatura infantil y juvenil*. No. 1. (January-June, 1995): 24–31.

Munoz, Manuel Pena. "De 'El Peneca' a 'Papelucho.'" (From El Peneca to Papelucho). *Revista latinoamericana de literatura infantil y juvenil*. No. 3. (January-June, 1996): 26–33.

Robledo, Beatriz. "El torno a la obra de Ivar da Coll." (Around the work of Ivar da Coll). *Revista latinoamericana de literatura infantil y juvenil*. No. 4. (January-June, 1996): 36–41.

Rodriguez, Gloria Maria. "Una literatura 'en abstracto.'" (An Abstract literature). *Revista latinoamericana de literatura infantil y juvenil*. No. 4. (July-December, 1996): 6–7.

Schon, Isabel ed. *Contemporary Spanish-Speaking Writers and Illustrators for Children and Young Adults: A Biographical Dictionary*. Westport, Conn.: Greenwood, 1994.

This book is an indispensable resource, the only one of it's kind. Includes brief biographies and bibliographies on virtually every Latino children's author.

3 LATINO FOLKLORE AND FOLK RHYMES

In the previous chapter I made the point that in every case Latino children's literature begins with folklore—tales and rhymes. These are the foundation of any collection of Latino materials and of any programming with Latino children. They represent the basic cultural touchstones every child should know. In this chapter, I focus on these stories and poems and how they can be used in the classroom and library. While Latino children are familiar with much of the world's folklore in translation, here I focus on the most common Latino folktales. There are several major stories that seem to be common, and I list the various available retellings that are appropriate to share with children.

As far as folk rhymes are concerned, there is a wealth of Latino children's poetry that rivals Mother Goose for the delightful way the language sounds when read out loud. These rhymes are meant to be shared with children. I've provided a literal translation of many of the rhymes so that the person who does not speak Spanish can know what it is about. Note that when a translation is not provided it means that the rhyme is made up of primarily nonsense words that don't have much meaning beyond the sound of the language itself. In this chapter I've tried to cover some of the most common and important tales and rhymes, as well as some favorites I've enjoyed using in my library. Of course, many other books of folktales and folk rhymes can be found in the bibliography.

FOLKTALES: MAJOR STORY TYPES

Latino folktales can be grouped into four main types. First, there are animal stories such as Tío Conejo (Uncle Rabbit). Second, there are traditional fairy tales, some of which show European or Spanish influences. The Catholic faith brought to Latin America by the Spaniards has also been an important influence, and many folktales have distinctly religious content. This can present a problem in public schools and libraries where mention of religion is taboo. Religion is so deeply interwoven in these tales, however, that it cannot be separated. When sharing them with a Latino audience, it is generally not a problem because the religious element is quite deep-rooted in the culture and generally accepted. In both animal and traditional fairy tales, you will find many trickster characters. The clever animal or person who is able to outwit the supposedly smarter animal or person is a popular motif. The third major category is ghost stories. Finally, there are stories from the Indian oral tradition. I'll explore the most common tales from each of these types.

ANIMAL TALES

Perez and Martina

Top on the list of Latino tales that every child should know is "Perez and Martina." Originating in Cuba, it tells the story of a little cockroach who rejects all her suitors except the gentlemanly mouse Perez. As each suitor approaches Martina, who is fanning herself on her porch or balcony, he proposes marriage. To each in turn Martina coyly says: "Perhaps, but tell me how you will speak to me in the future." Each suitor in turn is turned down because his way of speaking is not to her liking. The beautiful voice of Perez enchants her, however. They are married in a lavish ceremony, but then later, when Martina is cooking a soup, Perez becomes too curious, falls into the pot, and is boiled to death. Martina mourns the loss of her beloved. In a number of versions of this tale, Perez is miraculously restored to health. In some versions, Martina is a butterfly or an ant instead of a cockroach. This tale is notable because it is the earliest Latino folktale to come to prominence in this country through the version written by Pura Belpré. Her version and others are listed below.

Belpré, Pura. *Perez and Martina : A Puerto Rican Folktale*. Illus. Carlos Sanchez. New York: Viking, 1960, 1991.
The classic original retelling complete with the tragic ending.

González, Lucía M. "Martina the Little Cockroach" from *Señor Cat's Romance: And Other Favorite Stories from Latin America*. Illus. Lulu Delacre. New York: Scholastic, 1997.
In this version, doctors bring Perez back to life, and all ends happily ever after.

Hayes, Joe. *Mariposa, mariposa*. Illus. Lucy Jelinek. Santa Fe, N.M.: Trails West, 1988.
A variation on "Perez and Martina." Mariposa finds some money and gets a beautiful dress (her wings). She asks various animals who want to marry her how they will talk when they are married. She likes the mouse, but the mouse gets eaten by the cat. Friends bring flowers; she likes them so much that she flies from flower to flower to this day.

Herrmann, Marjorie E. *Perez and Martina/Perez y Martina: Fables in English and Spanish/Fábulas bilingües.* Lincolnwood, Ill.: National Textbook Company, 1988.
A controlled vocabulary version of the story for children to read on their own.

Moreton, Daniel. *La cucaracha Martina: A Carribean Folktale.* New York: Turtle Books, 1997.
A hip version of the "Perez and Martina" story. In this version, Martina marries a cricket instead of the *ratoncito* Perez.

Soler, Carola. *El pájaro de nieve y otras lecturas para niños* (The snow bird and other texts for children). Madrid: Aguilar, 1967.
Includes "El ratón pelado," a version of "Perez and Martina." Martina is an ant, and the exchange between the ant and her beau which is nicely poetic:

> RATÓN: ¡Hormiguita, qué guapa estás! (Little Ant, how beautiful you are!)
> HORMIGA: Hago bien, que tu no me lo das. (I'm doing well, no thanks to you.)
> RATÓN: ¿Te quieres casar conmigo? (Will you marry me?)
> HORMIGA: ¿Cómo vas a arrullar al niño? (How will you sing the baby to sleep?)
> RATÓN: Con amor y cariño. (With love and caring.)
> HORMIGA: Bueno, me casaré contigo. (Then yes, I will marry you.)

Rooster and the Wedding

This cumulative tale is known by many different titles. It is a classic folktale form: Rooster is on his way to his Uncle Parrot's wedding when he sees a kernel of corn in the mud. He eats it, dirtying his beak. Not presentable to go to his uncle's wedding, he asks the grass to clean his beak. The grass refuses, and so Rooster petitions the goat to eat the grass to make it clean his beak. The goat, too, refuses. This chain of events continues until it reaches Rooster's friend the sun. This is a wonderful tale to use to introduce children to Latino folklore. The preferred version is the the bilingual Lucía González retelling with illustrations by Lulu Delacre. An effective way to share this story is to have a colleague read a section in either the English or Spanish after you have read the other language. Going back and forth between the two languages heightens the fun of this story. This is perfect to use in mixed-language groups and in programs where you are introducing the library to Latino users. The most readily available versions of this tale are:

Ada, Alma Flor. *The Rooster Who Went to His Uncle's Wedding: A Latin American Folktale.* Illus. Kathleen Kuchera. New York: Whitebird (Putnam), 1993.
This version of the traditional tale "*Gallo de Bodas*" has the rooster meeting a lamb and a dog who begin the chain of events through which Rooster's beak is clean just in time for his uncle's wedding.

González, Lucía. *The Bossy Gallito/El gallo de bodas: A Traditional Cuban Folktale.* New York: Scholastic, 1994.
This book was named a Purá Belpré honor book for both writing and illustration in 1996.

Hayes, Joe. *No Way, José/¡De ninguna manera José!* Illus. Lucy Jelinek. Santa Fe, N.M.: Trails West, 1986.
If you use this version, you can get everyone to call out "No way José" as you tell the story. The format of the book probably makes this version is probably more appropriate for telling.

Tricksters: Coyote and Tío Conejo

Among the most popular of folktales with Latino children, the stories of Tío Conejo (Uncle Rabbit), show how the smallest and weakest of the animals can defeat the strongest, and that cleverness can win out over brute force. Tío Conejo can be a rogue, but he is very creative and even wise. He is a figure with whom children can identify, which explains his popularity with Latino children. Tío Tigre (Uncle Tiger), is often a character in these stories, and usually is the object of Tío Conejo's tricks. Full of humor, these stories come from the African tradition, but they have become uniquely part of the Latino culture as they have been retold and passed down from one generation to the next.

González, Lucía M. "How Uncle Rabbit Tricked Uncle Tiger" from *Señor Cat's Romance: And Other Favorite Stories from Latin America.* Illus. Lulu Delacre. New York: Scholastic, 1997.
Tío Conejo tricks Tío Tigre and ties his tale into a knot. Then after a few days, he puts honey all over himself and then covers himself with leaves. Tío Tigre has been waiting at the watering hole, but doesn't recognize this little leafy animal. Tío Conejo has the last laugh again as he reveals himself to Tío Tigre.

Johnston, Tony. *The Tale of Rabbit and Coyote.* Illus. Tomie DePaola. New York: Putnam, 1994.
Coyote is tricked again and again by Rabbit. Johnston says this tale comes from the state of Oaxaca, Mexico. In a scene reminiscent of "Brer Rabbit," Rabbit gets stuck to a wax image a farmer has placed

in his field because Rabbit has been stealing his chiles. But despite this setback, Rabbit is able to get the better of Coyote—first by duping him into taking his place in a stew pot. In another familiar episode, Rabbit tricks Coyote into drinking a lake to reach the "cheese" that is actually the reflection of the moon in the water. The ending explains why Coyotes howl at the moon: This is where Rabbit has taken refuge.

TRADITIONAL FOLK TALES

Pedro de Ordimalas

Pedro de Ordimalas is known by many different names, but the stories are found throughout Latin America. Some of the variants I have seen are:

Pedro, el de Malas (Wicked Peter)
Pedro Remales
Pedro Malasartes (Peter Evilarts)
Pedro de Urdemales/Juan de Urdemalas (Peter or John Evilschemer)
Pedro Animales
Pedro Tecomate (Peter Gourd)

Regardless of under what name he masquerades, Pedro descends from the Spanish picaresque tradition of Don Quixote, a roguish hero going out on adventures. In fact, Cervantes wrote a play in which Pedro appears. In some stories Pedro is a hero trying to correct injustices. In others he is much more of a trickster. Some of Pedro's stories are also shared by other protagonists such as Tío Conejo and Juan Bobo. Pedro is always trying to get rich or get out of having to do work. He loves to trick the mostly foolish and greedy people with whom he comes in contact. He can make bandits believe that money grows on trees. He can even win a battle of wits with the Devil himself, and he gets Saint Peter to let him into heaven.

Versions of Pedro de Ordimalas:

Brusca, María Cristina, and Tona Wilson. *El Herrero y el diablo* (The blacksmith and the devils). Illus. María Cristina Brusca. New York: Holt, 1992.
This version closely follows the basic version of the story with the main character now called Juan Pobreza, or John the Poor One. The illustrations in this version are particularly delightful, especially the ones showing the rich, young Juan partying, riding elephants, and showering people with money from his airplane.

Brusca, Maria Cristina, and Tona Wilson. *Pedro Fools the Gringo and Other Tales of a Latin-American Trickster.* Illus. Maria Cristina Brusca. New York: Redfeather (Holt), 1995.
The collection includes the following stories:
"Clever Little Pedro." Pedro fools the priest into believing that he's read books in the library to teach him how to steal the priest's cheese. In reality, Pedro has simply stacked the books so he can climb up on them. He also convinces the priest that there are one-legged chickens.
"Painted Horses" Pedro paints horses in order to pass them off as something they are not, but the paint washes off in the rain.
"Golden Partridge." A sure gross-out. Pedro does his business by the side of the road, then covers it up with a hat when two men ride up. He convinces them that there's a valuable golden partridge under the hat.
"Magic Pot" and "Money Tree" are also Juan Bobo tales. Pedro tricks the same men who thought he had a golden partridge into thinking that he has all the things he says he has. Their greediness makes them easy targets.
"Pig Tails in the Swamp" Pedro's master asks him to sell some pigs at market. Pedro pockets the money, cut's off the pigs tails, and makes his master think they've drowned in the swamp.
"Helper Rabbit." Pedro fools a man into thinking a rabbit can deliver messages.
"Burro Gold." Another gross-out that is sure to get a response. Pedro feeds his Burro gold coins and cons a man into giving him everything he owns in return for the gold-producing burro.
"Pedro and the Devil." This is a Latin American version of the story that is known as "Tops and Bottoms." Pedro cheats the devil out of his crops.
"Pedro Fools the Gringo." Pedro fools a gringo into thinking that a squash is actually a mare's egg that will produce a racing colt.
"Good-bye to Your Machetes." Pedro escapes from his captors by putting their whips, machetes, pistols, and knives in a sack while they are sleeping. He then heaves it over the side of a cliff.
"Pedro Goes to Heaven." Pedro fools his way through the pearly gates.

Griego y Maestas, José, and Rudolfo A. Anaya. "Pedro de Ordimalas." *Cuentos: Tales from the Hispanic Southwest.* Santa Fe: Museum of New Mexico Press, 1980: 160–171.
Pedro cheats Death twice, but the third time he dies and is sent to hell. But even the devils there can't stand him. Because of a bargain he had made with the Lord earlier in life, he ends up in heaven, but as a rock.

JUAN BOBO

Juan Bobo tales are sometimes indistinguishable from those about Pedre de Ordimalas. "Bobo" means "stupid" or "dunderhead." And as this name indicates, his stories are more characterized by stupidity than by the cleverness of Pedro de Ordimalas. If Juan triumphs, it is generally by mistake. Children love Juan Bobo stories because they can see they are smarter than him. Here are some children's versions of his stories:

Belpré, Pura. *Juan Bobo and the Queen's Necklace: A Puerto Rican Folktale*. Illus. Christine Price. New York: Warne, 1962.
When the Queen's pearl necklace is stolen, Juan Bobo tells his mother that he wants to get the reward. He is accepted at the palace even though he is a Bobo because no one else has been able to find the necklace. While staying in one of the rooms of the palace he is waited on by three maids who believe that he has discovered that they stole the necklace. This is because he sings a nonsense song to nightingales flying by as he looks out the window. They confess to him, and he saves their skins by making it appear that the necklace was eaten by a goose that is cooked for dinner.

Bernier-Grand, Carmen T. *Juan Bobo: Four Folktales from Puerto Rico*. Illus. Ernesto Ramos Nieves. New York: Harper, 1994.
"The Best Way to Carry Water." Juan Bobo tries to carry water to his mother using a wicker basket. He thinks he is strong because the basket is so light, but of course all the water has seeped out.
"A Pig in Sunday Clothes." Juan Bobo dresses up the family pig in his mother's clothes in order to take it to church. It promptly rolls in the mud.
"Do Not Sneeze, Do Not Scratch, Do Not Eat." Literally following his mother's instructions about good manners, Juan Bobo doesn't get anything to eat.
"A Dime a Jug." Juan Bobo ends up selling his jugs to flies.

Ferré, Rosario. *Los cuentos de Juan Bobo* (The Stories of Juan Bobo). Río Piedras, Puerto Rico: Ediciones Huracán, 1981.
Five Juan Bobo stories. They include a story about Juan and young ladies from Manto Prieto, Juan going to mass, Juan making a fool of himself dining in a wealthy home, and Juan journeying to the capital city.

González, Lucía M. "Juan Bobo and the Three-Legged Pot" from *Señor Cat's Romance: And Other Favorite Stories from Latin America*. Illus. Lulu Delacre. New York: Scholastic, 1997.
Juan Bobo's mother asks him to retrieve a pot from his grandmother

so that she can make rice with chicken. Since the pot has three legs, Juan thinks that it will come home on its own.

Pitre, Felix. *Juan Bobo and the Pig: A Puerto Rican Folktale.* New York: Lodestar (Dutton), 1993.
A another version of the story where Juan Bobo dresses the pig to send it to church.

GHOST STORIES

La Llorona

Most Latino children have grown up being told the story of La Llorona (the crying woman) by their parents. In most cases it is used as a motivational tool to promote good behavior. La Llorona is said to haunt "rivers, lakes, and lonely roads" (Anaya, *Maya's Children*). It is said that she appears at night and is searching for her own lost children. In the original version, La Llorona has taken her children's lives, and this is the reason for her ghostly appearance. This story is found in many Latin American countries. Children are told that unless they are good, La Llorona will come and take them away.

Anaya, Rudolfo. *The Legend of La Llorona.* TQS Publications, 1984.
A straightforward retelling of the original legend.

Anaya, Rudolfo. *Maya's Children: The Story of La Llorona.* Illus: Maria Baca. New York: Hyperion, 1997.
Some may balk at this version in which a villain, Señor Tiempo (The God of Time), steals Maya's children instead of her killing them, causing her to become La Llorona. Maya is born with a mark that is known as a sign of immortality. Señor Tiempo becomes crazy with jealousy over this usurpation of his powers and so robs Maya of her dearest treasure, her children.

Anzaldua, Gloria. *Prietita and the Ghost Woman/Prietita y la Llorona.* Illus. Christina Gonzalez. San Francisco, Calif.: Children's Book Press, 1996.
"La Llorona helps Prietita find an herb that the curandera needs to heal Prietita's mother."

Hayes, Joe. *La Llorona/The Weeping Woman.* Illus. Vicki Trego-Hill. Cinco Puntos Press, 1986.
This version is the best for storytelling because it is basically a transcription of the version Hayes uses when he tells the story out loud.

María Angula

Librarian, author, and storyteller Lucia M. González says this is her favorite story to tell around Halloween. It comes from the oral traditions of Ecuador, but it is a story type similar to that of the more well-known "Tailypo." When María is married, her husband asks her to make various special dishes, but she has never done much to learn how to cook. After a major cooking disaster, María goes to the house of her neighbor, doña Mercedes, for advice. When Mercedes tells María how to prepare the dish her husband requested, María replies flippantly, "If that is all there is to making that dish, *I knew that*." María repeatedly returns to doña Mercedes for help, and each time gives the same reply, that she already knew how to make the dish in question. Finally, doña Mercedes becomes annoyed, and when María asks her about a dish that includes tripe, Mercedes tells her to obtain that ingredient, and others from a fresh corpse in the cemetery. María does so, but that same night the spirit whose entrails María took, comes to ask for them back. When her husband wakes, his wife has disappeared, never to be seen again.

"María Angula." *Cuentos de espantos y aparecidos* (Stories of ghosts and apparitions). Ed. Veronica Uribe. São Paulo, Brazil: Editorial Atica, Coedición Latinoamericana, 1984: 33–40.

INDIAN ORAL TRADITION

Macario

One of my favorite stories that arises out of the Indian oral tradition is "Macario." This story has appeared as a major Mexican feature film based on the adult novel by the mysterious B. Traven. Macario is a young peasant who cannot provide for his family and becomes despondent. On the Day of the Dead he meets Death himself, who comes disguised as a peasant like Macario. Death trades the power to cure for a portion of turkey that Macario has. Macario soon becomes famous for his magical skill. That is until he disobeys Death's instructions. A nice version of the story can be found in the book *Cuentos*.

Griego y Maestas, José, and Rudolfo A. Anaya. "La comadre Sebastiana/Doña Sebastiana." *Cuentos: Tales from the Hispanic Southwest*. Santa Fe: Museum of New Mexico Press, 1980: 14–21. In this version the poor woodcutter goes nameless. He denies help to the Lord and the Virgin Mary before meeting Death, who is portrayed as a woman, doña Sebastiana. When the man disobeys Death's direction never to cure a person if he saw him (Death) at the head of the bed, Death takes the woodcutter to a room with two candles, representing life. The woodcutter's candle goes out: "At that moment the flame of the short candle went out, and the curandero's soul was added to doña Sebastiana's cart as it slowly made it's way into eternity."

Macario. Dir. Roberto Gavaldon. Mexico, 1958. 91 Minutes. Available from Facets Video.

Our Lady of Guadelupe

The story of Our Lady of Guadelupe is one cherished by all Mexicans. The Virgin Mary appears to a poor man named Juan Diego and tells him that she wishes a church to be built on the site where they are standing. She then instructs him to go to the Bishop. This is a miracle accepted as truth by most Catholic Latinos and cherished because it shows how marvelous events happen to ordinary people. The following are two versions of this tale retold for children.

DePaola, Tomie. *The Lady of Guadelupe*. New York: Holiday House, 1980.
   Spanish Translation: *Nuestra Señora de Guadelupe*. Trans. Pura Belpré. New York: Holiday House, 1980.
   DePaola's simple and respectful illustrations enhance this retelling of the story of the appearance of the Virgin Mary to the peasant Juan Diego.

Parish, Helen Rand. *Our Lady of Guadelupe*. Illus. Jean Charlot. New York: Viking, 1955.
   This older version of the story is most appropriate for the storyteller who is going to tell the tale of Juan Diego and the Virgin Mary.

Poinsettia

Another legend involves that of the poinsettia flower, which is traditional during the Christmas season:

DePaola, Tomie. *The Legend of the Poinsettia*. New York: Putnam, 1994.
   Lucinda helps her mother weave a blanket to be used for the Baby Jesus in a Christmas procession. When her mother gets sick, Lucinda tries to finish the blanket but ends up only tangling the yarn. Lucinda fears that she has ruined the celebrations until an old woman appears to her and tells her that the Baby Jesus will accept any gift she gives because it comes from the heart.

Mora, Pat and Charles Ramãirez Berg. *The Gift of the Poinsettia/El regalo de la flor de nochebuena*. Illus. Daniel Lechhãon. Houston: Piñata (Arte Público), 1995.

In this story it is a little boy participating in las posadas festivities who worries about a gift to bring to the Baby Jesus.

PROGRAMMING FOLKLORE

STORYTELLING

The tales that I've mentioned above all lend themselves to oral telling without using a book. Stories like "Perez and Martina" and "The Bossy Gallito" have a cumulative structure that make them easy to tell. Find the version or combination of versions that you like best. Make the story your own, adding your own flourishes or style. Sometimes this happens over repeated tellings. You can adapt them to your level of proficiency in Spanish from using only a few Spanish words throughout to being able to tell the entire tale in Spanish. I find that with cumulative tales it is easier to begin with a 3-x-5-inch card as a "cheat sheet" with the salient points. For example, if telling "The Bossy Gallito" you could list each of the animals or things the Gallito encounters (i.e., the grass, the fire) to jog your memory.

PUPPET SHOWS

Puppet shows are always an excellent way to present the folklore of any culture. Most of the Latino folktales I've mentioned adapt themselves easily for theatrical presentation. If you don't feel comfortable with writing your own adaptation, just use the dialogue as it comes from your source material. You can make adaptations to fit the puppets you have on hand if necessary.

Two of the following puppet shows, "Señor Conejo, Señor Coyote, y el Espantapajaros" (Mr. Rabbit, Mr. Coyote, and the Scarecrow) and "Perez and Martina" were adapted by Mary Alice Cortez and Sandra McLean of the Dallas Public Library Children's Center. They are reprinted here with their permission. A third show, "Marinerito Juan Trombón" (Little Sailor John Trombone), adapted from a show by Elsa Lira Gaiero of Uruguay, was anthologized in Carmen Bravo-Villasante's *Historia y antologia de la literatura infantil Iberoamericana*, Volume 2. All of these can be duplicated for the purpose of presentation in a school or library, where admission is not charged. In addition to the three scripts, here are some other stories that work well as puppet shows.

"The Rooster Who Went to His Uncle's Wedding." Source: *The Rooster Who Went to His Uncle's Wedding: A Latin American Folktale.* Illus. Kathleen Kuchera. New York: Whitebird (Putnam), 1993.
This story makes an excellent puppet show, as well as an ideal story to tell aloud. Simple stick puppets will work just fine. Use red and orange tissue paper for fire and blue cellophane for water.

"La cesta magica" (The magic basket). Source: Gasset, Angeles. "La cesta magica." In Bravo-Villasante, Carmen. *Antologia de la literatura infantil en lengua española.* Vol. 2 Madrid: Editorial Doncel, 1973: 439–449.
A more ambitious puppet show. A gentleman with a feather in his hat finds a magic basket full of money. When you pull out a bill, another appears in it's place. Pelos takes the basket for Panchita, his wife, who wants a basket for shopping. The gentleman then schemes to get the basket back.

"Coyote Rings the Wrong Bell." Source: Mora, Francisco X. *Coyote Rings the Wrong Bell: A Mexican Folktale.* Chicago: Children's Press, 1991.
Coyote gets tricked by Rabbit. Rabbit avoids being eaten by Coyote by telling him that he can have all the tender, juicy young rabbits he wants by ringing a bell in a tree. When shakes the tree in an attempt to ring the bell, he is attacked by a swarm of bees.

"La Gran fiesta de la primavera" (The great spring festival). Source: Mora, Francisco X. *La Gran fiesta.* Fort Atkinson, Wis.: Highsmith Press, 1993.
Crow shows his bird friends how to celebrate spring by decorating a tree. This show can be adapted to take place during winter as well.

"The Hummingbird's Gift." Source: Czernecki, Stefan, and Timothy Rhodes. *The Hummingbird's Gift.* Illus. Stefan Czernecki: straw weavings by Juliana Reyes de Silva and Juan Hilario Silva. New York: Hyperion, 1994.
When Consuelo saves the hummingbirds' lives they, in return, show her how to save her family from the drought. This is a possibility for a *Día de los Muertos* program because Consuelo is inspired to sell her woven figures for that holiday.

CREATIVE DRAMATIZATION

One of the most effective ways of sharing folktales is through creative dramatization. Any of the tales I have mentioned would probably lend themselves well to dramatic treatment. Children can enjoy being Martina and her suitors or the Rooster.

In an after school program I shared a number of tales with a group of middle school students who had newly immigrated to this country. I asked them to choose their favorite to dramatize. They picked Pedro. Together, we wrote a script and put on the production, complete with costumes, for an appreciative audience of parents and friends. The script we used begins on page 77, followed by the English on page 81. If time to memorize lines is a problem, have the children carry the scripts. We did our production twice, once in Spanish, and then again in English. Since these children knew little English, it was a challenge, but one that they enjoyed.

Señor Conejo, Señor Coyote, y el Espantapajaros
(Mr. Rabbit, Mr. Coyote, and the Scarecrow)

CAST:
  COYOTE WITH VELCRO
  RABBIT WITH VELCRO
  FARMER
  MONO (SCARECROW WITH VELCRO)
  SUN/MOON
  NARRATOR (Use a puppet of your choice.)
PROPS:
  CORN PLANT
  RAKE
  HOE
  WATERING CAN
  SLIP WHISTLE
  MUSIC
  TURKEY BASTER WITH WATER
  BLUE BACKDROP
  THE END/EL FIN SIGN

NARRATOR: (*Welcomes audience*) In Mexican folktales the conejo (rabbit) and the coyote are favorite characters. Señor Conejo is known as the trickster who lives by his wits and Señor Coyote is always very greedy and hungry. So please join us for (give title of show).

FARMER: (*Enters whistling and holding rake/watering can*)
  Oh what a beautiful day for gardening! I think I'll plant some corn. (*Scratches around with rake and whistles; uses watering can.*) There, I'm finished; now we'll let Mother Nature take her course. (*Farmer exits; play music and pass moon and sun overhead a few times.*) (*Use slide whistle and push corn plant up slowly.*)

FARMER: Oh look at the beautiful corn; I think I'll let it ripen one more day and then come back and pick it for my dinner. (*Farmer exits.*)

RABBIT: Hola! What a beautiful garden and I'm hungry. (*Looks around and hams it up; eventually steals corn plant and gleefully leaves.*) (*Pass moon and sun once.*)

FARMER: (*Whistling*) How is my corn today? My mouth is watering for a corn on the cob dinner. Mmmmmm. (*Sees corn is missing and has a fit; looks everywhere; asks audience if they saw anyone.*) What should I do? I think I will replant it and put a scarecrow by it to protect it. (*Sets to work. First he hoes then he waters. For a good effect at this point squirt audience with turkey baster. He then sets out the mono (scarecrow) and leaves.*) (*Turn on music and pass moon/sun over set several times. Then use slip whistle and slowly bring up the corn.*)

RABBIT: Boy, am I hungry. I'd like some more of that corn! (*Bumps into mono.*) Hey, get out of my way!

(*Mono doesn't move.*) Didn't you hear me? Let me pass! (*Mono doesn't move; rabbit pushes doll with paw and gets stuck.*) Aiee, let go of me! (*Gets other paw stuck; milk this for all it's worth: ask audience for help.*)

FARMER: (*Enters whistling*) Hm! What do we have here? Mmm a tasty rabbit. I think I'll go home and start the pot of water boiling for my favorite dish, corn and and rabbit stew. (*Exits*)

RABBIT: (*Pleads with audience*) Help me get unstuck; do you think the farmer will really boil me into a stew??? (*Pass moon and sun over the stage once.*)

Next day . . . .

COYOTE: Hmm, what do we have here? (*Whispers to audience*) Tasty young rabbit for my dinner. (*To rabbit*) Señor Rabbit, what are you doing stuck up there?

RABBIT: Señor Coyote, I stole some corn from the farmer and for my punishment he tied me to this mono so that I would not run away. He said he's coming back to take me down and put me in his chicken house. He wants to lock me in there with all of those chickens. I hate chickens.

COYOTE: Hmmm! Did you say chicken house? (*To audience*) I love juicy little chickens (*slurp, drool, etc.*). Señor Conejo, I am always ready to do a favor for a friend. Let me change places with you.

RABBIT: Are you sure you wouldn't mind??? It's hot and noisy and crowded in that chicken house.

COYOTE: Anything for a friend. Here, let me help you down. (*Unsnap velcro*)

RABBIT: Thank you; I am most grateful. Here, let me help you up. (*Snap velcro*) There, are you all right???

COYOTE: Couldn't be better.

(*Rabbit runs off chanting*) Nyah, nyah, nyah, nyah, nyah!!!!

FARMER: My cooking pot is boiling and I'm ready to fix that corn and rabbit stew. Mm, Mm, Mm, I'm hungry.

(*Rabbit peaks up from behind the curtain and repeats*) Nyah, nyah, nyah nyah, nyahll!

(Hold up the end/El fin sign)

The following adaptation of Perez and Martina is very versatile. You can adapt the show by using whatever animal puppets you have on hand as Martina's suitors.

Perez y Martina

CHARACTERS:
    MARTINA A COCKROACH
    PEREZ THE MOUSE
    SEÑOR BORREGA (Sheep)
    SEÑOR ABEJA (Bee)
    SEÑOR PATO (Duck)
    SEÑOR SAPO (Frog)
PROPS:
    BROOM
    COOKING POT
    SUN
    MOON
    BLACK/WHITE MANTILLA OR SCARF
    POWDER PUFF
    MUSIC, WEDDING & FLAMENCO
    CHAIR
    ROSES
    CONFETTI
    PESETA

SCENE 1
(*Blue backdrop, roses, chair. Martina enters with broom, scarf over her head.*)

MARTINA: Que hermoso día! Me encanta tener my casita y jardín en orden y limpio. ¡Hm! ¿Que es esto? Una peseta brillosa. Debe ser mi día con suerte. ¿Que haré, la guardo o la gasto? Ya, ya me ejite. Gasto la peseta, si, iré a comprar polvo y una mantilla. (*Martina exits. Play flamenco music. She reenters wearing black mantilla and poofing herself with powder puff. She dances to the music.*) Mmmm ahora con esta fragancia y la mantilla nueva, me siento hermosa (*sigh*). Cuando vendrá el guapisimo Señor Perez, el Ratón? (*Martina sits in the white chair, music off.*)

BORREGA: Good day Señorita Martina. You're so pretty.

MARTINA: Gracias Señor Borrega.

BORREGA: Will you ma-a-a-arry me?

MARTINA: Oh, quizás, si me dices como me hablarás en el futuro.

BORREGA: Así: ¡Baaaaaaaaaaaaaa!

MARTINA: ¡No, no, Basta! ¿Ha visto al Señor Perez, el Ratoncito? El es un caballero.

(*Señor Borrega leaves crying and whining.*)

(*Music on, Martina dances until snake enters, music off*)

ABEJA: Good day, Señorita Martina.

MARTINA: Buenos dias Señor Abeja.

ABEJA: ZZZZZZZZZZZZZZZZZZ Will you marry me? ZZZZZZZZZZZZ

MARTINA: Oh, quizás, si me dices como me hablarás en el futuro.

ABEJA: zzzzzzzzzzzzzzzzzzzzzzzzzzzzzzzzzzzzzzzzzzzzzzzzzz

MARTINA: ¡Basta basta! No Señor Abeja. Lárgate de aquí.

(Bee buzzes off)

MARTINA: Nadie, nadie se compara al gran galán, Señor Perez.

MARTINA: Aye, aye, aye, aye (To the tune of Cielito Lindo) ¿Donde esta el guapisimo Señor Perez y cuando vendrá a visitarme?

(*Señor Sapo hops in noisily.*)

SAPO: Y yo? Will you marry me?

MARTINA: Tal vez si me dices como me hablarás en el futuro.

SAPO: Borom, borom, borom . . . . (*and hops all over the place.*)

MARTINA : No, no, no me casaré con usted. No me gusta su voz, y ademas, he oido decir que ustedes, los sapos, hablan constantemente día y noche.

(*Señor Sapo hops away loud and fast.*)

MARTINA: ¿O mi estimado Perez, cuando vendrá? Se hace tarde, tal vez es mejor ir a la cocina y preparar una sopa para la cena. (*Martina begins to exit just as singing is heard offstage.*) Aye, parece que escucho al Señor Perez, vale ir a ponerme chevere. (*Martina rushes off and returns with the powder puff.*) Uuu, uuu, debo verme hermosa para mi guapisimo Señor Perez. (*turns to the audience*) ¿Me miro bonita?

(*Perez enters singing to a tune.*)

PEREZ: Un ratoncito soy. A handsome mouse am I.

MARTINA: Oh Señor Perez, su canción mueve mi corazón.

PEREZ: ¡Gracias Señorita Martina! For sometime now, I've wanted to ask you something. Will you marry me?

MARTINA: Oh quizás si me dice como me hablarás en el futuro.

PEREZ: Certainly, I shall read to you, and sing like this: Chui, Chui, Chui, Chui. . . .

PEREZ and MARTINA: ¡Vamos a la recepcion! To the reception! (*Puppeteers say or hold up sign saying* "and they lived happily ever after/Viveron feliz para siempre." EL FIN.)

Marinerito Juan Trombón

Adapted from the Puppet Show by Elsa Lira Gaiero

CHARACTERS:
JUAN TROMBÓN
CAPTAIN TORNADO

PROPS:
BROOM
CAPTAIN'S CAP

JUAN: (*Appears singing and dancing*)
Juan Trombón,
Juan Trombón
Marinerito,
Juan Trombón
I sail the seven seas
In my little cardboard boat

CAPTAIN: (*From inside*) ¡Juan Trombón!

JUAN: Presente, Capitán Tornado.

CAPTAIN: What were you doing, Juan Trombón?

JUAN: Cantaba, Capitán Tornado.

CAPTAIN: You weren't cleaning the boat as I ordered you?

JUAN: No, Capitán Tornado.

CAPTAIN: (*Furious*) And what were you waiting for?

JUAN: (*Trembling*) Que usted me viera, Capitán Tornado.

CAPTAIN: You don't need to wait for me. Now get to it. ¡Pues, rápido! Scrub down the deck! Sweep, wash, dust, clean pronto! ¡Pronto!

(*While the Captain shouts, Juan Trombón runs around like a madman doing everything the Captain orders. Finally, when the Captain finishes his tirade, Juan leans over the side of the puppet stage breathing heavily.*)

CAPTAIN: ¡Juan Trombón!

JUAN: (*Back up at attention*) ¡Presente, Capitán Tornado!

CAPTAIN: ¡Rápido! ¡Siga lavando, fregando, barriendo! (*Juan Trombón begins to clean again, but after a moment falls over the side of the stage, heaving.*) ¡Juan Trombón!

JUAN: (*Trying to catch his breath*) ¡Presente, Capitán Tornado!

CAPTAIN: Scrub the deck, clean the windows, fold the sails, raise the anchor, recoja las cuerdas, sweep the cabin, cook the food, mend the clothes. (*Juan runs about again, doing everything the Captain orders, then leans over the side of the stage, exhausted.*)

CAPTAIN: Es usted un desobediente, Juan Trombón, I will punish you as you deserve . . . .(*The furious Captain drops his cap, which he has been holding. Juan Trombón picks it up.*)

CAPTAIN: Give me back my cap, Juan Trombón!

JUAN: Pues, no, señor, ahora soy yo el Capitán y puedo mandar.

CAPTAIN: (*Crying*) Tiene razón. Whoever has the cap is captain of the ship. ¡Ay mi gorra! Now I am no longer Captain. ¡Ay, ay!

JUAN: ¡Marinero Juan Tornado!

CAPTAIN: Presente, Capitán Trombón.

JUAN: Más firme, Marinero Tornado. !Mas derecho! Lift up your head, straighten those shoulders, suck in that gut. March now. Uno dos, uno dos, uno dos, left, right, left right, left, right. (*The Captain marches back and forth*). Now scrub the deck, clean the windows, fold the sails, raise the anchor, recoja las cuerdas, sweep the cabin, cook the food, mend the clothes! (*While the Captain is working, Juan Trombón begins to sing as he did in the beginning.*)
Juan Trombón,
Juan Trombón
Marinerito,
Juan Trombón
nevega por los mares
en su barco de cartón.

Pedro de Ordimalas

Escena 1

NARRADOR: Había una vez hace mucho tiempo, tanto tiempo que casi olvido que vivía un hombre llamado Pedro de Ordimalas.

PEDRO: Voy al casino. Tal vez hoy gane suficiente dinero para traer algo de comida a casa para ti y el bebé.

ESPOSA DE PEDRO: ¡Oh!, Pedro. Tu me tratas bien, mejor de lo normal, aunque los juegos en el casino son tu único vicio. Pareces un bribón. ¿Porque no podemos vivir honestamente? Teníamos dinero, pero ya no. Lo has perdido todo.

PEDRO: Dame una oportunidad. Estoy seguro que hoy será me día de suerte.

NARRADOR: En Éste día El Señor y San Pedro decidieron disfrazarse y venir a la tierra a ver que tan caritativa y bondadosa es la gente.

SEÑOR: Apiádense de Éste pordiosero. ¿Buen hombre, una limosna por favor?

PEDRO: No tengo dinero, pero espérame aquí y consigueré algo para ti.

NARRADOR: Pedro corrió hacia el casino y pidió a sus amigos que le prestaran cincuenta centavos. Ellos no le querían prestar nada, porque pensaron que el los utilizaría para darlos de limosna. Pedro insistió hasta convencerlos que no sería así, y prometió que se los devolvería tan pronto como pudiera. Entonces Pedro corrió hacia los dos pordioseros y les dio el dinero.

SEÑOR: Pedro, por haberte apiadado de los pobres he decidido gratificarte concediéndote un deseo.

PEDRO: Todo lo que quiero es mi cincuenta centavos. De otra manera mis amigos no confiarán nunca mas en mi.

SEÑOR: (En tono sarcástico) No, eso no es suficiente para alguien tan bondadoso y de buen corazón como tú, quien ha tenido que pedir a sus amigos algo para ayudar a los pobres. Pide algo más.

PEDRO: Bien. Una cosa que me gustaría mucho es que cuando vaya a un lugar y no quiero dejarlo, ni siguiera Dios todo poderoso puede hacerme abandonarlo.

SEÑOR: Eso no es suficiente. ¿No deseas algo mas?

PEDRO: Bien. . . . (*Sus ojos brillaron*) ¿Me podrías dar un paquete de cartas mágicas?

SEÑOR: Muy bien, pide algo mas.

PEDRO: Biiiieeeen . . . .Hmmmm . . . algo que siempre he querido es un tambor. Pero no un tambor común y corriente sino uno mágico. En el cual que se siente a tocar Éste tambor no puede pararse sin mi permiso. Y de la misma forma, ¿Porque no te haces cargo de toda mi familia, ellos no tienen porque sufrir nunca más. Ahora que soy tan pobre no puedo soportarlos como se les merecen.

SEÑOR: ¿Algo más Pedro? A pesar de tu renuencia creo que tienes anhelos en la vida.

PEDRO: Está bien. Cuando yo muera, prométeme que tomarás mi cuerpo y mi alma. ¡De esta forma no moriré!

SEÑOR: Te concederé todo cuanto has pedido. (A un lado a San Pedro). Hay que ver como el granuja de Pedro hace uso de sus nuevos dones.

NARRADOR: Desde entonces, Pedro siempre ganó con sus cartas mágicas. Creció rico pero desatendió a su familia, quienes eventualmente crecieron enfermos y murieron. Pedro estaba solo, aunque no realmente. Tenia caudales de dinero para mantenerse acompañado.

PEDRO: Tengo tanto dinero. No se que hacer, ya que no tengo familia.

Escena 2
NARRADOR: Una noche, después de haber transcurrido varios años, Pedro escucho pasos de alguien que se acercaba y entonces tocó a la puerta.

PEDRO: ¿Quien es?

LA MUERTE 1: La muerte, he venido a llevarte conmigo.

PEDRO: Si iré, pero primero me gustaría que te sentaras aquí a tocar mi tambor. Cuando la gente pobre lo escuche vendrá, y entonces les daré toda mi riqueza. Después me podrás llevar.

NARRADOR: Una vez que La Muerte se sentó a tocar el tambor, descubrió que no se podía parar.

MUERTE 1: ¡Me has engañado, no me puedo parar!

PEDRO: Me voy al casino.

NARRADOR: Pedro regresó ocho días mas tarde.

MUERTE 1: ¿Pedro, que vas a hacer conmigo?

PEDRO: Te dejaré ir, solo si prometes darme el doble de años de vida que me quedan.

MUERTE 1: Te concederé el deseo, todo lo que quiero es liberarme de Éste tambor mágico.

NARRADOR: La Muerte fue a reportar lo que sucedido al Señor.

MUERTE 1: Es imposible traer a Pedro.

SEÑOR: Enviare a la Muerte que carga la guadaña.

NARRADOR: Otra vez una noche, Pedro escucho pasos acercarse y de pronto a alguien que tocaba a la puerta.

PEDRO: ¿Quien es?

MUERTE 2: Soy la Muerte que carga una guadaña. He venido a llevarte conmigo.

PEDRO: Si iré, pero primero me gustaría que te sentaras aquí a tocar mi tambor. Cuando la gente pobre lo escuche vendrá y entonces les daré toda mi riqueza. Después tu podrás llevarme.

NARRADOR: Una vez que La Muerte que carga la guadaña se sentó a tocar el tambor, descubrió que no se podía parar.

MUERTE 2: ¡Me has engañado, no me puedo parar!

PEDRO: Ahora me voy al casino.

NARRADOR: Pedro regresó ocho días mas tarde.

MUERTE 2: ¿Pedro, que vas a hacer conmigo?

PEDRO: Te dejaré ir solo si prometes darme el doble de años de vida que me quedan.

MUERTE 2: Te concederé el deseo, todo lo que quiero es liberarme de Éste tambor mágico.

NARRADOR: La Muerte que carga la guadaña fue a reportar lo sucedido al Señor.

MUERTE 1: Es imposible traer a Pedro.

SEÑOR: Como te pudo hacer tonto, igual que la Muerte 1. Enviare a La Muerte del carruaje que lleva un arco y una flecha.

NARRADOR: Esta vez era mediodía. Pedro no solo escucho pasos, sino también el terrible galopar de los caballos tirando el carruaje de la muerte, Pedro salió a recibirla.

MUERTE 3: Yo soy la Muerte del carruaje que carga un arco y una flecha. He venido a llevarte conmigo. Cierra tus ojos.

NARRADOR: Pedro cerró los ojos sin pensarlo, y antes de que los pudiera abrir fue muy tarde. Sintió que la flecha de la muerte lo atravesó, y enfrente de el dijo las llamas del infierno. La muerte finalmente se llevó a Pedro de Ordimalas.

Escena 3

NARRADOR: Pedro llego al infierno en vísperas de la celebración de la fiesta anual. Los diablos del infierno le encomendaron cuidar de la leña. Mientras Éste la juntó, Pedro también recolectó un tarro de goma de árbol. El día de la fiesta lo enviaron a arreglar las sillas, y conforme las acomodaba les ponía goma. Los diablos llegaron y se sentaron, y justo cuando se preparaban a comer Pedro dijo . . . .

PEDRO: Momento, no podemos empezar a comer sin antes dar gracias a Dios.

DIABLOS: ¡No! ¡No menciones ese nombre!

PEDRO: Santo, Santo, Santo es el Señor Dios.

NARRADOR: Aquellas palabras infundieron pánico en el infierno. Los diablos aterrorizados intentaron correr pero ellos estaban pegados a sus sillas. Se tropezaban unos con otros en su afán por liberarse. La puerta estaba cerrada de tal manera que algunos aun pegados a sus sillas lograron saltar por la ventana. Entre mas fuerte cantaba Pedro mas consternación y pánico causaba.

PEDRO: Santa María, ¡Madre de Dios!

NARRADOR: Finalmente, uno de los diablos se escapó y fue a quejarse con San Pedro.

DIABLO: Pedro nos esta volviendo locos a todos allá en el infierno. ¿Porque no te lo traes?

SAN PEDRO: Lo reportaré. (*Y Éste fue al Señor*) Los diablos en el infierno no pueden soportar a Pedro de Ordimalas.

SEÑOR: Ya sabía de el, y he tenido suficiente de ese bribón.

NARRADOR: De tal forma que San Pedro, escoltando a Pedro lo trajo ante la presencia del Señor.

SEÑOR: Quizás si te enviamos lejos a cuidar ovejas ya no te meterás en tantos líos.

PEDRO: Pero Señor, no me iré. Recuerdas que uno de los deseos que me concediste consiste en que si yo no quiero abandonar un lugar ni siquiera Dios Padre pueda obligarme.

SEÑOR: Engañaste a dos de mis mejores muertes. Burlaste a los diablos mas diablos del infierno. Pero no conseguirás burlarte de mi. Permanecerás en la gloria pero lo harás en forma de piedra.

PEDRO: Si, Señor, pero al menos seré una roca con ojos.

Pedro of Ordimalas

Scene 1

NARRATOR: A long time ago, so long that it has almost been lost in the memory, there lived a man named Pedro de Ordimalas.

PEDRO: I'm going to the casino. Perhaps today I will win enough to bring some food home for you and the baby.

PEDRO'S WIFE: Oh Pedro. You treat me well, better than most, but the casino is your one vice. You are something of a rascal when it comes to that. Why is it that we cannot eat honestly? There used to be money but now there is none, you have squandered it all away.

PEDRO: Give me a chance, I'm sure today will be my lucky day.

NARRATOR: That very day the Lord and Saint Peter disguised themselves and came to earth to see who the charitable people were.

LORD: Alms for a poor crippled man. Good sir, can you spare any money?

PEDRO: I have none, but wait right here and I'll get something for you.

NARRATOR: Pedro ran back to the casino and asked his friends for fifty cents. They didn't want to give it to him because they thought he would give it to charity. He managed to convince them that he would not, and promised that he would return quickly. Pedro ran to the two beggars and gave his money to them.

LORD: Pedro, for having felt sorry for the poor I am prepared to grant you any wish.

PEDRO: All I want is my fifty cents back. Otherwise my friends won't believe me.

LORD: (*with a hint of sarcasm*) No, that is certainly not enough for someone as kind and bighearted as you, who would borrow from his friends in order to give to the poor. Ask for something more.

PEDRO: Well, one thing I would like a lot is that if I am in a place and I don't want to leave, not even God Almighty could make me go.

LORD: That is nothing. Don't you want anything more?

PEDRO: Well. . . . (*His eyes brighten*) Could I have a magical deck of cards?

LORD: Very well, ask for more.

PEDRO: Weeelll . . . .Uh . . . Something I've always wanted is a drum. Not just an ordinary drum, but a magical drum. Whoever sits down to play this drum won't be able to get up without my permission. And, by the way, why don't you take all my family. They don't need to suffer anymore. Now that I'm so poor, I haven't been able to support them very well.

LORD: Anything else, Pedro? Despite your reluctance you appear to have no lack of desires.

PEDRO: Okay. When I die, promise that you will take both my body and my soul. That way I won't die!

LORD: I will give you all that you have requested. (*aside to Saint Peter*) We shall see just how this rascal Pedro makes use of his new found riches.

NARRATOR: From then on, Pedro always won with his new deck of cards. He grew rich, but neglected his family, who all eventually grew sick and died. Pedro was alone, but not really. He had plenty of money to keep him company.

PEDRO: I have too much money. I don't know what to do with it all, now that I have no family.

Scene 2

NARRATOR: One night, many years later, Pedro heard footsteps, and then a knock at the door.

PEDRO: Who is it?

DEATH 1: Death. I have come to take you with me.

PEDRO: I will come, but first I would like you to sit here and play my drum. When the poor people hear it they will come and I will give them all my wealth. Then you may take me.

NARRATOR: When Death sat down at the drum she discovered that she couldn't move.

DEATH 1: You've tricked me, I can't move.

PEDRO: I'm off to the casino.

NARRATOR: Eight days later, Pedro returned.

DEATH 1: Pedro, what are you going to do with me?

PEDRO: I will only let you go if you promise to double the years of life left to me.

DEATH 1: I will grant your wish, all I want is to be free of this magic drum.

NARRATOR: Death went back to the Lord to make a report.

DEATH 1: It is impossible to bring Pedro.

LORD: I will send the Death that carries the scythe.

NARRATOR: Again one night, Pedro heard footsteps, and then a knock at the door.

PEDRO: Who is it?

DEATH 2: I am the Death who carries a scythe. I have come to take you with me.

PEDRO: I will come, but first I would like you to sit here and play my drum. When the poor people hear it they will come and I will give them all my wealth. Then you may take me.

NARRATOR: When the Death who carries a scythe sat down at the drum, she discovered that she couldn't move.

DEATH 2: You've tricked me, I can't move!

PEDRO: I'm off to the casino.

NARRATOR: Eight days later, Pedro returned.

DEATH 2: Pedro, what are you going to do with me?

PEDRO: I will only let you go if you promise to double the years of life left to me.

DEATH 2: I will grant your wish, all I want is to be free of this magic drum.

NARRATOR: The Death who carries a scythe went back to the Lord to make a report.

DEATH 2: It is impossible to bring Pedro.

LORD: How could you let yourself be fooled just like the first death? I will send the Death that rides a cart and carries a bow and arrow.

NARRATOR: This time it was midday. Pedro heard not only footsteps, but also the terrible creaking of Death's cart. Instead of waiting for her to knock, he went out to greet her.

DEATH 3: I am the Death who rides a cart and carries a bow and arrow. I have come to take you with me. Close your eyes.

NARRATOR: Pedro closed his eyes without thinking, and before he could open them it was too late. He felt the arrow of death pass through him, and in front of him he saw the flames of hell. Death had finally gotten the best of Pedro de Ordimalas.

Scene 3
NARRATOR: Pedro arrived in hell just in time for the annual *fiesta*. The devils put him in charge of the firewood. As he gathered it, he also collected a jar full of sticky pitch. On the day of the party they sent

him to arrange the chairs. As he set each chair, he put a lump of pitch on the seat. The devils came and took their places, and were just about ready to eat when Pedro said . . . .

PEDRO: We can't eat until we've said grace.

DEVILS: NO! Don't say His name!

PEDRO: Holy, holy, holy is the Lord God.

NARRATOR: The words spread panic throughout hell. The devils tried to jump up to escape but they were stuck to their chairs. They bumped and stumbled into each other in their mad dash to get out. The door was locked so some jumped out the windows. The more consternation and panic Pedro caused, the louder he sang.

PEDRO: Holy Mary, Mother of God!

NARRATOR: Finally, one devil escaped and went to complain to Saint Peter.

DEVIL: Pedro is driving us all crazy down there. Why don't you take him?

SAINT PETER: I will report it. (*He goes to the Lord*) The devils in hell can't stand Pedro de Ordimalas.

LORD: Have him brought before me. I have had enough of that rascal.

NARRATOR: So, Saint Peter had Pedro escorted into the presence of the Lord.

LORD: Perhaps if we sent you far away to tend sheep you would not get into so much trouble.

PEDRO: But Lord, I will not leave. Don't you remember that one of the gifts you gave me clearly states that if I don't want to leave a place, not even God the Father can make me.

LORD: You got the best of two of my deaths. You got the best of the devils in hell. But you will not get the best of me. You will remain in the glory, but you will do so as a rock.

PEDRO: Yes, Lord, but at least I will be a rock with eyes.

FOLK RHYMES AND *DICHOS*

The heritage of folk rhymes in Spanish is one that must be preserved for all children. Hearing these rhymes read aloud gives them a new appreciation of the beauty of the Spanish language. Some of these rhymes are virtually untranslatable because they depend so much on the sound of the Spanish cadences and rhymes. Some of them have English Mother Goose equivalents, such as "This little piggy went to market," which in Spanish becomes "*Éste niño compró un huevito*" (This child bought a little egg). Others are completely original.

All of these rhymes provide an excellent way to remind Latino children who are becoming more and more English dominant of the sounds of their mother tongue. Some of these have even been collected from Latino library patrons. As you do programs with Latino families you can be your own folklorist and gather new rhymes and riddles from your adult patrons that they may have learned as children. I've divided the rhymes into categories. First are rhymes that are used to begin a story, then rhymes to end a story. Following these are fingerplays, Spanish equivalents to Mother Goose rhymes, songs and games, nonsense and miscellaneous rhymes, goodnight rhymes, tongue twisters, and finally riddles.

TO BEGIN A STORY

El cuento
¿Quieres que te cuente un cuento?
Dime que si
y te lo contaré
dime que no
y no te lo diré.

The Story
Do you want me to tell you a story?
Say yes
And I'll tell you one
Say no
And I won't.

Otro cuento
¿Quieres que te cuente un cuento?
El burro está contento
¿Quieres que te cuente otra vez?
El burro está al revés.

Another Story
Do you want me to tell you a story?
The burro is contented
Do you want me to tell it to you again?
The burro is backwards.

Esto es verdad
Esto es verdad
y no me miento,
como me lo contaron
te lo cuento.

It's the Truth
It's the truth
And I'm not lying
As it was told to me
I am telling it to you.

TO END A STORY

Voy por un caminito
Y voy por un caminito,
y voy por otro,
y si éste cuento les gusto
mañana les cuento otro.

I Go on One Path
I go on one path
and go on another,
And if you liked this story
Tomorrow I'll tell you another.

El fin del cuento
Se acabo el cuento
y se lo llevó el viento
se fue . . . por el mar adentro.

The Story Is Over
The story is over
The wind carried it away
It's gone beneath the ocean.

Colorín colorado
Y colorín colorado
Éste cuento se ha acabado,
y pasó por un zapato roto
para que mañana te cuente otro.

Colorín Colorado
Colorín colorado
This story is over,
It passed by a broken shoe
So that tomorrow I can tell you another.

El cuento se acabo
Y el cuento se acabó
cuando lo vuelva
a encontrar
se lo volveré a contar.

The Story Is Over
And the story is over
When I meet you again
I'll tell it to you again.

FINGERPLAYS

The following are Spanish takes on "This little piggy went to market."

Hallando un huevo
Éste niño halló un huevo; (*hold up little finger*)
Éste lo coció; (*hold up ring finger*)
Éste lo peló; (*hold up middle finger*)
Éste le hecho la sal; (*hold up index finger*)
Éste gordo chaparrito se lo comió. (*hold up thumb*)

Le dio sed,
Y se fue a buscar agua . . . ,
Buscó y buscó . . . , (*Use fingers to look for water at elbow, then shoulder*)
¡Y aquí halló!
Y tomó y tomó y tomó . . . (*Tickle under the arm*)

Los niños traviesos
-Éste pide pan (*hold up thumb*)
-Éste dice: no lo hay (*hold up index finger*)
-Éste dice: ¿Que haremos? (*hold up middle finger*)
-Éste dice: ¡Lo robaremos! (*hold up ring finger*)
-Éste dice: ¡No, no, que nos castigara nuestro mamá! (*hold up little finger*)

Este, chiquitito y bonito
Este, chiquito y bonito, (*hold up little finger*)
éste, el rey de los anillitos, (*hold up ring finger*)
éste, tonto y loco, (*hold up middle finger*)
éste, se marcha a la escuela, (*hold up index finger*)
y éste, se lo come todo. (*hold up thumb*)

Finding an Egg
This little boy found an egg;
This one cooked it;
This one peeled it;
This one salted it;
This fat little one ate it.

It made him thirsty,
And he went to look for water…
He looked and looked…
And here he found it!
And drank and drank and drank…

The Mischevious Children
This one asks for bread.
This one says there is none.
This one asks "What shall we do?"
This one says "We'll rob some."
This one says "No, no, our mother will punish us!"

This One Pretty and Small
This one, pretty and small
This one, king of the rings
This one, silly and foolish
This one, goes to school
And this one, eats everything up.

Here are some other fingerplays.

Con los manos
Con los manos (*hold up both hands*)
aplaudo, aplaudo, aplaudo (*clap three times*).
Y ahora las pongo
En mi repaso. (*put both hands in your lap*)

With My Hands
With my hands
I clap, clap, clap.
And now I put them
In my lap.

La hormiguita
Andaba la hormiguita (*walk fingers up and down arm*)
juntando su comidita
le coge un aguacerito
¡Que corre pa' su casita! (*run fingers quickly down to hand*)
y se metió en su covachita. (*cup one hand around the other*)

The Ant
The little ant walked
Carrying her food
She gets caught in a rainstorm
How she runs to her little house!
And goes into her little hole.

El ratoncito
Poy ahí viene un ratoncito
que le cayó un aguacerito
y corriendo, corriendito (*run fingers up arm*)
se metió en un agujerito. (*end in the ear*)

The Little Mouse
There comes a little mouse
Caught by the rain
And runs
Into a hole.

Cinco lobitos
Cinco lobitos (*hold up five fingers*)
tiene la loba,
cinco lobitos
detrás de la escoba. (*make a sweeping motion with the hand*)
A los cinco los parió
y a los cinco los crió
y a los cinco lobitos
leche les dio.

Five Baby Wolves
Five baby wolves
Have their mother,
Five baby wolves behind the broom.
To the five she gave birth,
She raised them
And gave them milk to drink.

Los lobitos
Cinco lobitos, (*hold up five fingers to represent the five little wolves*)
tiene la loba,
blancos y negros
detrás de la toba
Uno le canta (*hold up one finger*)
todo el día
y otros le tocan (*hold up four fingers*)
la sinfonía.

The Baby Wolves
Five baby wolves
have their mother.
They are black and white
behind the tuba.
One sings
all day,
And the others play
a symphony.

Chocolate
Chocolate,
molinillo, (*move hand in a circle as if you are grinding chocolate*)
corre, corre, (*move hand as if it is running away*)
que te pillo. (*wag finger of your other hand at the "bad" hand*)

Rima de chocolate
Uno, dos, tres, cho- (*Count with the fingers for each line*)
Uno, dos, tres, -co-
Uno, dos, tres, -la-
Uno, dos, tres, -te-
Bate, bate chocolate. (*Use one arm to make a big bowl, and use the other hand to beat the chocolate*)

La gallinita napolitana
La gallinita napolitana
Pone un huevo cada semana (*hold up one finger*)
pone dos, (*hold up two fingers*)
pone tres, (*hold up three fingers*)
Ponce cuatro, (*hold up four fingers*)
pone cinco, (*hold up five fingers*)
pone seis, (*hold up six fingers*)
¡Pone siete a la semana! (*hold up seven fingers*)
pone ocho, (*hold up eight fingers*)
pone nueve, (*hold up nine fingers*)
pone diez, (*hold up ten fingers*)
la gallinita, ya lo ves,
quiere que escondas tus pies. (*cover your feet with your hands*)

Una gallina en un arado
Una gallina en un arado
puso un huevo colorado
puso uno (*hold up one finger*)
puso dos (*hold up two fingers*)
puso tres (*hold up three fingers*)
puso quatro (*hold up four fingers*)
puso cinco (*hold up five fingers*)
puso seis (*hold up six fingers*)
puso siete (*hold up seven fingers*)
puso ocho (*hold up eight fingers*)

Chocolate
Chocolate
grinder,
run, run
you are naughty.

Chocolate Rhyme
One, two, three, CHO.
One, two three, CO.
One, two three. LA,
One, two, three, TE
Beat the, beat the, beat the chocolate.

The Napolitan Hen
The Napolitan hen
Lays one egg a week
Lays two
Lays three
Lays four
Lays five
Lays six
Lays seven in the week!
Lays eight
Lays nine
Lays ten
The hen, now you see,
Wants you to hide your feet.

The Hen on a Plow
The hen on a plow
laid a colored egg,
laid one,
laid two,
laid three,
laid four,
laid five,
laid six,
laid seven,
laid eight,

puso nueve (*hold up nine fingers*)
puso diez (*hold up ten fingers*)
puso Puaff!! (*close hands, then open them quickly*)
La Luna.

laid nine,
laid ten
laid Puaff!
The Moon.

Cinco pollitos
Cinco pollitos (*hold up five fingers*)
tiene mi tía uno le canta, (*hold up one finger*)
otro le pía (*hold up two fingers*)
y tres le tocan la chirimía. (*hold up
    three fingers*)

Five Chicks
Five chicks
has my aunt
one sings
another cries
and three play the flute.

Pinguino
Pin-uno, pin-dos, pin-tres (*hold up fingers for each
    number*)
pin-cuatro, pin-cinco, pin-seis,
pin-siete, pin-ocho, pingüino! (*wiggle all eight fin-
    gers on "pingüino"*)

Penguin
Pin-one, pin-two, pin-three,
pin-four, pin-five, pin-six,
pin-seven, pin-eight, penguin!

Los pescaditos
Los pescaditos andan en el agua
nadan, nadan, nadan (*move hands apart in a slow
    swimming motion*)
Vuelan, vuelan, vuelan (*stretch out arms on either
    side, and make a flying motion*)
Son chiquititos, son chiquititos (*put thumb and fin-
    ger close together to indicate something small*)
Vuelan, vuelan, vuelan (*swimming motion again*)
Nadan, nadan, nadan. (*flying motion again*)

The Little Fish
The little fish swim in the water
They swim, swim, swim
They fly, fly, fly
They are little, they are little
They fly, fly, fly
They swim, swim, swim.

The following are two Spanish equivalents of "patty-cake."

Tortillitas
(*Pat hands throughout, alternating directions of fingers like a tortilla-maker*).
Tortillitas para mamá
Tortillitas para papá
Las quemaditas para mamá
Las bonitas para papá.

Tortillitas, tortillitas,
tortillitas para Papá;
tortillitas para Mama.
Tortillitas de salvado
para papa cuando está enojado;
tortillitas de manteca
para mamá que está contenta.

Papas y papas
Papas y papas para papá,
papas y papas para mamá.
Las quemaditas para papá;
las calientitas para mamá.

La araña
La araña pirulina
por la pared se subió (*make climbing motions with fingers*)
y mi tía, Catalina
con la escoba se barrió. (*make sweeping motions with hands*)

Tengo
Tengo, tengo, tengo (*point to self*)
Tu no tienes nada (*point to someone else*)
Tengo tres ovejas en mi manada (*hold up three fingers*)
Una me da leche (*point to first finger*)
una me da lana (*point to second finger*)
y otra mantequilla (*point to third finger*)
para la semana.

Tortillas
Tortillas for mother
Tortillas for father
The burnt ones for mother
The good ones for father.

Tortillas, tortillas
Tortillas for mother
Tortillas for father
Leftover tortillas
for father when he's angry
Tortillas of butter
So mother is happy.

Potatoes and Potatoes
Potatoes and potatoes for father
potatoes and potatoes for mother
The burnt ones for father
The hot ones for mother.

The Spider
The spider
climbed up the wall
and my Aunt Catalina
brushed it away with a broom.

I Have
I have, I have, I have
You don't have anything
I have three sheep in my flock
One gives me milk
One gives me wool
And the other butter
for the week.

Éste y éste

En la casa de éste y éste (*hold up one finger each time you say "éste"*)
condivadan a éste con éste
y dicen éste y éste
que sino va éste con éste
no irá éste sin éste.

This One and This One

To the house of this one and this one
They invite this one with this one
And this one and this one say
That if this one doesn't go with this one
This one will not go with this one.

Los animalitos

Detrás de doña Pata (*point behind*)
corren los patitos (*make running motion with fingers*)
por allí, por allá, (*point to left and right*)
cuá, cuá, cuá.

The Little Animals

Behind Mrs. Duck
run the ducklings
over here, over there…
quack, quack, quack.

Detrás de doña Gallina (*point behind*)
siguen los pollitos (*make running motion with fingers*)
por allí, por allá, (*point to left and right*)
pío, pío, pa.

Behind Mrs. Hen
follow the little chicks
over here, over there…
cheep, cheep, cheep.

Detrás de doña Cabra (*point behind*)
van las cabritos (*make running motion with fingers*)
por allí, por allá, (*point to left and right*)
baa, baa, baa.

Behind Mrs. Goat
come the the baby goats
over here, over there…
baa, baa, baa.

Abranlas, cierrenlas

Abranlas, ciérrenlas, (*open hands, close hands*)
Abranlas, ciérrenlas, (*open hands, close hands*)
Pla, pla, pla, pla, pla,
Abranlas, ciérrenlas, (*open hands, close hands*)
Abranlas, ciérrenlas, (*open hands, close hands*)
Pónglanlas acá. (*put hands in lap*)

Open Them, Close Them

Open them, close them,
Open them, close them,
Pla, pla, pla, pla, pla,
Open them, close them,
Open them, close them,
Put them here.

A, E, I, O, U

A, e, i, o, u, arbolito de pirú (*Point to a different child for each vowel or syllable*)
dime cuantos años tienes tú. (*The person you land on tells his or her age*)
A, e, i, o u, arbolito de pirú (*Point to different children again*)
dime el nombre que llevas tú. (*The person you land on tells his or her name*)

A, E, I, O, U

A, e, i, o u, little tree of Piru
Tell me your age.
A, e, i, o u, little tree of Piru
Tell me your name.

El pollito asadito

El pollito asadito (*curve fingers of left hand in a loose fist to look like a chicken*)
con su sal y su mojito. (*count fingers, raising them one by one*)
¡Por aquí pasó el pollito! (*surprise children by making chicken fly to your other hand and tickle it*)

Contando y cantando

Uno, dos, tres, cuatro y cinco, (*hold up each finger on one hand*)
Seis, siete, ocho, nueve, y diez. (*hold up each finger on other hand*)
Con esta mano cuento cinco (*hold up first hand*)
Y con la otra hasta diez. (*hold up other hand*)

Al subir una montaña

Al subir una montaña (*make climbing motions with arms*)
una pulga me picó; (*pinch arm*)
la cogí de las narices (*pinch tip of nose*)
y se me escapó. (*make flying motion with fingers*)
Botín, botero, y salió
rosa, clavel, y botón.

Cinco centavos cafes

Cinco centavos cafés en mi bolsa. (*hold up five fingers*)
Éste es para el chicle; (*point to thumb*)
Éste es para un anillo; (*point to index finger*)
Éste es para un tambor; (*point to middle finger*)
Éstos los guardaré en mi bolsa (*point to ring finger*)
Para otra cosa. (*point to little finger*)

¿Cuantos dedos son?

¿Cuantos dedos tengo aquí? (*hold up nine fingers; keep the little finger down*).
(*Children count*)
¡Nueve!
La colita se mueve. (*wiggle the little finger*)

The Roasted Hen

The roasted hen
with its salt and its little cake.
The little chick went this way!

Counting and Singing

One, two, three, four, and five,
six, seven, eight, nine, and ten.
With this hand I count five
With the other up to ten.

While Climbing a Mountain

While climbing a mountain
A flea bit me
I caught it by the nose
and it escaped.
boot, boot-maker, and left (*nonsense*)
rose, carnation, button. (*nonsense*)

Five Brown Pennies

I have five cents in my purse.
This one is for gum;
This one is for a ring;
This one is for a drum;
And these I'll keep in my purse
For something else.

How Many Fingers Are There?

How many fingers do I have here?
(*Children count*)
Nine!
The tail wags.

MOTHER GOOSE RHYMES

Children enjoy jumping over a small object, it doesn't have to be a candlestick, while saying this rhyme together.

Tengo una vela
Tengo una vela
en un candelero
la pongo en el suelo
y la brinco ligero.

Jack Be Nimble
Jack be nimble,
Jack be quick,
Jack jump over the
Candlestick.

This little miracle translates exactly as the English rhyme, except for changing the references to all the king's horses and all the king's men.

Humpty Dumpty
Humpty Dumpty se sentó en un muro,
Humpty Dumpty se cayó muy duro.
Ni la guardia civil (*Neither the civil guard*)
Ni la caballería (*Nor the cavalry*)
Supieron como se incorporaría.

Humpty Dumpty
Humpty Dumpty sat on a wall,
Humpty Dumpty had a great fall.
All the king's horses
And all the king's men
Couldn't put Humpty together again.

Un ratón
Un ratón, un ratón,
corriendo por aquí, corriendo por allí,
comiendo queso, comiendo pan
al fin los gatos lo agarrarán,
al ratoncito se comerán
¡qué caray! ¡qué caray!

One Mouse
One mouse, one mouse
Running here, running there
Eating cheese, eating bread
In the end the cats will kill him dead
They'll eat him whole
What a pity! What a pity!

SONGS AND GAMES

This song tells the story of Don Gato (Mr. Cat), who is engaged to be married, but then falls off a roof and is thought to be dead. In some versions of the song he calls for a doctor, in other versions a priest. Some versions give more details about his injuries, such as a broken head, spine, and ribs. When his funeral procession goes through the street where fish are sold, the odor revives him. This resurrection does not occur in all versions.

Estando el señor don Gato

Estando el señor don Gato
sentadito en su tejado
marramamiau, miau, miau,
sentadito en su tejado.

Ha recibido una carta
que si quiere ser casado
marramamiau, miau, miau,
que si quiere ser casado.

Con una gatita blanca,
hija de un gato pardo,
marramamiau, miau, miau,
hija de un gato pardo.

Don Gato por ir a verla
se ha caído del tejado,
marramamiau, miau, miau,
se ha caído del tejado.

Se ha roto siete costillas,
es espinazo y el rabo,
marramamiau, miau, miau,
el espianzo y el rabo.

Vengan, vengan pronto
médicos y cirujanos,
marramamiau, miau, miau,
médicos y cirujanos.

Mátenle gallinas negras
y denle tazas de caldo,
marramamiau, miau, miau,
y denle tazas de caldo.

There Was Mr. Cat

There was Mr. Cat
Sitting on his roof
Meow, meow, meow,
Sitting on his roof.

He had received a letter
Asking him if he wanted to be married
Meow, meow, meow,
Asking him if he wanted to be married.

To a white cat
Daughter of a brown cat
Meow, meow, meow,
Daughter of a brown cat.

Mr. Cat going to see her
Has fallen from his roof
Meow, meow, meow,
Has fallen from his roof.

He has broken seven ribs
His spine and his tail
Meow, meow, meow,
His spine and his tail.

Come, come quick
Doctors and nurses
Meow, meow, meow,
Doctors and nurses.

Kill some black hens
And give him spoonfuls of soup
Meow, meow, meow,
And give him spoonfuls of soup.

Y que haga testamento
de todo lo que ha robado,
marramamiau, miau, miau,
de todo lo que ha robado.

Ya lo llevan a enterrar
por la calle del Pescado,
marramamiau, miau, miau,
por la calle del Pescado.

Al olor de las sardinas
el gato ha resucitado,
marramamiau, miau, miau,
el gato ha resucitado.

Por eso dice la gente:
siete vidas tiene un gato
marramamiau, miau, miau,
siete vidas tiene un gato.

Y aquí se acaba la copla
de Don Gato enamorado,
marramamiau, miau, miau,
de Don Gato enamorado.

Si me dan pasteles
Si me dan pasteles . . .
démelos calientes,

Que pasteles fríos . . .
empachan la gente.

Si me dan pasteles
no me den cuchara,

Que mamá me dijo
que se los llevara.

And make a will
Of everything that has been taken
Meow, meow, meow,
Of everything that has been taken.

Now they're taking him to be buried
Along Fish Street
Meow, meow, meow,
Along Fish Street.

When he smells the sardines,
The cat wakes up
Meow, meow, meow,
The cat wakes up.

Because of this the people say:
A cat has seven lives
Meow, meow, meow,
A cat has seven lives.

And this is how the ballad ends
Of Mr. Cat in love
Meow, meow, meow,
Of Mr. Cat in love.

If You Give Me Pies
If you give me pies,
give them to me hot,

Because cold pies
people don't like.

If you give me pies
don't give me a fork,

Because my mama told me
to carry them.

This is a favorite song. You can have children hold up ten fingers as you begin the song, and then put a finger down as you begin losing dogs.

Los diez perritos

Yo tenía diez perritos, y uno se cayó en la nieve
ya no más me quedan nueve, nueve, nueve, nueve, nueve.

De los nueve que tenía, uno se comió un bizcocho,
ya no más me quedan ocho, ocho, ocho, ocho, ocho.

De los ocho que tenía, uno se golpeo su frente,
ya no más me quedan siete, siete, siete, siete, siete.

De los siete que tenía, uno se quemó los pies,
ya no más me quedan seis, seis, seis, seis, seis.

De los seis que tenía, uno se escapó de un brinco,
ya no mas me quedan cinco, cinco, cinco, cinco, cinco.

De los cinco que tenía, uno se metió en un teatro,
ya no mas me quedan cuatro, cuatro, cuatro, cuatro, cuatro.

De los cuatro que tenía, uno se cayó al revés,
ya no mas me quedan tres, tres, tres, tres, tres.

De los tres que tenía, uno sufrió de un tos,
ya no mas me quedan dos, dos, dos, dos, dos.

De los dos que tenía, uno se murió de ayuno,
ya no mas me queda uno, uno, uno, uno, uno.

Los pollitos

Los pollitos dicen
"Pió, pió, pió,"
Cuando tienen hambre,
Cuando tienen frío.

La gallina busca
El maíz y el trigo,
Les da la comida
Y les presta abrigo.

I Had Ten Puppies

I had ten puppies, one fell in the snow,
now I only have nine, nine, nine, nine, nine.

Of the nine that were left, one ate a biscuit,
now I only have eight, eight, eight, eight, eight.

Of the eight that were left, one banged his forehead,
now I only have seven, seven, seven, seven, seven.

Of the seven that were left, one burned his feet,
now I only have six, six, six, six, six.

Of the six that were left, one ran away,
now I only have five, five, five, five, five.

Of the five that were left, one went into a theater,
now I only have four, four, four, four, four.

Of the four that were left, one fell backwards,
now I only have three, three, three, three, three.

Of the three that were left, one caught a cold,
now I only have two, two, two, two, two.

Of the two that were left, one died of fasting,
now I only have one, one, one, one, one.

Baby Chicks

Baby chicks are singing
"cheep, cheep, cheep,"
When they are hungry
When they are cold.

Mamma looks for wheat,
Mamma looks for corn,
Mamma feeds them dinner,
Mamma keeps them warm.

Bajo sus dos alas	Under mamma's wings
Acurrucaditas	Sleeping in the hay
Hasta el otro día	Baby chicks all huddle
Duermen los pollitos.	Until the next day.

This game is played everywhere. It is similar to "London Bridge is Falling Down." Two children each choose a different fruit to be. They then form an arch. Everyone gets in a line and holds on to the waist of the person in front of them. Everyone moves under the arch. The person who happens to be under the arch when the song is completed is captured. The captured person chooses which side they wish to be on and gets behind the person they choose. When everyone has been captured, you have two long lines of children facing each other, and they play tug of war. In the version given here, the two fruits (sides) chosen are melón and sandía (cantaloupe and watermelon).

Víbora de la mar	**To the Serpent**
A la víbora, víbora	To the serpent, the serpent
de la mar, de la mar	Of the sea, of the sea,
por aquí puede pasar.	It can pass here.
Los de adelante corren mucho,	Those in front run fast,
los de atrás se quedarán	Those behind will stay
tras, tras, tras, tras.	Behind, behind, behind, behind.
Una mexicana	A mexican girl
de fruta vendida,	A fruit seller,
ciruela, chavacan, melón o sandia.	Plum, apricot, cantaloupe, or watermelon.
Será melón, será sandía,	It will be cantaloupe, it will be watermelon,
será la vieja del otro día.	It will be the old woman of the other day.
(*Spoken*) ¿Con quien te vas, con melón o sandia?	(*Spoken*) Who will you go with? Cantaloupe or watermelon?
(*After everyone has chosen sides they pull apart as they say:*)	(*After everyone has chosen sides they pull apart as they say:*)
El puente es de oro,	The bridge is made of gold,
el puente es de plata,	The bridge is made of silver,
el puente es de papel,	The bridge is made of paper,
el puente es de cáscara de plátano.	The bridge is made from a banana peel.

A game similar to "Ring around the Rosie."

Que llueva, que llueva
Que llueva, que llueva,
la Virgen de la Cueva,
los pajaritos cantan,
las nubes se levantan,
que si, que no,
que caiga el chaparrón,
que toquen los tambores
porro, porrón pon pon,
que rompan tus cristales
y los míos no.

It's Raining
It's raining, it's raining
The virgin of the cave
The birds sing
The clouds raise
Yes? No?
The rain pours
The drums pound
porro, porron pon pon (*nonsense*)
it breaks your glass
and not mine.

NONSENSE AND MISCELLANEOUS RHYMES

The following are versions of a rhyme that goes back to the seventeenth century. A game can be played as you say it. Since the words *"asserín, asserán"* connote a sawing sound and motion, two people can sit facing each other. They hold hands, and as they say the rhyme they rock back and forth. The object is to stretch as far back as possible without breaking the handclasp. If it is broken, the children tickle each other.

A remar
¡A remar, a remar,
marineros de San Juan!
¡A los chicos darles leche,
a los grandes darles pan!

Row
Row, row,
sailors of San Juan!
Give the little ones milk,
and the big ones bread.

Los maderos de San Juan
Aserrín, aserrán,
los maderos de San Juan;
piden pan y no les dan,
piden queso, les dan hueso,
piden ají
¡eso sí!

The Loggers of San Juan
Saw, saw,
the loggers of San Juan;
ask for bread and don't get it,
ask for cheese and get bones,
ask for chili pepper.
That yes!

Aserrín, aserrán
Aserrín, aserrán,
los maderos de San Juan;
piden queso,
piden pan.
Los de rique alfeñique,
los de roque alfandoque.
Los de trique,
triqui tran
triqui, triqui, triqui, tran
triqui, triqui, triqui, tran.

Saw, Saw
Saw, saw,
the loggers of San Juan;
they ask for cheese,
they ask for bread.
Los de rique alfeñique, (*the rest of the rhyme is all nonsense*)
los de roque alfandoque.
Los de trique,
triqui tran
triqui, triqui, triqui, tran
triqui, triqui, triqui, tran.

Asserín, asserán
Aserrín, aserrán
las sierras aquí están
las del rey, sierran bien,
las de la reina también,
las del duque
truque truque truque,
y las mías sierran en el río,
aunque hace frío.

Saw, Saw
Saw, saw
the saws are here,
the king's saws saw well
the queen's saw well as well
the duke's saws
truque truque truque (*nonsense*)
and my saws saw in the river
even though it's cold.

Aserrín, aserrán,
sierran todas las sierras
los piños de San Juan.

Saw, saw,
all the saws saw
the pines of San Juan.

¿Que te dijo el calderón?
Dique, dique,
dique don,
que te dijo el calderón
que comieras y bebieras
y en tu casa estuvieras
arrimadita en un rincón
Que dedo tienes en el corazón
el chiquito o el mayor
El chiquito.
Si hubieras dicho el mayor
no pasarías tanto dolor.
Dique, dique,
dique, don.

What Did the Cauldron Say?
Dique, dique, (*nonsense*)
dique don, (*nonsense*)
What did the cauldron tell you?
that you should eat and drink
and stay in your house
curled up in a corner.
What finger do you have in your heart,
the little one or the big one?
The little one.
If you had said the big one,
You wouldn't have been in such pain.
Dique, dique, (*nonsense*)
dique, don. (*nonsense*)

Las campanas de montalban
Las campanas de Montalban,
unas vienen y otras van;
las que no tienen badajo
van abajo, abajo, abajo!
Tente, chiquito;
tente, bonito;
que te vas a tierra,
a tierra, a tierra!

The Bells of Montalban
The bells of Montalban,
some come and some go;
those that do not sound
go down, down, down.
The little one,
the beautiful one,
are going to the earth,
to the earth, to the earth.

Here's a series of nonsense rhymes based on the words "*Tin marín*" or "*Pin marín*." These are used for choosing sides, or as counting out rhymes for circle games. The gist of the rhyme is "It wasn't me, it was someone else. Hit them." For some of these there is no English translation.

Tin marín de dos
Tin marín de dos
quien fue.
Cucara macara
títere fue.

Tin marín de dos pingüe
Tin marín de dos pingüe,
cucara macara titiri fue
Yo no fui, fue Teta
pégale, pégale que ella fue.

Another rhyme for choosing sides:

Al subir por la escalera
Al subir por la escalera
una mosca me pico.
La agarre por las orejas,
la tire por el balcón.
Taco, taco,
al que le toque
el numero cuatro
Una, dos, tres y cuatro.

While Going up the Stairs
While going up the stairs,
a fly bit me.
I took her by the ears
And threw her over the balcony.
Taco, taco,
the one who's picked
is number four.
One, two, three, and four.

This rhyme combines part of the "Napolitan Hen" with the nonsense words about a king passing by.

Pin, pin, San Agustín
Pin, pin, San Agustín,
la meca, la seca, la tortoleca,
el hijo del rey paso por aquí
comiendo maní
a todos les dio menos a mi
la gallina encluecada
puso un huevo en la granada
puso uno, puso dos,
puso tres, puso cuatro,
puso cinco, puso seis,
puso siete, puso ocho,
pan y bizcocho para el burro mocho,
palos con palos para los caballos,
tuturutu para que salgas tu.

Here are some fun animal rhymes.

Por aqui viene un gallo
Por aquí viene un gallo,
por aquí viene una gallina
cada uno se meta en su cocina.

Here Comes the Rooster
Here comes the rooster,
here comes the hen
each one will end up in my kitchen.

Los pollitos
Cinco pollitos tiene mi tía;
uno le salta, otro le pía
y otra le canta la sinfonía.

The Chickens
My aunt has five chickens,
one jumps, one clucks,
and the other one sings the symphony.

Tengo un gato
Tengo un gato en mi cocina
que me dice la mentira.
Tengo un gato en mi corral
Que me dice la verdad.

Perico tenía un gato
Perico tenía un gato,
lo mando a por tobacco,
le compro una corbata
que le llegaba hasta las patas,
una, dos y tres.

Chango, gorila
Chango, gorila,
¿Quien te hizo el pelo?
¡Ramón!
¿Cuanto costo?
¡Tostón!
¿Como te quedo?
¡Chueco!

Nadaban los patos
Nadaban, nadaban
nadaban los patos
nadaban, nadaban
y no se mojaban.

La ranita soy yo
La ranita soy yo
glo, glo, glo.
El sapito eres tú
glu, glu, glu.
Cantemos así
gli, gli, gli.
Que la lluvia se fue
gle, gle, gle.
Y la ronda se va
gla, gla, gla.

I Have a Cat
I have a cat in my kitchen
that tells me lies.
I have a cat in my corral
That tells me the truth.

Parrot Had a Cat
Parrot had a cat,
he sent it to get some tobacco,
the cat bought a tie instead
that went down to his paws,
one, two, and three.

Hey, Gorilla
Hey, gorilla,
who did your hair?
Ramon!
How much did it cost?
Alot!
How does it look on you?
Crooked!

The Ducks Swam
The ducks swam,
swam, swam.
The swam, swam
and didn't get wet.

I Am the Frog
I am the frog,
glo, glo, glo. (*nonsense*)
You are the toad,
glu, glu, glu. (*nonsense*)
We sing like this,
gli, gli, gli. (*nonsense*)
The rain went away,
gle, gle, gle. (*nonsense*)
And the round goes on,
gla, gla, gla. (*nonsense*)

These rhymes are like "The Song that Doesn't End."

Un barco chiquito
Había una vez un barco chiquito,
que no podía, que no podía navegar,
pasaron 1, 2, 3, 4, 5, 6, 7, semanas
y el barquito, y el barquito no podía navegar,
y si la historia no les parece larga,
y si la historia no les parece larga,
y si la historia no les parece larga,
volveremos, volveremos, volveremos a empezar.
Había una vez . . . .

The Small Boat
Once upon a time there was a small boat,
that couldn't, couldn't navigate,
1, 2, 3, 4, 5, 6, 7, weeks passed,
and the little boat, the little boat still couldn't navigate,
and if this story doesn't seem long,
and if this story doesn't seem long,
and if this story doesn't seem long,
we'll go back, go back, go back to the beginning.
Once upon a time....

Una hormiguita
Esta era una hormiguita
que salió de un hormiguero,
se robó un granito
y volvió a su hormiguero.
Y vino otra hormiguita
del mismo hormiguero
se robó un granito
y volvió al hormiguero
Y vino otra hormiguita . . . .

Little Ant
This was a little ant
who left his anthill,
he robbed a seed,
and returned to his anthill
There came another little ant
from the same anthill
he robbed a seed,
and returned to his anthill
There came another little ant....

This is a nonsense counting rhyme:

Una, dola
Una, dola,
trela, cuatrola,
quina, quinete,
estaba la reina
en su gabinete.
Vino Gil,
apago el candil
candil, candilon,
cuenta las veinte
que las veinte son.

This wonderful rhyme uses nonsense words to create the sound of scissors cutting hair.

Cuando me recorta el pelo
Cuando me recorta el pelo
la tijera de mama
va diciendo en su revuelo:
chiqui-chiqui-chiqui-cha . . . ,
aletea,
viene y va,
y a mi oido cuchichea,
chiqui-chiqui-chiqui-cha.
Cuando el pelo me recorta
la tijera de mama
charla mas de lo que corta:
chiqui-chiqui-chiqui-cha.

When I Get a Haircut
When I get a haircut
Mama's scissors
Say in their flight
chiqui-chiqui-chiqui-cha…,
aletea,
viene y va,
y a mi oido cuchichea,
chiqui-chiqui-chiqui-cha.
When I get a haircut
Mama's scissors
Sing more than they cut
chiqui-chiqui-chiqui-cha.

—German Berdiales

These are other rhymes that center on home and family.

Palmas, palmitas
Palmas, palmitas
que viene papá
y trae un perrito
que dice quá, quá.

Palm, Little Palm
Palm, Little Palm,
Papa's coming
with a dog
that says quá, quá.

Papá, mamá
Papá, mamá
me quiero casar
con un pajarito
que sepa bailar.

Father, Mother
Father, Mother,
I'd like to marry
A beautiful bird
Who can dance like a fairy.

This is a rhyme a mother will say if her child is ill.

Colita de rana
Sana, sana, colita de rana
Si no sanas ahora,
Sanarás mañana.

Frog's Tail
Get well, get well little frog's tail
If you don't get better today,
You'll get better tomorrow.

Azota manitas
Azota manitas,
que viene papá
azótalas bien,
que pronto vendrá.

Hammer It Handyman
Hammer it handyman,
because father is coming,
Hammer it well
because he'll be here soon.

Mi buena mamita
Mi buena mamita
Me lleva a la mesa
me da la sopita
y luego me besa.

Arroz con leche
Arroz con leche,
me quiero casar,
con una señorita
de éste lugar.
Que sepa escribir,
que sepa bordar,
que sepa abrir la puerta
para ir a jugar.
Con ésta sí,
con ésta no,
con esta señorita
me caso yo.

Don Melitón
Don Melitón era muy chato.
Le llamaban narices de gato.
Pero los gatos se le han escapado
comiendo ratones a medio bocado.

Luna
Luna, luna, dame una tuna
la que me diste
se cayó a la laguna.

La luna
Mira la luna
comiendo su tuna;
echando las cáscaras
en esta laguna.

Los dias de la semana
Lunes, martes, miércoles, tres.
Jueves, viernes, sábado, seis.
Y domingo siete.

My Good Mommy
My good mommy
Brings me to the table,
She gives me soup,
And then she kisses me.

Rice with Milk
Rice with milk,
I want to marry,
with a woman
from this place.
Who knows how to write,
who knows how to embroider,
who knows how to open the door
to go out to play.
To this one yes,
to this one no,
To this woman
I will get married.

Don Melitón
Don Melitón was very snub-nosed
They called him cat nose.
But the cats have escaped,
and are eating rats, their mouths half full.

Moon
Moon, moon, give me a tuna.
The one you gave me
fell in the lagoon.

The Moon
Look at the moon,
eating his tuna,
throwing the scales
into this lagoon.

Days of the Week
Monday, Tuesday, Wednesday, three.
Thursday, Friday, Saturday, six.
And Sunday, seven.

A-B-C-D
A-B-C-D
La burra se me fue por la calle de mi Tía Merced.

A-E-I-O-U
A-E-I-O-U
El burro sabe mas que tu.

Simon Bribón
Simon bribón,
comió mi melón
y luego me dijo
¡Que calveron!

A-B-C-D
A-B-C-D
The burro left me in my Aunt Merced's street.

A-E-I-O-U
A-E-I-O-U
The donkey knows more than you.

Lazy Simon
Lazy Simon
ate my melon
and later said to me
How greedy I was!

GOODNIGHT RHYMES

Sueño
Éste niño tiene sueño
y no se puede dormir
tiene un ojo cerrado
y el otro no puede abrir.

El día que tú naciste
El día que tú naciste
nacieron las cosas bellas
nació el sol, nació la luna
y nacieron las estrellas.

Arrorró mi nene
Arrorró, mi nene,
arrorró, mi sol,
duérmete pedazo de mi corazón.
Éste niño lindo no quiere dormir
porque no le traen
la flor del jardín.

Nanita
Nanita, nana,
duérmete lucerito
de la mañana.

Sleepy
This child is sleepy
But he can't go to sleep,
He has one eye closed
And he can't open the other.

The Day You Were Born
The day you were born
All the beautiful things were born,
The sun was born, the moon was born,
And the stars were born.

Lullaby
Go to sleep my child,
go to sleep my sun,
sleep little piece of my heart.
This beautiful child doesn't want to sleep
because no one is bringing him
a flower from the garden.

Lullaby
Lullaby, and goodnight
Sleep little light
of the morning.

TONGUE TWISTERS

These tongue twisters are fun to say, but virtually untranslatable!

El arzobispo (The Archbishop)

El arzobispo de Constantiopla
que quiere desarzobisconstantinopolitanizar;
el desarzobisconstantinopolitanizador
que lo desarzobisconstantinopolitanizare
buen desarzobisconstantinopolitanizador será.

Tengo una guitarilla (I have a guitar)

Tengo una guitarilla mal enguitarillada.
El que la enguitarillo no la supo enguitarillar.
Voy a buscar un eunguitarillador que la enguitarille
    mejor.

Tengo un guacalito (I have a crate)

Tengo un guacalito mal enguacalitado.
El que lo enguacalito no lo supo enguacalitar.
Voy a buscar un enguacalitador que lo enguacalite
    mejor.

Fui al perejil (I went to the parsley)

Fui al perejil
y me emperejilé
para desmperejilarme
cómo me desmperejilaré.

En un jucal de Junquier (In the rushes of Junquier)

En un jucal de Junquier
juncos juntaba Julián
Juntóse Juan a juntarlos
y juntos juncos juntaron.

Si cien sierras asseran cien (If one hundred saws saw one hundred)

Si cien sierras asserán cien
siprese, sescientas sierras
asserán seisceintos cipreses.

Un dicho (A saying)

Me han dicho que has dicho un dicho
que han dicho que he dicho yo,
el que lo ha dicho mintió
y en caso que hubiese dicho

ese dicho que tu has dicho
que han dicho que he dicho yo
dicho y redicho quedo
y estaría muy bien dicho,
siempre que yo hubiera dicho
que se dicho que tu has dicho
que han dicho que he dicho yo.

PIÑATA RHYMES

Dale, dale, dale
Dale, dale, dale, no pierdas el tino.
Mide la distancia que hay en el camino.

Bolita
Bolita, bolita
te llaman piñatita
eres muy redondita,
y yo con esta varita
te destrozaré ahorita.

Hit It, Hit It, Hit It
Hit it, hit it, hit it, don't loose your skill.
Measure the distance there is in the path.

Little Ball
Little, ball, little ball
they call you piñata
you are very round,
and with this stick
I will break you right now.

ADVINANZAS (RIDDLES)

This book would not be complete without mentioning an extremely popular form of Latino folklore: the riddle. Almost every book that has collected Latino folklore includes some *adivianzas*. Here are some examples:

Blanca por dentro,
verde por fuera;
si quieres saber mi nombre,
espera.

White inside
Green on the outside.
If you want to know my name,
wait.

Solution: *Pera* (pear)
This riddle is a play on words, since the letters that make the word "espera" (wait), form the phrase "es pera" or "it's a pear."

Oro parece,
plata no es,
el que no lo acierte
bien bobo es.

It looks like gold,
Silver it's not,
He who doesn't know this
is a dolt.

Solution: *Plátano* (Banana)
Again, a play on words. "plata no es" means, "silver it is not," but if you combine "plata" and "no" you get "plátano" or banana!

Some adivinanzas are more poetic:

Un pajarito voló, voló,
pasó por los ojos
y nadie lo vio.

A bird flew, flew
Past in front of our eyes
And no one saw it.

Solution: *El sueño* (A dream).

¿Que cosa es?
Una cosa muy bonita
que tiene alas
y se pone en la cabeza.

What is it?
A very beautiful thing
it has wings
and you put it on your head.

Solution: *El sombrero* (A hat).

Tito, tito, capodito
sube al cielo y pega un grito.

Tito, tito, with a little cap
rises to the sky and shouts.

Solution: *Triquictraque* (Firecrackers).

SOURCES FOR FINGERPLAYS

Many of the above fingerplays were gathered from colleagues, miscellaneous handouts, and copies that have come into my possession over the years. The following are some of the published sources for fingerplays that I have found most useful. In the bibliography, I have noted which books have included any of the fingerplays and rhymes mentioned here.

Bravo-Villasante, Carmen. *Colorín colorete*. Madrid: Ediciones Didascolia, 1983.
    A book of riddles, rhymes, tongue twisters, lullabies, carols, and prayers.

Ebinger, Virginia Nylander. *Spanish Songs, Games, and Stories of Childhood*. Santa Fe, N.M.: Sunstone, 1993.
    Particularly notable for its explanations of how to play the various games. Includes the music for all the songs.

Fernández, Laura. *De tin marín: cantos y rondas infantiles* (Children's songs and rhymes). Mexico: Editorial Trillas, 1983. (picture book)
    Nursery rhymes and songs enhanced by Fernández's delicate illustrations.

Flint Public Library. *Ring a Ring o' Roses: Fingerplays for Preschool Children*.
    This book includes 25 Spanish-language fingerplays. The cost is approximately $7.00 and the book can be ordered from
    Flint Public Library Business Office
    1026 East Kearsley
    Flint, MI 48502–1994
    810–232–7111

Griego, Margot C. and Betsy L. Bucks, Sharon S. Gilbert, and Laurel H. Kimball. Selected and translated. *Tortillitas para mama and Other Nursery Rhymes/Spanish and English*. Illus. Barbara Cooney. New York: Holt, 1981. (picture book)
    This classic should be in the collection of any librarian or teacher working with Latino children. It includes some of the most common rhymes.

Jiménez, Emma Holgun, and Chonchita Morales Puncel. *Para chiquitines: cancionciats, versitos y juegos meñiques* (For little ones:

Songs, verses, and fingerplays). Illus. Gilbert T. Martinez. Glendale, Calif.: Bowmar, 1969.
A book of songs, poems, and fingerplays with colorful illustrations. Includes music and guitar chords for the songs. Some are traditional, others are new creations of the authors.

Llimona, Mercedes. *Juegos y canciones para los niños* (Stories and songs for children). Barcelona: Ediciones Hymnsa, 1984.
A selection of fingerplays with illustrations that suggest how to act them out. Includes *"Este niño tiene sueño," "Cinco lobitos," "Éste compró un huevito," "Que llueva," "La gallina ponicana," "Arroz con leche,"* and many others.

Lubbock Public Schools. *Kindergarten Bilingual Resource Handbook.* Austin, Tex.: Dissemination and Assessment Center for Bilingual Education, 1973.
Includes a fairly large selection of nursery rhymes and fingerplays.

Medina, Arturo. *Pinto maraña: juegos populares infantiles* (Popular children's games. Illus. Carmen Andrada. Valladolid, Spain: Editorial Miñón, 1987.
This collection includes children's games, such as hopscotch, and accompanying rhymes for some. There are also some song lyrics at the end.

Orozco, José-Luis. *De colores and Other Latin-American Folk Songs for Children.* Illus. Elisa Kleven. New York: Dutton, 1994. (music)
Selected, arranged, and translated by José Luis Orozco. Orozco includes background on the origins of the songs as well as some related games. Among the songs are *"El chocolate," "La araña pequeñita/*The Eensy, Weensy Spider," *"Los Pollitos* (The baby chicks)."

———. *Diez deditos and Other Play Rhymes and Action Songs from Latin America.* Illus. Elisa Kleven. New York: Dutton, 1997. (picture book)
This is the book that teachers and librarians have been waiting for forever. It includes rhymes in Spanish and English, with line drawings that show how to do the actions. Includes *"Este compró un huevito,"* and many others.

Sandoval, Rubén. *Games, Games, Games/Juegos, juegos, juegos: Chicano Children at Play—Games and Rhymes.* Illus. David Strick. New York: Doubleday, 1977.
Black-and-white photos of children illustrate this collection of traditional rhymes used in children's games such as jump rope.

Schon, Isabel. *Tito, tito: Rimas, adivinanzas y juegos infantiles* (Tito, tito: Rhymes, riddles, and children's games) Illus. Victoria Monreal. Mexico D.F.: Editorial Everest, 1995. (poetry 7–11)
Isabel Schon collects the rhyme games she loved the best as a child. The text is complimented by beautiful watercolor illustrations.

El silbo del aire: Antología lírica infantil—1 (A breath of air: Anthology of children's songs). Barcelona: Editorica Vicens-Vivas, 1985. A collection of songs in Spanish that caregivers, teachers, and librarians can use with children. Includes music.

Zwick, Louise Yarian, and Oralia Garza de Cortés. *Rimas y cancioncitas para niños (Rhymes and songs for children).* Houston Public Library, 1984.
A small pamphlet with rhymes and songs gathered by these librarians.

4 BEYOND FOLKLORE: OTHER TYPES OF LATINO CHILDREN'S LITERATURE AND ART

For the most part, the books discussed so far have been fiction. But, in any discussion of library materials for children we must include nonfiction, as well as nonprint materials. In this chapter we talk briefly about categories of nonfiction as well as other art forms, specifically plays and music, that are relevant in working with Latino children. I'll also mention some Latino children's magazines that might be appropriate for a collection.

NONFICTION

Most of the nonfiction available in Spanish is translated from English. The Eyewitness books, for example, as well as other Dorling Kindersley titles are all available in Spanish. Nonfiction in Spanish can be used in libraries and schools in the same way as any English-language book. Since the bulk of this material does not relate strictly to Latino cultural concerns it falls outside of the scope of this manual.

A type of nonfiction more in keeping with the purpose of this manual is nonfiction directly related to Latino culture and issues. This includes biographies of prominent Latinos as well as books specifically about Latino culture or history. The following is a selected bibliography of a few of the more notable titles. The intended age group for these books is indicated in parentheses after the citation.

LATINO CULTURE AND HISTORY

Almada, Patricia. *From Father to Son.* Illus. Marianno de López. Crystal Lake, Ill.: Rigby, 1997. (Ages 7–11)
Spanish edition: *De padre a hijo.*
A father and son carry on a family tradition that began in Mexico and is now established in Los Angeles. The photographs demonstrate the different steps in the preparation of dough and a variety of different kinds of breads. Includes a map and some riddles.

Ancona, George. *Barrio: José's Neighborhood*. New York: Harcourt, 1998. (Ages 7–11)
José lives in San Francisco's mission district. Ancona photographs him engaging in his daily activities, as well as some significant cultural celebrations. Ancona evokes the feeling of growing up Latino.

———. *Fiesta Fireworks*. New York: Lothrop, Lee and Shepherd, 1993. (Ages 7–11)
A family prepares fireworks in the Mexican town of Tultepec to celebrate the fiesta honoring the town's patron saint, San Juan de Dios.

———. *Mayeros: A Yucatec Maya Family*. New York: William Morrow, 1997. (Ages 7–11)
Armando and his family are descendants of the Mayas. The book follows Armando and his family through a week of preparations for the town's fiesta, and gives some idea of their daily life as well. In this photograhic essay Ancona demonstrates connections between past and present Mayan culture.

Anderson, Joan. *Spanish Pioneers of the Southwest*. Illus. George Ancona. New York: Lodestar (Dutton), 1989. (Ages 7–11)
Ancona's photos portray a re-enactment of family and village life in New Mexico in the 1700s.

Ashabranner, Brent. *Children of the Maya: A Guatemalan Indian Odyssey*. Illus. Paul Conklin. New York: Dodd Mead, 1986. (Ages 8–14)
Describes the struggles of Guatemalan Indians who have relocated to Florida to escape political oppression. Illustrated with black-and-white photographs.

———. *Dark Harvest: Migrant Farmworkers in America*. Illus. Paul Conklin. New York: Shoe String, 1993. (Ages 8–14)
Discusses the very real social problems encountered by migrant farmworkers.

———. *Our Beckoning Borders: Illegal Immigration to America*. New York: Cobblehill, 1996. (Ages 8–14)
This book offers both sides of the immigration argument. While it focuses on the Mexican border and Latino immigrants, it also covers the whole spectrum of immigration from all nations.

———. *Still a Nation of Immigrants*. New York: Cobblehill, 1993. (Ages 8–14)

Presents a historical overview as well as success stories of individual immigrants.

Atkin, S. Beth. *Voices from the Fields: Children of Migrant Farmworkers Tell Their Stories*. Boston: Little Brown, 1993. (young adult)
The author interviewed children ages 9–18, and they candidly tell what life is like for migrant farmworkers—the heat in the fields and other issues suchs as gangs and constantly having to move to different schools.

Cockroft, James D. *Latinos in the Making of the United States*. The Hispanic Experience in the Americas Series. New York: Watts, 1995. (Ages 8–14)
Cockroft shows the the many contributions Latinos have made to our country.

Cooper, Martha, and Ginger Gordon. *Anthony Reynoso: Born to Rope*. New York: Clarion, 1996. (Ages 7–11)
Anthony is a nine-year-old whose father is teaching him how to become a rodeo performer in the Mexican tradition.

Garcia, Guy. *Spirit of the Maya: A Boy Explores His People's Mysterious Past*. Illus. Ted Wood. New York: Walker & Co., 1995. (Ages 7–11)
Kin is a direct descendent of the Maya. He learns to appreciate his heritage through his father's traditional artwork and through a visit to the ancient ruins of temples and pyramids.

González-Jensen, Margarita. *Mexico's Marvelous Corn*. Crystal Lake, Ill.: Rigby, 1997. (Ages 7–11)
Spanish edition: *El maravilloso maiz de México*. Corn is described in all its variety and flavors in this book, with brief, descriptions of various ancient and modern methods of preparation.

Haskins, Jim. *Count Your Way through Mexico*. Illus. Helen Byers. Minneapolis, Minn.: Carolrhoda, 1989. (Ages 3–7)
With this counting book, Haskins relays some basic information about Mexico and its culture, such as food and holidays.

Hewett, Joan. *Hector Lives in the United States Now: The Story of a Mexican-American Child*. Illus. Richard R. Hewett. New York: HarperCollins, 1990. (Ages 7–11)
Hector Almaraz is ten years old. This book shows some of the everyday events in his life, from playing sports to attending first holy communion.

Horenstein, Henry. *Baseball in the Barrios*. New York: Gulliver (Harcourt), 1997. (Ages 7–11)
Venezuelan boys hope to make it into the big leagues in the United States. Photos show the real poverty of the people.

Jordan, Tanis. *Angel Falls: A South American Journey*. Illus. Martin Jordan. New York: Kingfisher, 1995. (Ages 7–11)
The fauna of the Angel Falls region of southeast Venezuela is portrayed with beautiful illustrations. There is a glossary of all the animals discussed.

King, Elizabeth. *Chile Fever: A Celebration of Peppers*. New York: Dutton, 1995. (Ages 7–11)
Color photos demonstrate the history and cultivation of chile peppers.

Krull, Kathleen. *The Other Side: How Kids Live in a California Latino Neighborhood*. Illus. David Hautzig. New York: Lodestar (Dutton), 1994. (Ages 7–11)
Kids tell why they left Mexico with their families and what is different about their lives in California.

Lankford, Mary. *Quinceñera: A Latina's Journey to Womanhood*. Illus. Jesse Herrera. New York: Millbrook, 1994. (Ages 7–11)
Lankford describes the preparations and the ceremony of a young girl's quinceñera, or 15th birthday. This is a major rite of passage for Latinas, celebrating their journey from childhood to adulthood.

Marrin, Albert. *Empires Lost and Won: The Spanish Heritage in the Southwest*. New York: Atheneum, 1997. (Ages 8–14)
Marrin details the influence of Spanish explorers and conquistadores on what is now the southwestern United States.

Meltzer, Milton. *The Hispanic Americans*. New York: HarperCollins, 1982. (Ages 8–14)
Meltzer profiles ordinary people and shows the problems they faced in immigrating to this country.

Perl, Lila. *Piñatas and Paper Flowers: Holidays of the Americas in English and Spanish/Piñatas y flores de papel: Fiestas de las Américas en inglés y español*. Trans. Alma Flor Ada. New York: Clarion, 1983. (Ages 7–11)
Perl describes the Latino holidays celebrated in the United States as well as those observed in Latin America.

Presilla, Maricel E., and Gloria Soto. *Life around the Lake: Embroideries by the Women of Lake Patzcuaro*. New York: Holt, 1996. (Ages 7–11)
The book relates how the traditional embroidery of the women of the Lake Patzcuaro region of Mexico continues and adapts to changing times.

———. *Mola: Cuna Life Stories and Art*. New York: Holt, 1996. (Ages 7–11)
Mola art is created by women who live in the San Blas Islands off Panama. The text describes the method through which these colorful fabric designs are created as well as history, customs, and even songs that relate to this art form.

Silverthorne, E. *Fiesta! Mexico's Great Celebrations*. Brookfield, Conn.: The Millbrook, 1992. (Ages 8–14)
An excellent book that not only gives the cultural and historical background for Mexican celebrations, but also provides activity ideas with instructions for making crafts and foods. This book has separate sections on religious, patriotic, and other celebrations.

Solá, Michéle. *Angela Weaves a Dream: The Story of a Young Maya Artist*. Illus. Jeffrey Jay Fox. New York: Hyperion, 1997. (Ages 7–11)
The story of how Angela practices weaving the seven sacred designs of the Maya is interspersed with Mayan myths regarding these signs. Angela wins first prize in the weaving competition.

Viesti, Joe, and Diane Hall. *Celebrate! In Central America*. Illus. Joe Viesti. New York: Lothrop, 1997. (Ages 7–11)
This useful and welcome book combines beautiful photography with descriptions of how various holidays are celebrated in particular Latin American countries. Holidays covered include the Day of the Dead and the Dance of the Conquistadors in Guatemala; Carnival and Holy Week in El Salvador; the San José Fair in Honduras; the Virgin of Masaya Celebration in Nicaragua; Columbus Day in Costa Rica; and Carnival in Panama.

Wolf, Bernard. *Beneath the Stone: A Mexican Zapotec Tale*. New York: Orchard, 1994. (Ages 7–11)
Leo is a Zapotec boy. He and his family weave rugs and wall hangings that are sold throughout Mexico. Illustrated with color photographs, this book tells the story of Leo and his family throughout the year. In doing so it conveys information about the important holidays and culture. It includes a map and a note about the Zapotecs.

BIOGRAPHY

Morey, Janet Nomura, and Wendy Dunn. *Famous Hispanic Americans*. New York: Cobblehill, 1996. (Ages 8–14)
A collective biography of 14 notable Hispanic Americans including math teacher, Jaime Escalante; astronaut Ellen Ochoa; singer Gloria Estefan; and actor Andy Garcia.

Sinnott, Susan. *Extraordinary Hispanic Americans*. Chicago: Children's Press, 1991. (Ages 8–14)
Short biographies of Latinos from virtually every walk of life beginning with the age of exploration. This book impressively shows the real contributions Latinos have made.

Winter, Jonah. *Diego*. Illus. by Jeanette Winter. Trans. Amy Prince. New York : Knopf, 1991. (Ages 3–7)
A bilingual picture book that discusses the childhood of Diego Rivera and how it influenced his art.

Winter, Jeanette. *Josefina*. San Diego: Harcourt, 1996. (Ages 3–7)
Inspired by Josefina Aguilar, this is a kind of counting book in which Josefina makes clay figures in the family tradition. Use in a storytime with *Diego*.

NOTABLE SPANISH-LANGUAGE NONFICTION

Armella de Aspe, Virginia. *La lana* (Wool). Illus. Noé Katz. Mexico D.F.: Editorial Patria, 1983. (Ages 3–7)
Colleción Piñata. Series: *Las materias primas* (Primary materials)
Hilario is a shepherd. This is the story of how wool is made from his sheep.

Castelló, Beatriz de Maria y Campos. *Tres colorantes prehispanicos* (Three prehispanic coloring agents). Illus. Pascuala Corona. Mexico D.F.: Editorial Patria, 1985. (Ages 3–7)
Colleción Piñata. Series: *Las materias primas* (Primary materials)
Three methods the Indians used for coloring fabric: cactus, shells, and plants.

Girón, Nicole. *El barro*. (Clay). Illus. Abraham Mauricio Salazar. Mexico D.F.: Editorial Patria, 1983. (Ages 3–7)
Colleción Piñata. Series: *Las materias primas* (Primary materials).
Making pottery and other objects from clay.

———. *El azúcar*. (Sugar). Illus. Ana Villaseñor. Mexico D.F.: Editorial Patria, 1985. Colleción Piñata. (Ages 3–7)

Colleción Piñata. Series: *Las materias primas* (Primary materials).
A little boy narrates the story of how his father makes cane sugar.

Jacob, Esther. *Las tortugas de mar* (The sea turtles). Illus. Felipe
Dávalos. Mexico D.F.: CONAFE (Consejo Nacional de Fomento
Educativo), 1984. (Ages 3–7)
A science book about turtles that also includes Mexican legends
concerning the turtle. This book brought illustrator Felipe Dávalos
to wider attention and earned him the Ezra Jack Keats Award.

Sánchez, Isidro. Series: "Un día en la escuela." (One day at school).
Illus. Irene Borday. Barcelona: Parramón, 1992. (Ages 3–7)
Titles in this series include: *Mi primer día de colegio* (My first day
at school), *La clase* (The class), *El recreo* (Recess), and *Salimos de
la escuela* (We leave school).

————. Series: *Mis plantas.* (My plants) Illus. Carme Peris. Barcelona:
Parramón, 1991. (Ages 3–7)
Titles in this series include *El bosque* (The forest), *El jardín* (The
garden), *El huerto* (The vegetable garden), and *Los aborles frutales*
(Fruit trees).

Sánchez, Isidro. Series: *Mis animales preferidos.* (My favorite animals).
Illus. María Rius. Barcelona: Parramón, 1992. (Ages 3–7)
Mi perro (My dog), *Mi gato* (My cat), *Mi pájaro* (My bird), and *Mi
hámster* (My hamster).

Any of the above books can be used to support teaching in the associated curriculum units that cover these topics. Some of the books,
such as Lila Perl's *Piñatas and Paper Flowers*, give excellent background information on holidays, which can be very useful when planning celebrations and in helping children who are assigned reports on
special days. Many of these books are also useful for introducing children of all cultures to various aspects of the Latino culture.

REFERENCE BOOKS AND MEDIA IN SPANISH FOR CHILDREN

There is always a need for reference works in Spanish when Latino
children are doing reports. The following is a list of encyclopedias
and other reference works that might be useful. They are all suitable
for elementary and middle school-age children. There are now some
encyclopedias and reference works for children on CD-ROM as well.
These are also included in this list. A helpful Web site that contains
information on CD-ROM reference works is maintained by the library
in Valladolid, Spain. The address is bpval.bcl.jcyl.es/CDRef.html.

Atlases

Atlas geográfico (Geographical atlas). Madrid: SM, 1994.

Atlas histórico (Historical atlas). Madrid: SM, 1994.

Dictionaries

Diccionario didáctico de español: Elemental (Didactic Spanish dictionary: Elementary). Madrid: SM, 1994.

Diccionario didáctico de español: Intermedio (Didactic Spanish dictionary: Intermediate). Madrid: SM, 1993.

Raventós, Margaret H., and David L. Gold. *Random House Spanish-English, English-Spanish Dictionary*. New York: Random House, 1995.

Encyclopedias

Descubrir: la enciclopedia de la edad escolar (Discover: The School-age encyclopedia). Barcelona: Salvat, 1994.

Diccionario enciclopédico Espasa (Espasa encyclopedic dictionary). Madrid: Espasa Calpe, 1994. 2 vols.

Enciclopedia basica escolar VOX (The Vox basic school encyclopedia). Barcelona: Bibliograf, 1994. 13 vols.

Enciclopedia escolar (Children's encyclopedia). Madrid: Editorial Everest, 1994.

Enciclopedia juvenil illustrada (Illustrated juvenile encyclopedia). Madrid: Susaeta, 1994.

Enciclopedia juvenil Oceano (Oceano juvenile encyclopedia). Barcelona: Oceano, n.d., 6 vols.
An excellent choice for upper elementary- and middle-school-aged children. Contents are divided into general areas of study like natural sciences, geography, and history. Each area is designated by a color bar across the top of the page. Includes full-color illustrations, an index, and a list of vocabulary words.

Gran Enciclopedia Larousse (Grand Larousse encyclopedia). Barcelona, Planeta, 1990. 12 vols.

El mundo mágico de los niños: Mi primera enciclopedia (The Magical

world of children: My first encyclopedia). Barcelona: Oceano, n.d., 6 vols.
One of the best encyclopedias in Spanish for younger elementary school-age children. It is full of appealing full-color illustrations and includes a glossary of more difficult words.

Norma diccionario enciclopédico ilustrado (Norma illustrated encyclopedic dictionary) Barcelona: Editorial Norma, 1994. 7 vols.

Oceano color: Diccionario enciclopedico universal (Oceano in color: Universal encyclopedic dictionary) Barcelona, Oceano, n.d., 6 vols. Comes highly recommended. Check with publisher or distributor for the most recent update. Incluldes excellent color photos and diagrams.

¿Que es que? El gran libro de consulta (What is what? The big reference book). Madrid: Altea, 1996.

Saber saber junior: enciclopedia juvenil. (Junior know know: Juvenile encyclopedia). Barcelona: Larousse, 1995.

Reference Works on CD-ROM
Atlas mundial Encarta. (Encarta World Atlas). Microsoft, 1996.

Encarta 97. (in Spanish) Microsoft, 1996.

LATINO CHILDREN'S THEATER

Theater has always been an particularly popular Latino art form, especially suited to the culture. Throughout Latin America you will find many examples of religious folk plays. These dramas depicting religious stories hinge on interaction between the audience and the actors and are acted out in spaces other than the traditional proscenium. This type of theater, which is really almost a pageant, brings a community together and forms an important part of Latino culture.

In Latin America, theater has also provided a voice for the disenfranchised. This is especially apparent in the *Teatro Campesino,* or farmworkers' theater, which was born out of the Chicano movement and farmworkers' strike led by Cesár Chavez in the 1960s. Teatro Campesino was founded by Luis Valdez, who also became its principal playwright. Their initial efforts were known as *Actos,* or acts. These short plays were often very political in nature and were meant to motivate the audience to social action. Valdez later gained fame as the author of *Zoot Suit*, a full scale musical that was produced to great acclaim.

The following are some sources of plays that might be presented in school and library settings. When performing these plays, please pay close attention to copyright notices. Even if you are presenting a reading or staging for which no admission is charged, most playrights still require written permission. Addresses of agents or other parties from whom this permssion may be obtained are usually found on the copyright page.

Armijo, Consuelo. *Bam, bim, bom, arriba el telon* (Up goes the curtain). Valladolid, Spain: Editorial Miñón, 1984.
Plays for kids to present:
"Gorros y Botas" (Caps and boots)
"Cumpleaños de Verano" (A summer birthday)
"Una Historia de Sacos" (A history of sacks)
"Pájaros de Invierno" (Birds in winter)
"Un Duende en Palacio" (A goblin in the palace)
"Disimulando" (Hiding)

Otero, Clara Rose. *La cena de tío Tigre y otras obras de teatro para niños* (Uncle Tiger's dinner and other theater pieces for children). Caracas, Venezuela: Ediciones Ekaré, 1993.
This useful book includes four easy-to-produce plays based on Uncle Lion and Uncle Rabbit folktales. In the title play, Rabbit helps Turtle when Uncle Lion comes into Turtle's house and takes over his bed. The book includes delightful illustrations that provide costume and set ideas for productions by young people.

Rosenberg, Joe ed. *¡Aplauso!*: Hispanic Children's Theater. Houston: Piñata (Arte Público), 1995.
This anthology of plays by Latino authors includes three plays in English and Spanish versions, one Spanish play, one English play and two bilingual plays.
Fred Menchaca and Filemón/Fred Menchaca y Filemón by José G. Gaytán
The Caravan/La caravana by Alvan Colón
Bocón by Lisa Loomer
The Day They Stole All the Colors/El día que robaron todos los colores by Héctor Santiago
The Legend of the Gold Coffee Bean by Manuel Martín Jr.
*El gato sin amigos/*The Cat Who Had No Friends by Joe Rosenberg
Song of the Oak/El canto del roble by Roy Conboy

La lente maravillosa (The Marvelous lens) by Emilio Carbadillo.
This play teaches the principal of personal hygiene in an amusing way and makes teaching science concepts fun.

Rivera, José. "Maricela de la Luz Lights the World." *American Theater*. 13, no. 10 (December 1996): 25–38.
Based on bedtime stories this well-known Puerto Rican playwright told his daughter, the play tells the story of Maricela and her brother Riccardo, who become involved in an apocalyptic conflict involving figures from many of the world's mythologies. Set in present day Los Angeles, this play presents a magically realistic blend of elements. These recognizably contemporary Latino young people become heroes and save the world from the cold grip of snow creatures.

Soto, Gary. *Novio Boy: A Play*. San Diego, Calif.: Harcourt, 1997.
Rudy doesn't believe it when an older girl (11th grade) accepts a date with him. Now he needs to know what to say, how to behave, and he needs money. And then, everyone shows up at the restaurant during the date itself. Could be presented fully staged, or as a reading.

Valdez, Luis. "*Los Vendidos*." *Luis Valdez—Early Works: Actos, Bernabe and Pensamiento serpentino*. Houston: Arte Público, 1971, 1990.
This would be an excellent play for young teens to present, although since it was written in 1967 and refers to Governor Reagan, you might update it or make some mention of the historical context. It satirizes various Mexican stereotypes such as the migrant farmworker, the zoot-suited Pachuco, the sombrero-clad revolucionario Pancho Villa clone, and the business-suited Mexican American. The setting is Honest Sancho's Used Mexican Lot and Mexican Curio Shop. A secretary from Governor Reagan's office enters seeking a "Mexican type" for the administration. Sancho shows off his models. The humor hits home, as when Sancho describes the farmworker model to the secretary: "Economical? Señorita, you are looking at the Volkswagon of Mexicans. Pennies a day is all it takes. One plate of beans and tortillas will keep him going all day. That, and chile. Plenty of chile. Chile jalapeños, chile verde, chile colorado. But of course, if you do give him chile, then you have to change his oil filter once a week" (42, 43). The twist ending is that Honest Sancho is really a robot; the models are fully alive and simply pulling a scam.

Vigil, Angel. *¡Teatro! Hispanic Plays for Young People.* Englewood, Colo: Teacher Ideas Press (Libraries Unlimited), 1996.
This book provides scripts for plays that are easy to produce. Especially nice are the scripts for holidays and Cinco de Mayo.

LATINO CHILDREN'S MUSIC

Happily there are numerous recordings available featuring Latino artists that can be used either on their own or as part of other programming. These recordings help reinforce and celebrate Latino cultural heritage. On a more practical level they can be used to teach children how a particular rhyme or song should be sung or as a resource for the librarian or teacher who wishes to perform some of these traditional songs themselves. Many of the traditional songs provide a tune for folk rhymes and for Mother Goose rhymes as well. They are a wonderful vehicle through which Latino children and families can celebrate their cultural heritage and traditions. I have found that many adults say that they don't remember any rhymes, but when they hear them, they smile and all of a sudden remember something from their childhood they had nearly forgotten. The recordings mentioned should strike a chord in children, especially those who are new immigrants. I have noted where an album includes songs or poems or fingerplays that are mentioned elsewhere in this manual.

FIESTA MUSICAL

Fiesta Musical: A Musical Adventure through Latin America for Children (Music for Little People; 9 42533–4). This is a good way to begin a journey through the different musical styles of Latin America. The album is narrated by Emilio Delgado who plays "Luis" on Sesame Street. A number of different Latin artists appear on the record and the songs are delightful, representing numerous countries and many styles of Latin music. An excellent booklet accompanies this album with lyrics, notes about the types of instruments played, and even some ideas for activies such as making your own instruments and dances.
> *Fiesta musical* (Musical party)—María Medina Serafín
>   (Puerto Rico—Bilingual Rap)
> *A la escuela* (To school)—Bobí Céspedes (Cuba—Rumba)
> *La acamaya* (The crawdad)—Eugene Rodriguez and Artemio
>   Posadas Jimenez (Mexico—Huapango)
> *Tonadas de quitiplas* (Sounds of *quitiplas* drums)—Jackeline Rago
>   (Venezuela)
> *Salaque*—Sukay (Bolivia)

Happy Bomba—Carolyn Brandy (Puerto Rico—Bomba)
Los pollitos (The Little chicks)—María Márquez (Venezuela)
De la puna—Sukay (Peru)
Los enanos (The Little people)—Eugene Rodriguez and Artemio Posadas Jimenez (Jarojcho region of Mexico)
El gallo pinto (The Painted rooster)—Claudia Gomez (Argentina)
Una melodía (A Melody)—Bobí Céspedes (Cuba)
No llora má (Don't cry anymore)—María Márquez (Carribean)

Available from
Music For Little People
P. O. Box 1460
Redway, CA 95560

TISH HINOJOSA

Tish Hinojosa is an Austin, Texas-based artist. Her parents came to this country from Mexico. Her work, primarily for adults, reflects her bicultural heritage. Her one children's album is a gem.

Cada Niño/Every Child
This CD contains 11 bilingual songs for young children. There are playful songs, story songs, and lullabies. They are all about "the rich mixture of Latino and American culture and traditions." Lyrics in both languages are available.
Cada niño/Every Child
Escala musical/Music Scale
Siempre abuelita/Always Grandma
Baile vegetal/Barnyard Dance
Nina violina/Magnolia
Simplemente por amor/Simply for Love
Hasta los muertos salen a bailer/Even the Dead Are Rising Up to Dance
Quien/Who
Las fronterizas/The Frontier Woman
Señora Santa Ana

Cada Niño is put out by
Rounder Records
One Camp Street
Cambridge, MA 02140

JOSÉ-LUIS OROZCO

José-Luis Orozco is a native of Mexico City. He perhaps has made the single greatest contribution to Latino children's music through his continuing series of CDs and cassettes of children's songs, rhymes, and singing games. They include some of the classic rhymes mentioned in Chapter 3. If you are not bilingual, you could perhaps play Orozco's renditions for your children.

Latin American Children's Songs, Games, and Rhymes
José-Luis Orozco
Vol. 1: *Lírica infantil* (Children's Lyrics)
Chocolate
Pin Una . . .
Sana, sana
Aserrín
Los pollitos
Vol. 2: *Lírica Infantil* (Children's Lyrics)
Nanita nana
La vibora de la mar
Vol. 3: Latin American Children's Songs, Games, and Rhymes
Vol. 4: *Animales y bailes* (Animals and dances)
Vol. 5: *Letras, Numeros y Colores* (Letters, numbers, and colors)
Chocolate
Diez Perritos
Vol. 6: *Fiestas*/Holidays
Vol. 7: *Navidad y Pancho Claus* (Christmas)
Vol. 8: *Arrullos*/Lullabies
Vol. 9: *De Colores* (accompanies the book *De Colores*)
El chocolate
La vibora de la mar
Los pollitos
Vol. 10: *Corridos Mexicanos y Chicanos* (Mexican and Chicano Ballads)
Vol. 11: *Esta es mi tierra* (This land is my land)
Vol. 12: *Diez Deditos*
Tortillitas
Esté compró un huevo
Asserín, asserán

Orozco's recordings are available through
Arcoiris Records
P. O. Box 7428
Berkeley, CA 94707
510–527–5539

Jose Luis Orozco also now has a Web site that lists all the tracks for each of his albums and through which they can be ordered. The address is:
www.joseluisorozco.com.

SUNI PAZ

Suni Paz is an Argentine singer, composer, and guitarist. She has worked extensively with Alma Flor Ada, creating the accompaniment for a series of books and accompanying tapes that were especially designed as readers for schools. She has also produced other book and cassette pairs in conjunction with the Santillana publishing company. These contain many songs and rhymes taken from Latino sources.

Canciones para el recreo (Children's songs for the playground). FC7850. 1977.

Alerta Sings: Children's Songs in Spanish and English from Latin America, the Carribean, and the United States. FC7714. 1980.

These recordings are available from
Folkways Records
Distributed by Birch Tree Group
180 Alexander Street
Princeton, NJ 08540

MARIA ELENA WALSH

Maria Elena Walsh has delighted generations of Argentine children with her music, which sadly has been difficult to obtain in the United States. It is now possible to purchase a number of her CDs on the Internet at the "Music and More" site:
www.w3ar.com.ar/mmore/dbmore/Mus0063.htm.

This is a good site to find Latino children's music other than Walsh as well. It is available in English.

OTHER NOTABLE RECORDINGS

Here are some other notable recordings for children in Spanish:

Arroz con leche (Rice with milk): Popular Songs and Rhymes from Latin America. Selected by Lulu Delacre. Performed and produced by Carl and Jennifer Shaylen. New York: Scholastic, 1992. Item number 0590600354.
This recording accompanies Delacre's outstanding book.

LATINO CHILDREN'S MAGAZINES

The following is a representative list of Latino-oriented children's magazines. These are an essential part of a balanced collection and provide popular reading for Latino children. For some, they may help to keep in touch with what is popular in their home countries. Many of these magazines can be obtained through a subscription service such as EBSCO. ISSN, where available, and publishers' addresses of for these titles are listed. However, it is generally easier to obtain them through a jobber than directly from the publisher. A good reference source for magazines in Spanish, including children's, is the reference work *Magazines for Libraries* by Bill Katz. Note that the international phone numbers are in the following format: (Country Code) City Code seven-digit phone number.

Billiken
Editorial Atlántida, S. A.
Azopardo 579
1307 Buenos Aires
Argentina
Editor: Carlos Silveyra
(54) 1–130–7040
ISSN: 0006–2553

Chispa (Spark)
Tlacopac No 6, Col Campestre
C. P 01040, Mexico, D. F.
or Apartado Postal 19–456
C. P. 03910, Mexico, D. F.
(52) 5–662–6046
(52) 5–662–7791 fax
ISSN: 0185–1756

Eres (For young adults. Similar to *Tiger Beat* or *People*)
Bi-weekly
Editorial Eres, S. A.
Andres Bello, 45, piso 14
Polanco
11560 México, D. F.
(52) 5–709–7302
(52) 5–281–3200 fax
No ISSN

Skipping Stones (A multicultural children's magazine with frequent
   articles in Spanish)
   P.O. Box 3939
   Eugene, OR 97403–0930
   503–342–4956
   ISSN: 0899–529X

Tu Internacional (Similar to *Seventeen*. Covers health, beauty, fash-
   ion, relationship, entertainment, and psychology)
   Editorial America, S. A.
   6355 N.W 36th Street
   Virginia Gardens, FL 33166
   Subscription address: Box 10950
   Des Moines, IA 50347–0950
   305–871–6400
   ISSN: 0746–9691

Zoo Books (Spanish-language edition of this familiar kids magazine)
   Wildlife Education Ltd.
   9820 Willow Creek Suite 300
   San Diego, CA 92131–1112
   800–477–5034

FURTHER READING

Zwick, Louise Yarian. "Recordings in Spanish for Children." *School Library Journal*. 35, no. 6 (February, 1989): 23–26.

5 SCHOOL AND LIBRARY PROGRAMS

STARTING PROGRAMS

Now we come to actual programs that you can do in a school or library setting with Latino children. In preparing programs, it is important to remember, as I have emphasized throughout this book, that not all Latino kids speak Spanish, and if they do, they may not speak it as their first language. The conflict this presents can be solved. To use storytime as an example, if two storytimes are offered, do one in English and one in Spanish or bilingual. If you speak Spanish, then it's easy. If you don't, find a volunteer, such as a parent, who can help you. Working with parents is crucial. Latino parents are very concerned for the welfare of their children. Since the culture is so family oriented, you must have them on your side to reach the children. Latino parents can be a wealth of knowledge—they may know stories, rhymes, or games from their childhoods, but before they can share their culture with you, you must reach them.

OUTREACH AND PUBLICITY

Whether you are working in a school or a library, outreach should be second-nature when working with Latinos. Since there is no tradition of public library service in Mexico and other Latin American countries, often a Latino immigrant will have no practical experience with a library and its standard services, such as story hour programs. There is no question as to whether outreach in the Latino community is necessary; it should just be done. Children will not come to programs unless their parents bring them. The sort of outreach I'm talking about cannot be done by putting up signs advertising a program. Parents must be reached on a more personal basis. School librarians can reach out during monthly PTA meetings or when there are parent-teacher conferences. For the public library it can be a little more difficult.

Public librarians can visit PTA meetings. Many schools have special educational programs that involve parents and children together. Seek these groups out. I have visited groups of parents with younger children who met in a school cafeteria. Other groups have brought parents and children into the library. Usually these are stay-at-home moms with preschool-age children. Libraries can be a great resource for these types of groups. One school year, we sponsored meeings for the HIPPY (Home Instruction Program for Preschool Youngsters) program, which teaches parenting skills to young Latino mothers while providing enrichment activities for their infants and toddlers. I knew a kindergarten teacher who, on his own initiative, took the time to invite all the parents of the children in his class to a tour of the library. The people in this group had never been to the library before. Encourage this sort of thing—otherwise many of these parents and children might never come to the library. It's a good idea to visit, or even better sponsor, English-as-a-second-language and citizenship classes.

The Latino media are also a great place to reach your audience and publicize your programs. If you live in an area where there are Latino media outlets such as newspapers, radio, or T.V. stations, this is one of the best ways to promote the school or library. Arrange for an interview on radio or T.V. Make sure your news gets sent to all of these outlets. Press releases should include the following information:

Elements of a Good Press Release

Event:

Date:

Time: Place:

Who Is Sponsoring the Event?:

Who Can Participate?:

How Many are Expected?:

Purpose of Event:

Deadline for Reservations (If Applicable):

What Else Do People Need To Know about Your Event?:

Phone Number That Can Be Publicized for Event Information:

Name and Phone Number of Contact Person:

The information regarding the contact person should be in the upper left or right hand corner of the news release. A news release should have a specific date of release, or the words "For Immediate Release" at the top. The first paragraph should summarize in one or two sentences what the release is about, using the five-point method: "who, what, when, where, why." After the first paragraph, continue to develop your story in more detail. Use the "inverted pyramid" structure, moving from general information to more detail. Limit the release to one page if possible. If you must use more than one page, put "more" at the bottom of each page but the last. Use the ### symbol at the very bottom of your release. The release should be double-spaced with wide margins on letter-sized paper. Use short sentences with action verbs. Keep it simple. Check for correct spelling and grammar. Know and meet any deadlines set by media outlets. Don't write a headline for your release. All abbreviations must be understood, so write things out. Spell numbers from one to ten. Use numerals for numbers from 11 up.

STORYTIMES AND THEME PROGRAMS

The following are suggested bilingual storytimes that can be used individually or in a series. A second section includes ideas for special occasions and holidays. A third section describes intergenerational programs that can involve both parents and children. These storytimes include stories primarily in English. Where the stories are available in both English or Spanish, this is noted. Full bibliographic information for the books can be found in the bibliography.

TODDLER TIME (AGES 18 MONTHS TO 2 YEARS) AND PRESCHOOL STORYTIME (AGES 3–5 YEARS)

It is difficult to to have specific theme programs for toddlers since the titles in Spanish for this age group are so limited. To present bilingual or Spanish-language storytimes for toddlers you have to think beyond books in Spanish. Most toddler-appropriate books in English have simple enough texts that they can easily be translated. You can also use wordless books and describe them in Spanish. The following are suggestions of poems and fingerplays that could be combined for toddler times. These can also be used effectively with groups of older preschoolers as well. Remember that with the toddler age group, 15 minutes is usually the maximum attention span. For preschoolers you can usually go up to 30 minutes.

Suggested Books for Toddler Time and Preschool Storytime:

Aragon, Jane Chelsea. *Cancion de cuña* (A lullaby).

Barberis, Franco. *¿De quien es este rabo?* (Whose tail is this?)
This is a simple story where children simply have to guess which animal's tail they are seeing. This could be paired with *Una Cola Especial* (A special tail) by Margarita M. Robleda, a story about a hen who doesn't like her tail and looks for another. It could also be used with *El rabo del gato* (The cat's tail) by Clarita Kohen, a story about a cat that chases another cat's tail.

Brusca, María Cristina. *Three Friends: A Counting Book/Tres amigos: un cuento para contar*.
Here is a counting book with cowboy characters.

Culla, Rita. *Marta y sus amigos* (All the animals are Marta's friends).
You can use puppets and have children make the animal sounds.

Lee, Héctor Viveros. *Yo tenía un hipopótamo*.
In this predictable tale, the narrator tells the fate of each of his pets. At the end he comes to the cat, which he keeps.

Menéndez, Margarita. *Un abrigo crecedero* (The overcoat that got bigger).
Rita has a slightly-too-big-for-her overcoat that grows. She uses it to create shadows that make her look like an elephant or a ghost. She can hid all her toys in it. When it rains she doesn't need an umbrella. She can hide in it when she doesn't want to see anybody. And she can jump without a parachute.
This board book is told in rhyme.

Mora, Pat. *1, 2, 3*.

Suárez, Maribel "Concept Books."
Las formas (Shapes).
Los números (Numbers).
Los colores (Colors).
Los contrarios (Opposites).
Las letras (Letters).
Mis primeras palabras (My first words).

Tabor, Nancy. *El gusto del mercado Mexicano* (A taste of the Mexican market.) Show toddlers the different foods. Then do some of the food-related rhymes.

Suggested Fingerplays for Toddlers:

Simón Bribón
(Children pretend they're eating a melon)
Simón bribón
comió me melón
y luego me dijo
¡Que calveron¡

Lazy Simon
Lazy Simon
ate my melon
and later said to me
How greedy I was!

Los niños traviesos
A Latin equivalent of Eeny, Meny, Miny, Moe
—Este pide pan
—Este dice: no lo hay
—Este dice: ¿Que haremos?
—Este dice: ¡Lo robaremos!
—Este dice: ¡No, no, que nos castigara
nuestro mamá!

The Mischevious Children
This one asks for bread.
This one says there is none.
This one asks "What shall we do?"
This one says "We'll rob some!"
This one says "No, no, our mother will punish us!"

Hallando un huevo
Este nino halló un huevo;
Este lo coció;
Este lo peló;
Este le hechó la sal;
Este gordo chaparrito se lo comió.

Le dio sed,
Y se fue a buscar agua . . . .
Buscó y buscó . . . .
¡Y aqui halló!
Y tomó y tomó y tomó . . . .
(Count on the fingers for each "Este." Look for water
    with the fingers, first at elbow, then at shoulder.
    End with a tickle under the arm.)

Finding an Egg
This little boy found an egg;
This one cooked it;
This one peeled it;
This one salted it;
This fat little one ate it.

He became thirsty,
And he went to look for water . . . .
He looked and looked . . . .
And here he found it!
And drank and drank and drank . . . .

Rima de chocolate
Uno, dos, tres, cho-
(Count with the fingers.)
Uno, dos, tres, -co-
Uno, dos, tres, -la-
Uno, dos, tres, -te-
Bate, bate chocolate

Chocholate Rhyme
One, two, three, CHO.
One, two three, CO.
One, two three. LA.
One, two, three, TE.

Chocolate, chocolate, beat the chocolate.

Tortillitas

"Tortillitas" is a Spanish equivalent of "patty-cake."

(Pat hands, alternating directions of fingers like a
    tortilla-maker.)
Tortillitas para mamá
Tortillitas para papá
Las quemaditas para mamá
Las bonitas para papá

Tortillitas, tortillitas,
tortillitas para papá;
tortillitas para mamá.
Tortillitas de salvado
para papá cuando está enojado;
tortillitas de manteca
para mamá que está contenta.

Tengo una vela
Tengo una vela
en un candelero
la pongo en el suelo
y la brinco ligero
(Children enjoy jumping over a small object, it
    doesn't have to be a candlestick, while saying
    this rhyme together.)

Song: Un Ratón
Un ratón, un ratón,
corriendo por aqui, corriendo por alli,
comiendo queso, comiendo pan
al fin los gatos lo agarrarán,
al ratoncito se comerán
¡qué caray! ¡qué caray!

Tortillas

Tortillas for mother
Tortillas for father
The burnt ones for mother
The good ones for father.

Tortillas, tortillas,
Tortillas for mother
Tortillas for father
Leftover tortillas
for father when he's angry
Tortillas of butter
So mother is happy.

Jack Be Nimble
Jack be nimble
Jack be quick
Jack jump over the
Candlestick.

One Mouse
One mouse, mouse
Running here, running there
Eating cheese, eating bread
In the end the cats will kill him dead
They'll eat him whole
What a pity! What a pity!

PRESCHOOL STORYTIME THEME PROGRAMS (3–8 YEARS)

Program 1: *Conozcandote*/Getting to Know You

Books:
    Keats, Ezra Jack. *My Dog is Lost.*
    Reiser, Lynn. *Margaret and Margarita/Margarita y Margaret.*
    Roe, Eileen. *Con mi hermano/With My Brother.*

Notes:
This is a perfect storytime for the librarian who is unsure about speaking Spanish. The Spanish required for these stories is minimal. The themes of these stories are Spanish and non-Spanish-speaking children working together and getting to know each other. In *Margaret and Margarita*, Margaret speaks only English and Margarita speaks only Spanish. They find a way to communicate when they meet in a park.

Song:
Los Diez Perritos (Sing after reading *My Dog is Lost*.)
    This is a favorite song. You can have children hold up ten fingers as you begin the song, and then put a finger down as you begin losing dogs.

Los diez perritos

Yo tenía diez perritos, y uno se cayó en la nieve
ya no más me quedan nueve, nueve, nueve, nueve,
nueve.

De los nueve que tenía, uno se comió un bizcocho,
ya no más me quedan ocho, ocho, ocho, ocho,
ocho.

De los ocho que tenía, uno se golpeo su frente,
ya no más me quedan siete, siete, siete, siete, siete.

De los siete que tenía, uno se quemó los pies,
ya no más me quedan seis, seis, seis, seis, seis.

De los seis que tenía, uno se escapó de un brinco,
ya no mas me quedan cinco, cinco, cinco, cinco,
cinco.

De los cinco que tenía, uno se metió en un teatro,
ya no mas me quedan cuatro, cuatro, cuatro, cuatro,
cuatro.

De los cuatro que tenía, uno se cayó al reves,
ya no mas me quedan tres, tres, tres, tres, tres.

De los tres que tenía, uno sufrió de un tos,
ya no mas me quedan dos, dos, dos, dos, dos.

De los dos que tenía, uno se murió de ayuno,
ya no mas me queda uno, uno, uno, uno, uno.

The tune for this song can be found in
Yurchenko, Henrietta. *A Fiesta of Folk Songs from
Spain and Latin America*. Illus. Jules Maidoff.
New York: Putnam, 1967.

Ten Puppies

I had ten puppies, one fell in the snow,
now I only have nine, etc.

Of the nine that were left, one ate a biscuit
now I only have eight, etc.

Of the eight that were left, one banged his forehead,
now I only have seven, etc.

Of the seven that were left, one burned his feet,
now I only have six, etc.

Of the six that were left, one ran away,
now I only have five, etc.

Of the five that were left, one went into a theater
now I only have four, etc.

Of the four that were left, one fell backwards,
now I only have three, etc.

Of the three that were left, one caught a cold,
now I only have two, etc.

Of the two that were left, one died of fasting,
now I only have one, etc.

Program 2: *Los libros y la biblioteca*/Books and the Library

Books:
  Balzoa, Asun. *Guilliermo, un ratón de biblioteca.*
  Mora, Pat. *Tomás and the Library Lady.*
  Nizri, Vicki. *Un asalto mayusculo.*
  Robles Boza, Eduardo. *Cuatro letras se escaparon.*

Activity:
For the story *Cuatro letras se escaparon* make small signs, one with each of the letters "P" "R" "O" "E" "Z" "A." Child volunteers can hold these letters and move around spelling the different words created by the escaped letters as the story progresses.

Poem:
"Las palabras son pájaros/Words are Birds" from *Laughing Tomatoes and Other Spring Poems/Jitomates risueños y otros poemas de primavera* by Francisco X. Alarcon. Illustrated by Maya Christina Gonzalez. Children's Book Press, 1997.

Program 3: *Ranas y peces*/Frogs and Fishes

Books:
Lionni, Leo. *Suimi.*
Mistral, Gabriela. *Crickets and Frogs: A Fable.*
tell "Un Cuento de Sapos." (See below)

Poems:

Los pescaditos
Los pescaditos nadan en el agua
nadan, nadan, nadan
Vuelan, vuelan, vuelan
Son chiquititos, son chiquititos
Vuelan, vuelan, vuelan
Nadan, nadan, nadan.

The Little Fish
The little fish swim in the water
Swim, swim, swim
They are little, they are little
They fly, fly, fly
They swim, swim, swim.

La ranita soy yo (I Am the Frog)
La ranita soy yo (I am the frog)
glo, glo, glo
El sapito eres tú (You are the toad)
glu, glu, glu
Cantemos así (We sing like this)
gli, gli, gli
Que la lluvia se fué (The rain went away)
gle, gle, gle
Y la ronda se vá (And the round goes on)
gla, gla, gla.

I Am the Frog
I am the frog
glo, glo, glo
You are the toad
glu, glu, glu
We sing like this
gli, gli, gli
The rain went away
gle, gle, gle
And the round goes on
gla, gla, gla.

Un Cuento de Sapos

Resulta que hace muchos años vivía un matrimonio de sapos que se querían grandamente y lo pasaban bien a la orilla de una charca. Las casa era de dos pisos, con terraza y todo, y en el verano salían de excursión en un bote hecho con una table y un pedazo de lona vieja. Y eran muy felices con sus trajes de seda verde y sus pecheras blancas y sus ojos que parecían bolitas negras que se les fueran a salir de la cara.

Por la única cosa que a veces peleaban era porque al señor Sapo le gustabe quedarse conversando con sus amingos de la gran ciudad Anfibia, y llegaba a lamorzar a las mil y tantas, y entonces la señora Sapa se enojaba mucho y discutían mucho más aún, y a veces las cosas se ponían harto feas.

Un día llegó el señor Sapo con las manos metidas en los bosillos del chaleco, silbando una canción de moda, muy contento. Y ya habían dado las tres de la tarde. ¡En verdad, no era hora para llegar a almorzar!

Como nadie saliera a recibirlo, en señor Sapo dijo, llamando:

—Sapita Cuacua . . . ,Sapita Cuacua . . .

Pero la señora Sapita Cuacua no apareció. Volvió a llamarla y volvió a obtener el silencio por respuesta. La fue a buscar el comedor, al salón, al dormitorio, al baño, a la cocina, al prepostero. Hasta se asomó a la terraza. Pero en ninguna parte estaba su mujercita vestida de verde.

De repente, el señor Sapo vio sobre una mesa del salón un papel que decía:
ALMORCE Y SALI. NO ME ESPERES EN TODA LA TARDE.

Al señor Sapo le pareció pésima la noticia, ya que no tendria quein le siriviera el almuerzo. Se fue entonces a la concina; pero vio que las ollas estaban todas vacías, limias y colgando de sus soportes. Se fue al repostero y encontró todos los cajones y estantes con llave.

El señor sapo comprendió que todo aquello lo había hecho la señora Sapita Cuacua para darle una lección. Y sin mayores aspavientos, se tovo que ir a donde la señora Rana, que tenía un despacho cerca del sauce de la esquina, a comprarle un pedazo de arrollado y unos pequenes para matar el hambre.

Pero como este señor Sapo era muy porfiado y no entendía lecciones, en ve de llegar esa noche a come a las nueve, como era lo habitual, llegó nada menos que un cuarto para las diez.

La señora Sapita Cuacua estaba tejiendo en el salón, y sin saludarlo siquiera, le dijo de muy mal modo:

—No hay comida.

—Tengo hambre—contestó el señor Sapo de igual mal humor.

—Yo, no.

—Yo, si.

—Yo, no.

—Yo, si.

Y como eran un par de porfiados y ninguno de ellos quería dar su brazo a torcer—como vulgarmente se dice—, a medianoche estaban todavía repitiendo:

—Yo, no.

—Yo, si.

—Yo, no.

—Yo, si.

Y cuando apareció el sol por sobre las montes, el matrimonio de los señores Sapos seguía empecinado, diciendo:

—Yo, no.

—Yo, si.

—Yo, no.

—Yo, si.

Y todo eso pasabe poco después que Noe echó a los animales del Arca, porque el diluvio había terminado. Ese día Noe había salido muy temprano a ver sus viñedos, y al pasar cerca de la charca oyó la discusión y movió la cabeza en señal de disgusto, porque le gustaba muy poco que los animales se pelearan. Y cuando por tarde pasó de regreso a su casa, le llegaron de nuevo las mismas palabras:

—Yo, no.

—Yo, si.

—Yo, no.

—Yo, si.

A Noe ya le dio un poco de fastidio, y acercándose a la puerta de las casa de los señores Sapos, les dijo:

—¿Quieren hacer el favor de callarse?

Pero los señores Sapos, sin oirlo, siguieron diciendo:

—Yo, no.

—Yo, si.

—Yo, no.

—Yo, si.

Entonces a Noe le dio rabia de veras, y les gritó, enojado:

—¿Se quieren callar los bochincheros?

Y San Pedro—que estaba asomado a una de las ventanas del cielo tomando el aire—le dijo a Noe, también medio enojado, porque hasta allá arriba llegaban las voces de los discutidores porfiados.

—Los vamos a castigar, y desde ahora, cuando quieran hablar, sólo podrán decir esas dos palabras estúpidas.

Y ya saben ustedes, mis queridos niños, por qué los Sapos de todas las charcas del mundo sólo pueden deci a toda hora y a propósito de toda cosa:

—Yo, no.

—Yo, si.

—Yo, no.

—Yo, si.

—Brunet, Marta. In "Bravo-Villasante, Carmen." *Historia y Antología de la Leteratura Infantil Iberoamericana.* Vol 1: 185–7.

A Frog Story

Synopsis: A long time ago there lived Mr. and Mrs. Frog. Mr. Frog liked to stay out late with his friends and would not come home for diner, which made Mrs. Frog angry.

One day he arrives home, expecting food, but finds a note from Mrs. Frog saying, "I've already eaten and left. Don't wait up." He goes out to find something to eat and doesn't come home till even later than usual. He finds Mrs. Frog knitting in the living room. She asks him where dinner is. Mr. Frog replies that he's the one who's hungry. Mrs. Frog, of course, just wants to get his goat and has already eaten, so she replies:

"I'm not."

"I am," replies Mr. Frog.

"I'm not."

"I am."

They go back and forth like that all night long and into the morning. Their racket catches the attention of Noah, who tries to get them to shut up without success. (This was, you see, just after all the animals had descended from the ark.) Noah enlists the aid of St. Peter and together they decide to punish the frogs, so that from then on they would only be able to say those two stupid words. And that is why to this day, frogs say "Ribbit, Ribbit."

Program 4: *Comida*/Food

Books:
> Bertrand, Diane Gonzalez. *Sip, Slurp, Soup/Caldo, caldo, caldo.*
> Hayes, Joe. *The Day It Snowed Tortillas.*
> Hayes, Joe. *A Spoon for Every Bite.*
> Paulsen, Gary. *La Tortilleria/The Tortilla Factory.*
> Soto, Gary. *Chato's Kitchen.*

Notes:
This can also be a tortilla storytime by omitting *Chato's Kitchen.*

Poems:

Tortillitas
Tortillitas
(Pat hands, alternating directions of fingers like a
   tortilla-maker).
Tortillitas para mamá
Tortillitas para papá
Las quemaditas para mamá
Las bonitas para papá

Tortillitas, tortillitas,
tortillitas para papá;
tortillitas para mama.
Tortillitas de salvado
para papa cuando está enojado;
tortillitas de manteca
para mamá que está contenta.

Tortillas
Tortillas for mother
Tortillas for father
The burnt ones for mother
The good ones for father.

Tortillas, tortillas
Tortillas for mother
Tortillas for father
Leftover tortillas for
father when he's angry
Tortillas of butter
So mother is happy.

Program 5: Pollitos/Chickens

Books:
Ada, Alma Flor. *Mediopollito/Half-Chicken.*
Barbot, Daniel. *Rosaura en bicicleta/A Bicycle for Rosaura.*
Delacre, Lulu. *The Bossy Gallito/El gallito de bodas.*

Poems:

Doña Pata
Detrás de doña Pata (*Point behind*)
corren los patitos (*Make running motion with fingers*)
por allí, por allá, (*Point to left and right*)
cuá, cuá, cuá
Detrás de doña Gallina
siguen los pollitos
por allí, por allá,
pío, pío, pa
Detrás de doña Cabra
van las cabritos
por allí, por allá,
baa, baa, baa

Mrs. Duck
Behind Mrs. Duck
run the ducklings
over here, over there . . .
    Behind Mrs. Hen
follow the little chicks
over here, over there . . .
    Behind Mrs. Goat
come the the baby goats
over here, over there . . .

Fingerplays:

La gallinita napolitana
La gallinita napolitana
Pone un huevo cada semana
pone dos,
pone tres,
pone cuatro,
pone cinco,
pone seis,
¡Pone siete a la semana!
pone ocho,
pone nueve,
pone diez,
la gallinita, ya lo ves,
quiere que escondas tus pies.

The Napolitan Hen
The Napolitan hen
Lays one egg a week
Lays two
Lays three
Lays four
Lays five
Lays six
Lays seven in the week!
Lays eight
Lays nine
Lays ten
The hen, now you see,
Wants you to hide your feet.

Song:

Los pollitos	**The Baby Chicks**
Los pollitos dicen	Baby chicks are singing
"Pio, pio, pio,"	"Pio, pio, pio,"
Cuando tienen hambre,	"Mamma we are hungry
Cuando tienen frio.	"Mamma we are cold."
La gallina busca	Mamma looks for wheat,
El maíz y el trigo,	Mamma looks for corn,
Les da la comida	Mamma feeds them dinner,
Y les presta abrigo.	Mamma keeps them warm.
Bajo sus dos alas	Under mamma's wings
Acurrucaditas	Sleeping in the hay
Hasta el otro dia	Baby chicks all huddle
Duermen los pollitos.	Until the next day.

The tune for this song can be found in Orozco, José Luis. *De Colores: and Other Latin-American Folk Songs for Children*. Illus. Elisa Kleven. New York: Dutton, 1994, 32.

Variations:
You could use *El sancocho del sábado* by Torres.

Program 6: *Abuelos*/Grandparents

Books:
Dorros, Arthur. *Isla.*
————. *Abuela.*
Mora, Pat. *Pablo's Tree.*
Reiser, Lynn. *Tortillas and Lullabies/Tortillas y cancioncitas.*

Activity:
Have the children draw a picture of themselves with their grandparents, doing whatever they like to do best together. If grandparents are there, have them draw a picture, too.

These books would an intergenerational program. Make sure the grandparents are there with the children.

Program 7: *Bodas y familias*/Weddings and Families

Books:
Belpré, Pura. *Perez y Martina.*
Soto, Gary. *Snapshots from the Wedding.*
Van Laan, Nancy. *La boda: A Mexcan Wedding Celebration.*

Program 8: *Piratas*/Pirates

Books:
Gusti/Ricardo Alcántara. *El pirata valiente.*
Rohmer, Harriet and Mary Anchondo. *The Headless Pirate/El Pirata sin cabeza.*
Zaton, Jésus. *Mi papá y yo somos piratas.*

Program 9: *El sol y la luna*/The Sun and the Moon

Books:
Aardema, Verna. *Borrguita and the Coyote.*
Ada, Alma Flor. *The Lizard and the Sun/La lagartija y el sol.*
Balzoa, Asun. *Munia y la luna.*
Ehlert, Lois. *Moon Rope/Un lazo a la luna.*
Gollub, Matthew. *The Moon Was at a Fiesta.*
Johnston, Tony. *The Tale of Rabbit and Coyote.*

Poem:

El día que tu naciste
El día que tú naciste
nacieron las cosas bellas
nació el sol, nació la luna
y nacieron las estrellas.

The Day You Were Born
The day you were born
All the beautiful things were born
The sun was born, the moon was born
And the stars were born.

Activities:
Both the Aardema and Johnston books retell the folktale where Coyote is tricked into thinking that the reflection of the moon in the water is a cheese. Use whichever you prefer. Either of these stories provide excellent opportunities for creative dramatization. A great art project to go along with this storytime would be to have the children draw and color an Aztec-style sun, complete with a face. All you need are crayons and paper.

Program 10: *Pesadillas*/Nightmares
Books:
    Balzoa, Asun. *Munia y el crocolilo naranja.*
    Belpré, Pura. *Oté: A Puerto Rican Folktale.*
    Da Coll, Ivar. *Tengo miedo.*
    Hayes, Joe. *El Terrible Tragadabas/The Terrible Tragadabas.*
    Sanromán, Susana. *Señora Regañona: A Mexican Bedtime Story.*

Activities:
The Terrible Tragadabas can be told effectively without the book. After reading *The Terrible Tragadabas* and *Señora Regañona*, have the children draw a picture of what they think these characters might look like.

Program 11: *Compleaños*/Birthday Party
Books:
    Guy, Ginger Fogelsong. *¡Fiesta!*
    Kleven, Elisa. *¡Viva! ¡Una piñata!*
    López, Loretta. *Que sorpresa de cumpleaños.*

Activity:
This would be the perfect program at which to break a piñata.

Program 12: *Arte*/Art
Books:
    Pellicer Lopez, Carlos. *Julieta y su caja de colores.*
    Winter, Jeanette. *Diego.*
    ———. *Josefina.*

Activity:
After these stories, spread a piece of butcher paper out over a table. Have the children gather around it. Have plenty of crayons. Have them illustrate a scene from their own lives and sign their names. The resulting mural can be hung on a library bulletin board.

Program 13: *Pelo/* Hair

Books:
Calders, Pere. *Brush.*
Cisneros, Sandra. *Hairs/Pelitos.*
Fernandez, Laura. *Pajaros en la cabeza.*

Note:
Brush could be paired with *The Iguana Brothers: A Tale of Two Lizards* by Tony Johnston to build a storytime on friendship.

UPPER ELEMENTARY PROGRAMS (AGES 9–12 YEARS)

Booktalk *My Name is María Isabel* by Alma Flor Ada

On her first day of school in the United States María is told that since there are already two Marías in her class, that she will be called Mary Lopez. María Isabel doesn't recognize herself in this "strange new name" (12). She has always loved her name because she was named for her father's mother and for her Puerto Rican grandmother. María's has to write a theme for her teacher on the subject: "My Greatest Wish." She writes:

> " . . . I think my greatest wish is to be called María Isabel Salazar López. When that was my name, I felt proud of being named María like my papás mother, and Isabel like my Grandmother Chabela. She is saving money so that I can study and not have to spend my whole life in a kitchen like her. I was Salazar like my papá and my Grandpa Antonio, and López, like my Grandfather Manuel. I never knew him, but he could really tell stories. I know because my mother told me.
> "If I was called María Isabel Salazar López, I could listen better in class because it's easier to hear than Mary López" (49–51).

Have children ask their parents the background of their name. Were they named after a relative? Children can share the meaning of their name.

Video Program—Gary Soto

Use one or both of the following Gary Soto videos:

———. *No Guitar Blues.* New York: Pheonix/BFA, 1991. 27 min.
A video of a story taken from *Baseball in April.* Fausto gets ridden with guilt over the dishonest way he obtains money to buy the guitar he wants. Later he receives a present of a bass *guitarrón* that has been in the family.

————. *The Pool Party*. Soto, 1993. 29 min.

A video based on Soto's book of the same name. Rudy Herrera gets invited to Tiffany Perez's pool party. Tiffany is one of the richest kids in school. His family tries to help him get ready and select a gift. Winner of the Andrew Carnegie Medal for Excellence in Children's Video.

Animal Folktales

Books:

Ehlert, Lois. *Cuckoo/Cucú*.

————. *Moon Rope/Un lazo a la luna*.

Kouzel, Daisy and Earl Thollander. *The Cuckoo's Reward/El premio del Cuco*.

Activity:

Compare and contrast the Ehlert and Kouzel versions of the Cuckoo legend. Note that the two Lois Ehlert books are connected by the appearance of the mole character in both.

Pedro de Urdemalas Tales

Books:

Aardema, Verna. *Pedro and the Padre*.

Brusca, María Cristina and Tona Wilson. *The Blacksmith and the Devil*.

Meet Josefina

Books:

Tripp, Valerie. *Meet Josefina*.

————. *Josefina Learns a Lesson*.

————. *Josefina's Surprise*.

————. *Happy Birthday, Josefina*.

————. *Josefina Saves the Day*.

————. *Changes for Josefina*.

Activities:

1. Have girls make salsa, tortillas (or both), using traditional methods. Get a parent to help you. For salsa, you can find a stone grinder.
2. Learn the traditional dances that Josefina and her family would have done at parties at their Rancho.
3. Have parents or other adults bring in traditional apparel and explain the significance of these clothes.

Notes:

Josefina Montoya is an American Girl in the series published by the Pleasant Company. She lives on a Rancho in New Mexico in 1824 with her father and sisters. This is just as the Santa Fe trail is bringing more people to her part of the world. Her mother has passed away, and she struggles to be loyal to her mother's memory while still learning to love the woman who will become her stepmother. The books examine the deep Latino roots of the Southwest.

HOLIDAY PROGRAMS

Program 1: *El Día de los Muertos*/Day of the Dead
Books:
   Ancona, George. *Pablo recuerda/Pablo Remembers*.
   Hayes, Joe. *La Llorona*.
   Levy, Janice. *The Spirit of Tío Fernando/El espiritu del Tío Fernando*.
   Johnston, Tony. *Day of the Dead*.

Poems:

Calavera I
Calaveras (skulls) can be spooky poems or songs
   for the Day of the Dead

Por aquí pasa la muerte
con su aguja y su dedal
remendando sus naguas
para el día del carnaval.

Skull I

Here passes Death
with his needle and his thimble,
mending his petticoat
for carnival day.

Calavera II
(This calavera is a skull made of sugar candy, colorfully decorated with the child's name on it.)

Ahí viene el agua
por la ladera
y se me moja
mi calavera.

Skull II

There comes the water
down the slope
and my calavera got wet.

Chumba la cachumba
If you wish, you can use the illustrated version of this poem published by Ediciones Ekaré.

Cuando el reloj marca la una,
los esqueletos salen de la tumba.
¡Chumba la cachumba
la cachumbambá!
Cuando el reloj marca las dos,
los esqueletos cantan a una voz.
¡Chumba la cachumba

(When the clock strikes one)
(The skeletons leave their tomb.)

(When the clock strikes two)
(The skeletons sing in one voice.)

la cachumbambá!
Cuando el reloj marca las tres,   (When the clock strikes three)
los esqueletos mueven los pies.   (The skeletons move their feet.)
¡Chumba la cachumba
la cachumbambá!
Cuando el reloj marca las cuatro,   (When the clock strikes four)
los esqueletos juegan al teatro.   (The skeletons play at theater.)
¡Chumba la cachumba
la cachumbambá!
Cuando el reloj marca las cinco,   (When the clock strikes five)
los esqueletos pegan un brinco.   (The skeletons jump.)
¡Chumba la cachumba
la cachumbambá!
Cuando el reloj marca las seis,   (When the clock strikes six)
los esqueletos nombran al rey.   (The skeletons name a king.)
¡Chumba la cachumba
la cachumbambá!
Cuando el reloj marca las siete,   (When the clock strikes seven)
los esqueletos lanzan un cohete.   (The skeletons launch a rocket.)
¡Chumba la cachumba
la cachumbambá!
Cuando el reloj marca las ocho,   (When the clock strikes eight)
los esqueletos comen bizcocho.   (The skeletons eat biscuits.)
¡Chumba la cachumba
la cachumbambá!
Cuando el reloj marca las nueve,   (When the clock strikes nine)
los esqueletos ven como llueve   (The skeletons look like rain.)
¡Chumba la cachumba
la cachumbambá!
Cuando el reloj marca las diez,   (When the clock strikes ten)
los esqueletos corren una res   (The skeletons chase a cow.)
¡Chumba la cachumba
la cachumbambá!
Cuando el reloj marca las once,   (When the clock strikes eleven)
los esqueletos tocan los bronces.   (The skeletons play the cymbals.)
¡Chumba la cachumba
la cachumbambá!
Cuando el reloj marca las doce,   (When the clock strikes twleve)
los esqueletos se ponen en pose.   (The skeletons strike a pose.)
¡Chumba la cachumba
la cachumbambá!
Cuando el reloj marca la una,   (When the clock strikes one)
los esqueletos van a la luna.   (The skeletons go to the moon.)
¡Chumba la cachumba
la cachumbambá!

Story:
"The Laughing Skull" from *Golden Tales* by Lulu Delacre.

Activities:
1. Have the children draw a skeleton. Use chalk on black paper.
2. Make a Day of the Dead altar. Read about the altar in Ancona's book and then have children make objects to place on an altar. For this activity you could bring out all your miscellaneous craft materials.
3. For refreshments, eat sugar candy caleveras.

Program 2: *Cinco de Mayo*/5th of May
Book:
    Beherens, June. *¡Fiesta! Cinco de Mayo.*
    Riehecky, Janet. *Cinco de Mayo.*

Poem:
    "Las palabras son pájaros/Words are Birds" from *Laughing Tomatoes and Other Spring Poems/Jitomates Risueños y otros poemas de primavera* by Francisco X. Alarcon. Illus. by Maya Christina Gonzalez. San Francisco: Children's Book Press, 1997.

Activity:
Make some of the recipes from Janet Riehecky's book.

Program 3: *Las Navidades*/Christmas
Books:
    Anaya, Rudolfo. *The Farolitos of Christmas.*
    Ciavonne, Jean. *Carlos, Light the Farolito.*
    Soto, Gary. *Too Many Tamales.*

Songs:
from *Las Navidades* by Lulu Delacre.

Refreshments:
Serve tamales or *buñuelos*, fried tortillas sprinkled with cinnamon.

INTERGENERATIONAL PROGRAMS

Since the family unit is so integral to Latino culture, many schools and libraries have found success in doing programs with parents or grandparents and children together. This programming goes beyond traditional storytimes to bring families together. There are many examples of successful programs, but the one thread they have in common is parent and child involvement. At the most basic level, bilingual or Spanish storytime should be done at a time when children and parents can attend together. Building on this foundation, more instructional programs can be held for parents, teaching them how to read to their children and how to model a reading habit. Librarians or teachers can demonstrate how to read a book with a child and suggest activities to be used with particular books.

One format that has worked for me is to involve at least two people, and to have a meeting with parents in one area of the library, while a storytime is being held for the children in another. At the end of the program, parents and children are brought back together. Obviously, this requires two staff people to work. It can be done based on staff or volunteer availability. You can also seek out guest speakers, such as Latino artists or storytellers from the community. This sort of programming can be organized as a one-time-only program or as a series of workshops. If you do a one-time only program you could choose any children's storytime mentioned here for the children. You might want to have some additional craft activities so that you don't have to fill up all the time with stories. Prepare a story, such as Eduardo Robles Boza's *Cuatro letras se escaparon* that children could present for their parents. The following is a possible format for the adult part of the program.

Library Program for Parents

Welcome (from library manager or other person in charge.)

Introduction to Library Services

Discussion of the types of children's literature available in Spanish, and different ways they can be shared. Discuss the importance of reading to children, focusing on the educational aspect.

Bring children back in and have them help tell a story to their parents.

Create a book display with books from your collection and give out a printed booklist. Serve refreshments afterwards, and offer parents a tour of the library. The key to making a program like this work is getting parent involvement, and the key to that is reaching the parents in a way that will make them want to participate. Some libraries have used variations on the "Born to Read" format: reaching pregnant women before babies are born and giving them instruction and materials. As the women apply for library cards they are provided with incentives such as "Born to Read" t-shirts or rompers for their children. Library programs are held in which child interaction with books can be modeled by librarians.

Another type of outreach can be found in a program done by the Bensenville, Illinois, public library: "A Community of Readers." This grant-funded program sent librarians to Latino homes to do a program with the families. Families received a bag with books, a puppet or finger play, and library publicity materials. Staff then talked to the parents about the importance of reading themselves and of reading to their children (Rodriguez, 332). This led to increased literacy and use of the library. The next step was bring these people to programs in the library. The programs were initiated for the families contacted through the Community of Readers program, but they were open to all. A program called "Stories and Songs for Babies" was created for infants. This program was designed for parent and toddler interaction. Some of the suggested storytimes in this chapter could be used in programs of this sort. "Stories and Songs with Grands" was a program designed for grandparents and preschoolers.

Another excellent model for an intergenerational program is "Gente y Cuentos" or People and Stories developed by Sarah Hirschman, which is a program where young adults and senior citizens meet to read and discuss short stories and poetry that have significant cultural content. The simple idea of reading stories and then discussing them can be adapted to work in many different group situations. The following is a list of stories and books that work very well when read aloud in group settings. They are a bit longer, but not too long to be read in one session. They could serve as the basis for programs with any mix of older children and families or other adults. They are all great catalysts for discussion. Complete information for the books can be found in the bibliography.

El caballito que queria volar by Marta Osorio.
A wooden carousel horse in this beautiful story wants to become a bird so that he can fly. He finally gets his wish. He is a different sort of horse from the beginning—the only horse on the carousel who is different. He was made from the carpenters' last piece of tree trunk, which had a large open gash. Two church bells overhear his wish and dispatch an owl to work some magic.
"Yo quiero volar—dijo más arriba aún de donde pueden ver mis ojos, cantar libremente y vivir en los jardines y en los parques, aunque existen el frío y el hambre, el calor y la sed . . . ." ("I want to fly. I want to fly higher that even my eyes can see, sing freely and live in the gardens and in the parks, even though I may be cold and hungry, or hot and thirsty . . . .")

La calle es libre by Kurusa.
English translation: *The Streets are Free.*
This is a true story of a group of kids who, with support from the

neighborhood librarian, take matters into their own hands when the government won't supply them with a park where they can play instead of in the streets.

"The Circuit" by Francisco Jiménez from *Leaving Home*. Eds. Hazel Rochman and Darlene Z. McCampbell.
This story is an unflinching look at the lives of migrant farmworkers. Just when the narrator finds a sympathetic teacher who will help him to learn to play the trumpet, he goes home to find that his family is packed and ready to move on to the next field.

Elena by Diane Stanley.
In a story based on tales passed down through her family Stanley writes in the voice of a young Mexican-American girl who recalls how her mother was forced to take their family to the United States because of the events of the Mexican Revolution.

"Tuesday Siesta" by Gabriel Garcia Marquez from *Collected Stories*. Trans. Gregory Rabassa and J. S. Bernstein. New York: HarperCollins, 1984, 1991: 99–106.
A mother and daughter take a train ride into a town that has shut down for the afternoon siesta. They find the priest, and ask to see the grave of a thief who was killed in that town. It is revealed that the woman is the mother of the thief. This story is notable for what is *not* said, and can spark discussion of many aspects of Latino culture.

Poem:
"La United Fruit Company" by Pablo Neruda. From *Canto general* (General song) Trans. Jack Schmitt. Berkeley: University of California Press, 1991.
This poem, which details how Jehova divided the earth between Coca Cola Inc., Ford Motors and other entities, as well as the United Fruit Company, will spark discussion of how Latin America has been affected by American industry.

Any of Gary Soto's books of poetry would also be effective in this type of setting. Both parents and young adults could write poems or recollections about their own neighborhood or growing up using Soto's poems and essays as inspiration. The point is that, ultimately, the most successful programming done with Latinos will be that which focuses on and involves families.

WORKS CITED

Rodriguez, Jill, and Maria Tejeda. "Serving Hispanics through Family Literacy: One Family at a Time." *Illinois Libraries* 75, no. 5 (1993): 331–335.

6 COLLECTION DEVELOPMENT ISSUES

General collection development policies remain the same regardless of the language in which a piece of material is written or the ethnicity of the author. There are, however, several issues that are unique to dealing with Latino literature. Chief among these is figuring out where to actually find Latino children's books.

REVIEWS/WHERE TO FIND

School Library Journal, Booklist, and *The Horn Book* all publish semiregular lists of Spanish-language books for children. I've made a habit of keeping these on file. Isabel Schon's periodic pieces for *Booklist* are especially helpful, because she also mentions books that are not recommended because of poor, inaccurate translations or other reasons. This is extremely useful for the librarian who is not familiar with Spanish. Isabel Schon is the director for the Center for the Study of Books in Spanish for Children and Adolescents based out of the University of California at San Marcos, which maintains a Web site with an extensive list of recommended titles and includes complete bibliographic information as well as grade levels and subject headings. They update titles monthly. Another excellent source for recommended books is the Consortium of Latin American Studies Programs' (CLASP) annual "Americas" award for children's and young adult literature. These can be books in English or Spanish, but must be United States works. Available on their Web site are lists of each year's awards with brief reviews. Don't forget to peruse the catalogs of the mainstream New York publishers for their Spanish-language titles, as well as titles in English that relate to Latino culture. Following is an annotated list of review sources. Note that international telephone numbers are in the following format: (Country Code) City Code-7 digit number.

Banco del Libro
Office address:
Avenida Luis Roche
Altamira Sur, Apartado 5893
Caracas 1010-A, Venezuela
(58) 2–265–3990/265–5017/267–6101
(58) 2–264–1391 (fax)

e-mail: blibro@reaccuin.ve

Banco del Libro, or "Bank of the Book," is a Venezuelan institution that is a model for Latin America in terms of conceiving, implementing, and diffusing programs and services related to the promotion of children's literature. Banco del Libro sponsors a publication, "*Tres estrellas y más*" (Three Stars and More), which is a bulletin published twice a year (in September and March) with reviews of recommended Spanish-language books. This includes critical reviews that rate books with three to five stars. An annual subscription can be obtained for $5.

Booklinks: Connecting Books, Libraries, and Classrooms
434 W. Downer

Aurora, IL 60506

(subscription address)

Booklinks occasionally includes bibliographies that relate to Latino interests.

Booklist
434 W. Downer

Aurora, IL 60506

(subscription address)

Internet: www.ala.org/booklist

Occasional features found in *Booklist* are bibliographies of "Books in Spanish from Spanish-Speaking Countries," "Books in Spanish Published in the U.S.," and "Recommended Reference Books in Spanish for Children and Adolescents." As mentioned above, the author of these columns, Isabel Schon, includes a helpful "Caveat Emptor/Inferior Translations" to assist librarians in building the best possible Spanish-language collections. Distributor addresses are included.

Center of the Study of Books in Spanish for Children and Adolescents
California State University, San Marcos

San Marcos, CA 92096–0001

760–750–4070

760–750–4073

e-mail: ischon@mailhost1.csusm.edu

(Isabel Schon, Director)

Internet: www.csusm.edu/campus_centers/csb/

This center is a major clearinghouse for information related to children's books in Spanish.

CLIJ (*Cuadernos de literature infantil y juvenil*)

ISSN 0214–4123
Amigó 38
08021 Barcelona, Spain
(34) 93–414–1166
(34) 93–414–4665 (fax)
e-mail: arce@infonet.es
Internet: www.infornet.es/ARCE/Clij.html
Editor: María Victoria Fernández

This is the most important Spanish-language magazine regarding children's books. It began publication in 1988 and its purpose is to dignify children's literature and to defend the cultural importance of reading from infancy. If you read Spanish, this is essential. *CLIJ* is a published monthly, with one issue each year devoted to various awards given in Spanish-speaking countries. An annual subscription is $120.

The Horn Book Magazine

11 Beacon Street, Suite 1000
Boston, MA 02108

The Horn Book publishes occasional review articles by Isabel Schon under the title "Noteworthy Children's Books in Spanish."

Las Américas Award List

Internet: www.uwm.edu/Dept/CLA/

The list is prepared annually by the national Consortium for Latin American Studies Programs.

Libros de México (Magazine)

Cepromex (Centro de Promoción del Libro Mexicano) (Center for the Promotion of Mexican Books)
Cámara Nacional de la Industria Editorial Mexicana
Holanda 13
04120
México, D. F.
(52) 5–688–2011/688–2221/688–2434
(52) 5–604–3147 (fax)

Published by an organization devoted to the promotion of Mexican books, this magazine provides articles of interest about Mexican literature, and a comprehensive list of new books presented by publishing house, as well as in Dewey Decimal order. Also available from this organization is a booklet called *Cómo comprar libros y publicaciones periódicas de México/How to Obtain Mexican Books and Periodicals.*

Libros en español para los pequeños (Pamphlet)
Office of Branch Libraries
New York Public Library
455 Fifth Avenue
New York, NY 10016
A copy of this pamphlet (*Books in Spanish for Little Ones*) can be
ordered for $5 from the New York Public Library.

Libros en venta
National Information Services Corporation
NISC USA
Wyman Towers
3100 St. Paul Street
Baltimore, MD 21218
410–243–0797
410–243–0982 (fax)
e-mail: sales@nisc.com
Internet: www.nisc.com
The Spanish-language equivalent of *Books in Print*.

Multicultural Review
Greenwood Press, Inc., Subscription Publications
88 Post Road W., Box 5007
Westport, CT 06881
203–226–3571
203–222–1502 (fax)

PUBYAC listserv
Address to post messages to listserv:
pubyac@nysernet.org
Subscription address:
listserv@nysernet.org
The text of the message should read:
subscribe PUBYAC
This is a discussion forum for children's and young adult librarians
in public libraries.

REFORMA Newsletter/REFORMANET **listserv**
Subscription address:
listproc@lmrinet.gse.ucsb.edu
The text of the message should read
subscribe reformanet [your first name] [your last name]
Internet:
latino.sscnet.ucla.edu/library/reforma/index.htm
REFORMA is the National Association to Promote Library Service

to the Spanish Speaking and an affiliate of the American Library Association. The quarterly newsletter is available only to members. The listserv discusses a myriad of topics related to library services for Latinos. If you have a question about Spanish-language books, someone here can probably help you.

Revista latinoamericana de literatura infantil y juvenil
(Latin American Magazine of Children's and Young Adult Literature).
A publication of IBBY Latinoamérica. Edited by Fundalectura, Columbian Section of IBBY
Av. (Calle) 40 N° 16–46
Apartado 048902
Bógata, Columbia
(57) 1–320–1511
(57) 1–287–7071 (fax)
A relatively new magazine that fills a real void. Contains reviews and informative articles about Latin American authors. In Spanish only.

School Library Journal
Subscription address:
P. O. Box 57559
Boulder, CO 57559
800–456–9409
800–824–4746 (fax)
School Library Journal publishes occasional reviews of children's books in Spanish.

DISTRIBUTORS

There is a growing number of distributors who deal either exclusively or extensively in Spanish-language books. Virtually all of these companies have catalogs from which materials can be selected and ordered. It is difficult, of course, to order sight unseen. Some vendors will bring materials to your location for first-hand inspection before your purchases are made. Some distributors will say that they can provide any title you request, but make sure they can fulfill their promises before you commit. You may be limited by the purchasing procedures dictated by your agency. Some require a contract to be made with a vendor and allow purchases only from those distributors with whom there are contracts.

Local Spanish bookstores, if there are any in your community, are a good source for actually seeing books before you buy. Larger chain bookstores such as Borders Books and Music and Barnes and Noble have begun carrying Spanish-language titles where the market and sales warrant. However, the bulk of books available in these stores are translations of books that appeared originally in English. If you have the money or resources, the best option is to travel to conventions and book fairs. A large number of Latino book publishers and distributors display at the American Library Association meetings and at some state library association conventions as well.

There are also fairs devoted exclusively to Latino books. The most prestigious of these is FIL, or the Feria Internacional del Libro (International Book Fair), held annually in Guadalajara, Mexico. This fair is an eye-opener in terms of the number and variety of books on display. For anyone seriously intrested in collection development and seeing books before purchasing, FIL is the place to do it. However, it is not necessarily the best place to buy unless you work through a distributor. To get the most out of attending FIL, it is extremely helpful to have a relationship with a distributor who has a presence at the fair. Distributors can get catalogs, price lists, and other information from publishers who are reluctant to give the same to librarians. Distributors may also provide services such as personal consultation regarding your collection needs and shipping to librarians shopping at the fair. Shipping is especially important given the complicated nature of importing books into this country. If a publisher ships directly to you and something goes wrong you generally have no recourse, whereas you do have possibility for resolution when working through a distributor based in the United States. A list of distributors and vendors as well as Spanish-language publishers is included in Chapter 7.

Information on FIL Guadalajara is available from
Information Center
Francia 1747
Col. Moderna A. Postal 39–130
Guadalajara, Jal. 44100 Mexico
(52) 3–810–0331/810–1374
(52) 3–810–0379/812–2841 (fax)
e-mail: Fil@Udgserv.cencar.udg.mx

INTERNET RESOURCES

The Internet has been a boon to the teacher and librarian looking for Spanish-language books. International communication has been greatly facilitated through e-mail and Web sites. Many Spanish and Latin American publishers as well as children's book organizations are now on the Internet. A list of Internet resources including online bookstores and catalogs appears in Chapter 7. The Internet addresses of distributors with an online presence are included with the distributor list under the individual distributor or vendor.

COLLECTION DEVELOPMENT POLICIES

I've talked about some general issues to help you find books to select. But selection is haphazard unless there are some rules to follow. The temptation with Spanish-language materials can be to grab up anything you can get your hands on, since they are often so difficult to find. Rather than making random, careless, thoughtless purchases, teachers and librarians must use some discrimination in the materials they select. To guide selection there must be some guidelines in place. The American Library Association's Library Services to the Spanish Speaking Committee, part of the Reference and User Services Association (RUSA), has adopted official guidelines for the collection and selection of materials. These appeared in the Summer 1988 edition of *RQ*, pages 491–493. They apply to both adult and children's selection. The following are some ideas that should help establish some general guidelines for the selection of Spanish-language materials specifically for children, taking the unique issues of these books into account.

COMMUNITY

Before you can know what to buy, you need to know for whom you are buying. This means that you need to know your community. Who lives in it? What kind of materials do they need? For teachers in schools the children are in front of you every day, and their language abilities and needs are readily apparent. In library settings, you can get a sense of your clientele as you work the reference desk on a regular basis. But, in order to make intelligent purchases, you have to be able to go on more than just a gut feeling based on the children you've talked to. There is also the issue of how to serve those who are not coming into the library. The first step is to check census information. This will probably confirm what you've already guessed in terms of the concentration of Latinos in your community. This data becomes the core of any collection development policy.

Other things that can be done to get a better sense of community needs is do outreach in the community, whether it be in a school, grocery store, or recreation center. It's particularly important to find out the language skills and preferences of the children in your community. Are they fully bilingual or Spanish-dominant? Do they prefer reading in Spanish or English? What do they want to read about? What are their informational reading needs? What are their reading ability levels? What are the primary Latino cultures represented in the community? This information will help you balance the collection between Spanish-language materials, bilingual books, and books in English with cultural relevance. It can be obtained by formal or informal surveys which can be done both in-house or through schools—with children in the classroom as well as parents in P.T.A. settings.

GOALS AND OBJECTIVES

What goals and objectives do you want to meet in building your Spanish-language children's collection? Your collection development goals should be congruent with your institution's mission statement, or the overall goals of your organization. Certainly, the overall goal will be to meet and respond to the changing recreational and informational reading needs of Latino children and to acknowledge and provide validation for their cultural heritage and background. Any selection policy should recognize the tremendous diversity in the Latino community and strive to reflect that diversity in the collection. A good Spanish-language collection for children, like any collection, should include standard titles, such as the ones I identified in Chapter 2. Isabel Schon has said "Just as any Anglo child grows up appreciating the language of Shakespeare, so should Spanish-speaking children grow up appreciating the language of Cervantes" (120). The classics in Spanish have a place in the collection. In addition to the standard titles, there should be titles that meet specific community needs. The ability to achieve collection development goals is limited by available budget, so you will have to exercise considerable discretion.

Some additional issues to consider in this goal setting are the availability of Spanish-speaking staff to articulate the collection and provide services to the Spanish-speaking community, as well as staff to process the materials. If bilingual catalogers are not available, then distributors who offer precataloged materials should be sought. Bilingual access to the collection should be considered. There should be Spanish tools within the library bibliographic databases as well as Spanish signage and printed materials in the facilities themselves.

Once the general goals have been defined, you can set objectives to meet them. Methods of acquisition need to be approved. The budget parameters need to be specific. The actual age levels for which materials will be acquired need to be defined. Make sure you have a mechanism for including community needs, desires, and requests in your selection decisions. This can be as simple as a box at the information desk for requests. Weeding should also be a part of the policy, and effort should be made to keep the collection up-to-date.

SELECTION CRITERIA

Binding

Binding quality is a constant complaint whenever there is a discussion of books from Latin American publishers. This has been a legitimate concern for a long time, because Latin American publishers have lacked the resources their North American counterparts have had to produce books with quality library bindings. This, however, is changing. According to Sally Taylor in *Publisher's Weekly*, "printing technologies have improved enormously in the last three years, in Mexico and elsewhere in Latin America. Lifting of tariffs on printing equipment under NAFTA and the presence of a number of U.S. printers in these markets helped spur the upgrade, as did the need to compete against editions from Spain" (S4). This means that more and more, the books imported from Latin America will be equal in quality to books published here.

In the case of poor bindings that will not last more than a precious few circulations, one option is to send the books, upon receipt, to a commercial binder for a library binding. This way quality books, marred only by the binding, can be added to library collections.

Translations

When considering the issue of translations as part of book selection, I am speaking primarily of bilingual books where the text appears in English and Spanish as well as materials with Latino cultural content that have been translated into Spanish. There are two issues involved when considering translations. First, there is the quality of the translation itself. It is important that there be no grammatical, spelling, or typographical errors. The text should be clear and readily understood and free of awkward or incorrect sentence constructions. I have seen books translated into "Spanish" where a Spanish-sounding suffix has simply been added to the English words. There are also translations in which the Spanish makes no real sense whatsoever; this problem becomes especially apparent when you attempt to read the book aloud. If you are not qualified to make this sort of judgment, then use review sources such as *Booklist* that take these issues into consideration, or find someone who has Spanish-language skills to review the translation for you.

The other issue is that of regional and national dialects. While most current Spanish-language publishing attempts to use a neutral dialect, there are still many books that use a form of Spanish more closely tied to a particular country. You can find regionalisms that are difficult to understood by someone who is not from a particular country. You will probably come across books written using the *vosotros* form of address. An otherwise excellent book does not have to be rejected because of this problem. If you choose to read a book that uses the *vosotros* form, you can simply substitute *ustedes*, the mode of address that is more widely used.

For the definitive treatment of this issue, the selector should consult Isabel Schon's article "Spanish Language Books for Young Readers— Great Expectations, Disappointing Realities," which appeared in the October 1, 1995, issue of *Booklist* magazine.

Cultural Sensitivity

In selecting books to use with Latino children, you need to be sensitive to cultural issues. First of all, find books that represent the cultures of the children you are working with. Find folktales that come from their native lands. As I noted in Chapter 3, there are some tales that have spread throughout the Latin American world. However, there have also been collections published that contain tales from specific countries. Some of the best are in the bibliography in Chapter 10.

Books should build up the child's sense of cultural identity. Avoid books that present a stereotyped view of Latino life. I call this the sombrero and tortilla school: books that portray only a world of poverty and traditional costumes. Books should respect the Latino culture and not portray it as inferior to Anglo culture. Using these guidelines, you can develop Spanish-language and bilingual collections that will nourish the souls of Latino children.

WORKS CITED

Schon, Isabel. "Spanish-Language Books for Young Readers—Great Expectations, Disappointing Realities." *Booklist.* 92, no. 3 (October 1, 1995): 318–19.

Taylor, Sally. "Big Changes South of the Border." *Publisher's Weekly.* September 23, 1996: S3–S20.

PART II:
PLANNING AND
PROGRAMMING RESOURCES

7 FINDING LATINO MATERIALS

ONLINE RESOURCES

Due to the constantly fluctuating nature of the World Wide Web, this portion of the manual is the one most apt to out-of-date soon. These sites were all checked just before this book went to press and at that point the information was accurate. Most of the sites will be somewhat stable, and if they move, a holding page will be left at the old URL to direct you to the new site.

WEB SITES

Azteca Web Page
www.azteca.net/aztec/
> Useful mainly for its links to Chicano-oriented sites. The literature section does not cover children's books.

Baja Global
www.bajaglobal.com
Children's page is at www.bajaglobal.com/ninos/index.htm
> The children's page includes the magazine *Super Niños* as well as fairy tales and other stories.

Bilingual Webquest Page
www.unm.edu/~judyk
> Bilingual science activities from an elementary school teacher.

Busquedas de Información (Information Searches)
www.scienceacademy.com/ssearch.html
> Links to sites in Spanish for students, parents, and teachers.

Center for the Study of Books in Spanish for Children and Adolescents
www.csusm.edu/campus_centers/csb/
> Isabel Schon's site is the the best one for a librarian or teacher looking for lists of recommended books. Schon gives complete bibliographic information and updates her list with recent titles.

Chasque
www.chasque.apc.org
  Includes a link to the magazine *Charona*.

Cibercentro
www.cibercentro.com
  A Yahoo-type search engine in Spanish, with the added feature of links for individual countries.

Cyber Spanglish
www.actlab.utexas.edu/~seagull/spanglist.html
  Computer terms in Spanish.

Escuela Virtual (The Virtual School)
www.cice.mx/esp/escuela
  Homework help in Spanish.

Hispanic Online-Latino Links
www.hisp.com/links.html
  A search engine in English from *Hispanic* magazine.

The Hispanic/Latino Telaranya
www.latela.com
  Provides links to numerous sites in Spanish.

Internet Familia
www.familia.cl
  A colorful site suitable for families, with links of interest to both children and parents.

Internet Educativa
www.ieducativa.com.ar
  An Argentine site dedicated to providing resources for educators.

Jardin Mundial Kindergarten
www.geocities.com/Athens/Acropolis/4616
  The Web site of a Kindergarten class in Aurora, Illinois, that includes project ideas, curriculum ideas, and a booklist of interest to bilingual educators.

Juegos y Canciones (Games and Songs)
www.hevanet.com/dshivers/juegos
  Songs and games that can be used in an elementary school classroom from the Summer FLES (Teachers of Foreign Languages in the Elementary School) conference in Forest Grove, Oregon.

Latin American Network

lanic.utexas.edu

Another good set of links for individual countries and a number of links grouped by subject that includes an excellent set of links for grades K-12. This is one of the best sites for teachers.

Latin World

www.latinworld.com

A directory of resources for Latin American and the Caribbean.

La Red Latina

www.inconnect.com/~rvazquez/sowest.html

Regional links for Latinos living in the Intermountain West.

Latino Literature

www.ollusa.edu/alumni/alumni/latino/latinoh1.htm

Excellent background cultural resources that help put Latino literature in context. It now includes a children's book home page.

Libromex

www.libromex.com.mx/

Includes lists of titles published by Mexican publishers such as Editorial Trillas.

Mundo Latino

www.mundolatino.org/

This site contains links to children's sites in its "Rinconcito" section.

National Latino Children's Institute

www.nlci.org

A Web site for an organization that promotes an agenda to improve the lives of Latino children. Includes a list of and links to a few sites of endorsing agencies.

REFORMA Web Page

lantino.sscnet.ucla.edu/library/reforma/index.htm

The Web site for this national association that promotes library service to the Spanish-speaking.

LISTSERVS

Listservs are accessed through your e-mail account. When you subscribe to a discussion list, you receive all the mail that anyone sends to the group. Depending upon the nature of the message, you can respond to any message privately to the sender or to the group itself.

Listservs are a way of communicating worldwide with colleagues with similar interests. This has been made possible by the growth of Internet.

Reformanet

Reformanet is the listserv of REFORMA, the national association to promote library service to the Spanish-speaking. It is a very active group, and useful if you want to communicate with colleagues facing similar challenges in providing library service to the Latino population.

> To subscribe to REFORMANET, send a message to:
> listproc@lmrinet.ucsb.edu
> Leave the "subject" line blank.
> In the body of the message, type subscribe REFORMANET and your first and last name.

Example:
> subscribe REFORMANET Tim Wadham

After you have sent your message you will receive confirmation of your subscription. You will then be able to send mail to the group at REFORMANET@lmrinet.ucsb.edu. I always save the confirmation message in a file so that I have the subscription commands and other information needed should you, for example, need to unsubscribe from the group. Remember that any business (as opposed to discussions), such as leaving the listserv, needs to be sent to Listproc, not REFORMANET.

ORGANIZATIONS

Note:
In the following sections, international phone numbers are listed in a standardized format: (Country Code) City Code-7 digit phone number. All city codes with the exception of Spain are one digit. All international calls from the United States must be proceeded by 011.

CERLALC
(Centro Regional para el Fomento del Libro en America Latina y Caribe or the Regional Information Center on Books, Reading, and Copyright in Latin America and the Caribbean).
Based in Bogota, Columbia, this organization has a CD-ROM list-

ing publishing houses, distributors, bookstores, and public libraries in its member countries.

CERLALC
Cll 70 No. 9–52
Santafé de Bogotá, D.C.
Columbia
(57) 1–321–7501 /321–7502
(57) 1–321–7503 (fax)
www.cerlalc.com
e-mail: info@cerlalc.com

CIDCLI
Centro de información y Desarollo del la Comunicación y la Literatura Infantiles (Center of Information and Development of Communication and of Children's Literature)
Av. México, 145–601
Col. del Carmen, Coyoacán
México, D. F. C. P. 04100
(52) 5–659–7524
(52) 5–659–3186 (fax)

Mexican Section IBBY (International Board on Books for Young People)
Assn. Mexicana Para el Fomento del LIbro Intantil y Juvenil
Parque España 13–A
Col. Condensa
México D.F. 06140
(52) 5–211–0492

SPANISH LANGUAGE BOOK AND MEDIA VENDORS AND DISTRIBUTORS

Astran, Inc.
591 S. W. 8th Street
Miami, FL 33130
305–858–4300
305–858–0405 (fax)
e-mail: sales@astranbooks.com

Baker and Taylor
251 Mt. Olive Church Road
Commerce, GA 30599
800–775–1100
800–775–7480

Bilingual Educational Services, Inc.
2514 South Grand Avenue
Los Angeles, CA 90007–9979
213–749–6213
800–448–6032
213–749–1820 (fax)
This catalog includes the core bilingual materials lists prepared by
the Los Angeles Unified School District, a separate list called "Focus on Books" from the Library Services Department of LAUSD,
and the State of California Department of Education list.

Bilingual Publications Company
270 Layfayette Street, Suite 705
New York, NY 10012
212–431–3500
212–431–3567 (fax)

Books on Wings
973 Valencia Street
San Francisco, CA 94110
415–285–1145
415–285–3298 (fax)
e-mail: casalibro@aol.com

Carvajal International
Barbara A. Starr/Len Koziuk
P. O. Box 460087
San Antonio, TX 78246–0087
800–888–8725
210–497–3886

Central Valley Video Distributors
910 W. Yosemite
Madera, CA 93638
800–771–0671
209–675–6829
209–675–3657 (fax)

Children's Book Press
  246 First Street, Suite 101
  San Francisco, CA 94105
  415–995–2200
  415–995–2222 (fax)
  e-mail: cbookpress@igc.apc.org

Children's Press
  5440 North Cumberland Avenue
  Chicago, IL 60656–1494
  800–621–1115
  800–374–4329 (fax)

Chulainn Publishing Corp
  244 Wagon Tongue Road
  Bailey, CO 80421
  888–525–2665
  303–838–4375
  303–838–4791 (fax)
  e-mail: editores@aol.com

Círculo de Lectores
  P. O. Box 970
  Hicksville, NY 11802–0970

The Spanish-language Book of the Month Club
  Publicaciones CITEM
  Av. Taxqueña 1798
  Co. Paseos de Taxqueña
  C. P. 04250
  Delegación Coyoacán
  México, D. F.
  (52)5–624–0100/60/62
  (52)5–624–0190/91 (fax)

Claudia's Caravan
  Multicultural/Multilingual Materials
  P. O. Box 1582
  Alameda, CA 94501
  510–521–7871

Continental Book Company
  625 E. 70th Avenue #5
  Denver, CO 80229
  303–289–1761
  800–279–1764 (fax)

Donars Spanish Books
P. O. Box 24
Loveland, CO 80539
800–552–3316
970–663–2124
800–708–8877 (fax)
970–667–5337 (fax)

EBSCO Subscription Services
5724 Highway 280 East
Birmingham, AL 35242
Internet: www.ebsco.com
A good source for Spanish-language magazines.

Educal S.A. de C.V.
Consejo Nacional para la Cultura y las Artes
Av. Ceylán No. 450
Col. Euzkadi, 02660
Mexico, D. F.
(52) 5–556–8315
(52) 5–355–6772 (fax)
Publishes a catalog "Dirección General de Publicaciones."

Fiesta Book Company
6443 N. W. 82nd Avenue
Miami, FL 33166
305–592–0171
305–592–7709 (fax)

Giron Spanish Book Distributors
1443 W. 18th Street
Chicago, IL 60608
800–40–LIBROS
312–226–1406
312–738–1997

Galivanes Books
P. O. Box 850206
New Orleans, LA 70185
504–866–3332
504–866–3332 (fax)

Hispanic Book Distributors
1328 West Prince Road
Tucson, AZ 85705
520–690–0643
520–690–6574 (fax)
e-mail: ntrejo@bird.library.arizona.edu

Howard Karno Books
P. O. Box 2100
Valley Center, CA 92087
760–749–2304
760–749–4390 (fax)
e-mail: karnobooks@cts.com

Imported Books
P. O. Box 4414
Dallas, TX 75208
214–941–6497

Latin American Book Source
48 Las Flores Drive
Chula Vista, CA 91910
619–426–1226
619–426–0212
Good source for music.

Latin American Book Store
204 N. Geneva Street
Ithaca, NY 14850
607–273–2418
607–273–6003 (fax)
e-mail: libros@americanbooks.com

Lectorum Publications Inc. (Subsidary of Scholastic)
111 Eighth Avenue, Suite 804
New York, NY 10011–5201
800–345–5946
212–929–2833 in New York and New Jersey
212–727–3035 (fax)
Internet: www.lectorum.com

Libros En Venta
Includes the publishing output of 20 Spanish-speaking countries and Spanish-language titles from 16 other non-Spanish-speaking countries.
NISC
Wyman Towers, Suite 6
3100 St. Paul Street
Baltimore, MD 21218
410–243–0797
410–243–0982 (fax)

Libros Hispanos del Mundo
1079–81 Allerton Avenue
Bronx, NY 10469
718–655–6558

Libros Sin Fronteras
P. O. Box 2085
Olympia, WA 98507–2085
800–454–2767 Orders
800–357–4332 Customer Service
360–357–4964 (fax)
e-mail: libros@wln.com

Libros U.S.A.
67 Meadow View Road
Orinda, CA 94563
510–254–2664
510–254–2668 (fax)

Madera CineVideo
311 South Pine Street, Suite 102
Madera, CA 93637
209–661–6000
800–828–8118
209–674–3650 (fax)
e-mail: Video@psnw.com
Internet: www.psnw.com/~video/

Mariuccia Iaconi Book Imports
970 Tennessee
San Francisco, CA 94107
415–821–1216
415–821–1596
e-mail: mibibook@ix.netcom.com

Multi-Cultural Books and Videos Inc.
28880 Southfield Road, Suite 183
Lathrup Village, MI 48076
810–559–2676
810–559–2465 (fax)

Multicultural Connection
Libros Bilingües Para Niños
P.O. Box 653
Ardsly, NY 10502–1020
800–385–1020 (phone and fax)
e-mail: bilngbk@mhv.net
Internet: www.mhv.net/~bilingbk

Nana's Book Warehouse, Inc./El Almacén de Libros de Nana
848 Heber Avenue
Calexico, CA 92231
800–737–NANA
760–357–4271
760–357–3226 (fax)
e-mail: nanas@quix.net

Niños
P. O. Box 1163
Ann Arbor, MI 48106–1163
800–634–3304

Playa del Sol Productos
12505 Beach Boulevard, Unit A4–198
Stanton, CA 90680
800–521–8949

Spama
267 4th Avenue
Brooklyn, NY 11225
718–788–1217
718–788–1217 (fax)

Spanish Super Bookstore
Libreria-Distribuidora & Ediciones Universal
3090 SW 8th Street
Miami, FL 33135
305–642–3234

T. R. Books
822 N. Walnut Avenue
New Braunfels, TX 78130
800–659–4710
830–625–2665
830–620–0470 (fax)
e-mail: trbooks@trbooks.com
Internet: www.trbooks.com

SPANISH-LANGUAGE BOOK PUBLISHERS/ IMPRINTS

The publishers listed here represent those most known for publishing quality children's books. The best way to obtain materials from foreign-based publishers is through a distributor, but information for these publishers is also provided should you wish to contact them directly. Some foreign-based publishers, like Santillana, have now established U.S. offices, making acquisitions less of a problem.

Arte Público Press
University of Houston
Houston, TX 77204–2090
800–633–ARTE
713–743–2847 (fax)

Charlesbridge Publishing
85 Main Street
Watertown, MA 02171
800–225–3214
800–926–5775

Children's Book Press
246 First Street, Suite 101
San Francisco, CA 94105
415–995–2200
415–995–2222 (fax)

CIDCLI (Mexico)
Av, México, 145–601, Col. de Carmen, Coyoacán
México, D. F. C.P. 04100
(52) 5–659–7524
(52) 5–659–3186 (fax)
e-mail: cidcli@data.net.mx
Internet: www.cidcli.com.mx

Clarion Books
  A Houghton Mifflin Companies Imprint
  215 Park Avenue South
  New York, NY 10003
  212–420–5883

Dominie Press, Inc.
  5945 Pacific Center Boulevard, Suite 505
  San Diego, CA 92121
  800–232–4570
  619–546–8822 (fax)

Ediciones Ekaré—Banco del Libro (Venezuela)
  Office address:
    Avenida Luis Roche
    Edificio Banco del Libro
    Altamira Sur
    Caracas 1062, Venezuela
    (58) 2–263–0080/0091
    (58) 2–263–3291 (fax)
  Postal address:
    Ediciones Ekaré
    Apartado 68284
    Caracas 1062, Venezuela

Overseas mailing address:
  Ediciones Ekaré
  11120 N. Kendall Drive
  Suite 207–1012
  Miami, FL 33176 USA

Ediciones Norte-Sur
  North South Books
  1123 Broadway, Suite 800
  New York, NY 10010
  800–282–8257
  212–633–1004

Ediciones SM
  Address in Spain:
    Joaquin Turina, 39
    28044 Madrid, Spain
    (34) 91–208–5145
  Address in Mexico:
    Calle Amores 1527

Colonia Del Valle Del Benito Juarez
Mexico, D.F. 03100
(52) 5–534–7779
(52) 5–534–7599 (fax)

Editorial Amaquemecan S. A. de C. V.
Galeana 111
Barrio del Niño Jesús
C.P. 14080
Mexico, D. F.
(52)5–573–7900
(52) 5–513–1086
(52) 5–573–7025
e-mail: Amaquemecan@compuserve.com

Editorial Atlantida S.A. (Argentina)
Florida 643
1005 Buenos Aires, Argentina
(54) 1–311–5416
(54) 1–312–9642
(54) 1–392–1453
Telex: 21163 EDIAT AR

Editorial Juventud (Spain)
Provenza, 101
08029 Barcelona, Spain
(34) 93–239–2000
(34) 93–321–7550
(34) 93–239–5099
(34) 93–239–8383 (fax)

Editorial Trillas (Mexico)
General Administration:
Av. Rio Churubusco 385
Col. Pedro María Anaya
Deleg. Benito Juárez, C.P. 03340
México, D.F.
(52) 5–688–4233
(52) 5–688–8388
(52) 5–604–1364 (fax)
Sales Division:
Calz. De la Viga 1132
Col. Apatlaco C. P. 09439
México, D.F.
(52) 5–633–0612/1122
(52) 5–633–0870/2221 (fax)

El Ateneo
  Pedro García S.A.L.E.I.
  Patagones 2463
  1282 Buenos Aires, Argentina
  (54) 1–942–9002/9052
  (54) 1–942–9162 (fax)
  e-mail: info@ateneo.com

Emecé Editores S. A. (Argentina)
  Alsina 2062
  1090 Buenos Aires, Argentina
  (54)1–953–4163/4038/4156

Fernández Editores S. A. de C. V. (Mexico)
  Eje 1 Pte. México Coyoacan 321 (Col. Xoco)
  C. P. 03330
  México, D.F.
  (52)5–605–2259/7819
  Internet: www.fesa.com.mex/

Fernández USA Publishing Co.
  1210 223rd Street, Suite 309
  Carson, CA 90745
  310–233–4920
  800–814–8080
  310–233–4926 (fax)

Fondo de Cultura Económica USA
  2293 Verus Street
  San Diego, CA 92154
  619–429–0455
  800–5–FCEUSA
  619–429–0827
  e-mail: fceusa@fceusa.com
  Internet: www.fceusa.com

Grolier Publishing Company
  Sherman Turnpike
  Danbury, CT 06816
  800–621–1115
  203–797–3657 (fax)

Harcourt Brace Children's Books
  525 B Street, Suite 1900
  San Diego, CA 92101–4495
  619–699–6431
  619–699–6220

Harper Arco Iris (imprint of HarperCollins)
10 E. 53rd Street
New York, NY 10022
212–207–7000
Internet: www.harpercollins.com

Henry Holt & Co.
115 West 18th Street
New York, NY 10011
212–886–9200
212–633–0748

Hyperion Books for Children/Disney Press
114 Fifth Avenue
New York, NY 10011
212–633–4433
212–807–5432

Lectorum Publications, Inc.
111 Eighth Avenue
New York, NY 10011
212–929–2833
800–345–5946
212–727–3035 (fax)
Internet: www.lectorum.com

Libros Mulberry en Español (imprint of William Morrow & Company, Inc.)
1350 Avenue of the Americas
New York, NY 10019
800–843–9389

Libros Rodríguez
P. O. Box 2854
Oxnard, CA 93034

Little, Brown and Company
34 Beacon Street
Boston, MA 02108
617–227–0730
617–624–9681 (fax)

Mariposa (imprint of Scholastic Inc.)
555 Broadway
New York, NY 10012
800–SCHOLASTIC

Mirasol (imprint of Farrar, Straus & Giroux)
  Books for Young Readers
  Farrar, Straus & Giroux
  19 Union Square West
  New York, NY 10003
  212–741–6900

Penguin Ediciones (imprint of Penguin U.S.A.)
  Penguin USA Children's Books
  575 Hudson Street
  New York, NY 10014
  212–366–2000
  212–366–2666 (fax)

Puvill Division Mexico
  Empresa 107, Mixcoac
  03920 México, D. F.
  (52) 5–611–1513
  (52) 5–598–4378 (fax)
  e-mail: 74173.1047@compuserve.com

Quality Books, Inc.
  1003 W. Pines Road
  Oregon, IL 61061
  800–323–4241
  815–732–4499

Rourke Publishing Group
  P. O. Box 3328
  Vero Beach, FL 32964
  561–465–4575
  561–465–3132 (fax)

Santillana USA
  2105 N.W. 86th Avenue
  Miami, FL 33122
  800–245–8584

Sierra Club Books for Children
  730 Polk Street
  San Francisco, CA 94109
  800–935–1056

Sitesa
   San Marcos 102, Tlalpan
   14000 México, D.F.
   (52)5–655–9144
   (52)5–573–9412 (fax)

Suromex Ediciones SA
   Distributed by Astran, Inc. (See p. 177.)

Susaeta Ediciones SA
   Distributed by Astran, Inc. (See p. 177.)

8 AWARDS AND PRIZES

There are numerous prizes awarded to Spanish-language children's books throughout the Spanish-speaking world. It is very difficult to keep track of all these awards—many are awarded by publishing houses rather than by organizations devoted to the promulgation of Spanish-language children's books. New awards sprout up, and others are discontinued. In general, you need to be careful of assigning any Spanish-language prize the same status as the Newbery and Caldecott awards in the U.S. Individual books need to be examined for their child appeal and quality. Selection decisions based solely on the fact that a book has won a prize can prove to be catastrophic. Many times these prizes are given for reasons other than child appeal, and focus on didactic or religious content. Titles that have won some of the more prestigeous and reliable awards are listed.

LAZARILLO

With the object of stimulating the production of good books especially for children and young people, the *Organización para el Libro Infantil y Juvenil* (OEPLI) (Organization for Children's and Young Adult Books), with the patronage of the Spanish Ministry of Culture, gives the "Lazarillo" prize annually to the best children's and young adult works written in Spanish and published especially for readers under the age of 15 years.

Since 1986 OEPLI has been charged with giving this prize annually, with the patronage of the Ministry of Education and Culture. This prize, the oldest and one of the most prestigious in children's literature was given for the first time by INLE (*Instituto Nacional del Libro Español*) (National Institute of the Spanish Book) in 1958, with the goal of stimulating the creation and production of good books for children and young people. Prizes are given to authors, illustrators, and publishing houses.

Lazarillo Award Recipients

1997
Author
Elacier Cansino for *El misterio de Velázquez.*
Honor
Concha Blanco for *A mi que me importa y Empar de Lanuza: Versos per a ossets.*
Illustrator
Manuel Barbero Richard for *El niño que dejó de ser pez.*
Honor
Angels Ruíz for *La pequeña costrurera.*
Montse Tobella for *El mond Rar de L'Estrafo.*

1996
Author
Miguel Fernández Pacheco for *Los zapatos de Murano.*
Illustrator
Isidro Ferrer for *El verano y sus amigos.*

1995
Author
José Zafra Castro for *Tres historias de Sergio.*
Honor
Isabel Molina for *El señor del cero.*
Honor
Santiago García-Clariac for *El señor que quería ser Tintín.*
Illustrator
Luis Farré Estrada for *Una casa com un cabás.*
Honor
Sofía Balzola for *La mariposa azul.*
Honor
Angels Ruiz for *Un domingo de perros.*

1994
Author
José Zafra Castro for *T'he agafat caputxeta.* Bruño.
Honor
Paloma Bardons for *Hojas de líneas rojas.*
Honor
Rafael Estrada Delgado for *El extraño caso de Comisario Olegario.* Bruño.

Illustrator
Samuel Velasco for *Chumplufated. . . .*
Honor
Josep Montserrat for *El viento del mar.*
Honor
J. A. Tassies for *Hora carabola.*

1993
Author
No Prize.
Honor
José Mª Plaza for *Que alguien me quiera cinco minutos.*
Honor
Ana Guillemi for *En la cola del aire.*
Illustrator
Gabriela Rubio for *Bzzz. . . . .* Grijalbo.
Honor
Monica Verena Kesuch for *Un curioso ratoncito.*

1992
Author
Francisco A. Díaz Guerra for *Nacido del verbo oscuro.* Bruño.
Honor
Eduardo Galán Font for *La silla voladora.*
Honor
Anton Cortizas for *Historias a algún percance, todas ditas en romance.*
Illustrator
José Mª Carmona for *Entre el juego y el frugo.*

1991
Author
Enrique Páez for *Devuelve el anillo, pelo cepillo.* Bruño.
Illustrator
Gusti for *La pequeña Wu-lli.* SM.

1990
Author
Agustín Fernández Paz for *Contos por palabras.* Xerais.

Illustrator
Marta Balaguer for ¡*Qina nit de Reis!*. Cruilla.

1989
Author
Miguel Angel Mendo for *Por un maldito anuncio*. SM.
Illustrator
Pablo Echevarría for *Camilón, comilón*. Destino.

1988
Author
Manuel Alfonseca Moreno for *El rubí del Ganges*. Noguer.
Illustrator
Francisco Giménez for *Historia de una receta*. Anaya.

1987
Author
Beatriz Doumercy for *Un cuento grande como una casa*. Anaya.
Illustrator
Montse Ginesta for *Gargantua*. Proa.

1986
Author
Fernando Martínez Gil for *El juego del pirata*. Noguer.
Honor
Manuel Alonso Erausquin for *Encuentro con los contrarios*.
Illustrator
Angel Esteban for *Los norks*.
Honor
Paula Reznickova for *El conqur i la nena*.

1985
Author
Francisco Climent Carrau for *El tesoro del Capitán Nemo*. Noguer.
Honor
Alfredo Gómez Cerdá for *El bloc de Timo*. Noguer.

Illustrator
Constantino Gatagán for *La Reina de las nieves*. Miñon.
Honor
Irene Bordoy for *El comillo*. Abaidía de Montserrat.

1984
Author
Concha Lópe Narvaez for *El amigo oculto y los espíritus de la tarrde*. Noguer.
Honor
Juan Antonio de Laiglesia for ¡*Chuic!*. Miñón.
Illustrator
Alfonso Ruano Martín for *El camino de Juan*.
Honor
Josep Montserrat for *El caballo fantástico*. SM.
Honor
Montse Ginesta Clavell for *El mag dels estels*. Juventud.

1983
Author
Miguel M. Fdez. de Velasco for *Las tribulaciones de Pabluras*. Noguer.
Honor
Rodolfo Guillermo Otero for *La travesía*. Noguer.
Illustrator
Juan Carlos Eguillor for *El saco de leña*.
Honor
Jesús Gabán Bravo for *El ciervo que fué a buscar la primavera*. Argos-Vergara.

1982
Author
Pilar Mateos for *Capitanes de plástico*. SM.
Honor
Enrique Gainza for *Wela y otros cuentos*.
Illustrator
Clara Pérez Escrivá for *La hija del sol*.
Honor
Constantino Gatagán for *Ping y pong y los animales* and *Ping y Pong navegantes*. Altea.

1981
Author
   José A. del Cañizo for *Las cosas del abuelo*.
   Noguer.
Honor
   Juan Gómez Saavedra for *Ristra de cuentos*.
Illustrator
   Carme Solé Vendrell for *Cepillo*. HYMSA.

1980
Author
   Joan Manuel Gisbert for *El misterio de la isla de
   Tokland*. Espasa-Calpe.
Honor
   María Puncel for *Abuelita Opalina*. SM.
Illustrator
   Viví Escrivá for *Dos cuentos de princesas*. Altea.

1979
Author
   No Prize.
Honor
   Graciela Montes for *Amadeo y otros cuentos*.
Illustrator
   Ulises Wensell for *Cuando sea mayor seré marino*
   and *Cuando sea mayor seré enfermera*. Altea.

1978
Author
   Hilda Perera for *Podría ser que una vez
   . . . .* Everest.
Illustrator
   José Ramón Sánchez for *Los libros del aprendiz
   de brujo*. Miñon.

1977
Author
   Fernando Alonso for *El hombrecito vestido de
   gris y otros cuentos*. Alfagura.
Illustrator
   No Prize.

1976
No Awards Given.

1975
Author
   Hilda Pereda for *Cuentos para chicos y grandes*.
   Miñon.
Illustrator
   Margarita Vazquez de Praga for *La ventana de
   María*.
Publisher
   Beginning in 1975, awarding this prize was dis-
   continued.

1974
Author
   Consuelo Armijo for *Los Bautautos*. Juventud.
Illustrator
   Miguel Calatayud for *Cuentos del año 2100*.
   Doncel.
Publisher
   No Prize.

1973
Author
   Carmen Vázquez Vigo for *Caramelos de menta*.
   Doncel.
Illustrator
   Miguel Angel Pacheco for *Maestro de la fantasía*.
   Santillana.
Publisher
   No Prize.

1972
Author
   Aaron Cupit for *Cuentos del año 2100*. Doncel.
Illustrator
   Manuel Boix for *El país de las cosas perdidas*.
   Doncel.
Publisher
   No Prize.

1971
Author
   María Puncel for *Operación pata de oso*. Doncel.
Illustrator
   Fernando Sáez for *Goya*. Verón.

Publisher
No Prize.

1970
Author
Fernando Sadot P'rez for *Cuentos del zodíaco*. Doncel.
Illustrator
Felicidad Montero for *Los músicos de Bremen*.
Publisher
Editorial Teide

1969
Author
José Javier Aleixandre for *Froilán, el maigo de los pájaros*. Marfil.
Illustrator
Fernando Sáez for *El Lazarillo de Tormes*. Susaeta.
Publisher
Editorial Verón

1968
Author
Jaime Ferrán for *Angel en Colombia*. Doncel.
Illustrator
María Rius for *¿Por qué cantan los pájaros?*. Teide.
Publisher
Editorial Cantábrica

1967
Author
Lita Tiraboschi for *Historia del gato que vino con Solís*. Aguilar.
Illustrator
Roque Riera Rojas for *El ingenioso hidalgo Don Quiote de la Mancha*. Credsa.
Publisher
No Prize.

1966
Author
Marta Osorio for *El caballito que quería volar*. La Galera.

Illustrator
Luis de Horna for *Gino, comino y el camello Moja-Jamón*. Marfil.
Publisher
No Prize.

1965
Author
Ana María Matute for *El polizónde Ulises*. Lumen.
Illustrator
Asunción Balzola Elorza for *Cancionero infantil universal*. Aguilar.
Publisher
Santillana S. A.

1964
Author
Carmen Kurtz for *Color de fuego*. Lumen.
Illustrator
Daniel Zarza Ballugera for *Fiesta en Marilandia*. Anaya.
Publisher
Ediciones Anaya

1963
Author
Angela C. Ionescu for *De un país lejano*. Doncel.
Illustrator
Celedonio Perellón for *Cuentos del ángel custodio*. Doncel.
Publisher
No Prize.

1962
Author
Concha Fernández-Luna for *Fiesta en Marilandia*. Anaya.
Illustrator
José Picó for *Fantasía*.
Publisher
Ediciones Gaisa

1961
Author
Joaquín Aguirre Bellver for *El juglar del Cid*. Miñon.

Illustrator
  José Narro Celorio for *Robinson Crusoe.*
  Juventud
Publisher
  Editorial Doncel

1960
Author
  Montserrat del Amo for *Rastro de Dios.* Cid.
Illustrator
  M. Jiménez Arnalot for *Yo soy el gato.* Gama.
Publisher
  Ediciones Gamma

1959
Author
  Miguel Buñuel for *El niño, la golondrina y el gato.*
  Doncel.
Illustrator
  Rafael Munoa for *Exploradores en Africa.* Aguilar.
Publisher
  Dalmau y Jover

1958
Author
  Alfonso Iniesta for *Dicen de las florecillas.* Dalmau.
Illustrator
  José Fª Aguirre for *El libro del desierto.* Aguilar.
Publisher
  Editorial Mateu

AMERICAS AWARD

"The Americas Award is given in recognition of U.S. works (picture books, poetry, fiction, folklore) published in the previous year in English or Spanish that authentically and engagingly present the experience of individuals in Latin America or the Caribbean, or of Latinos in the United States. By combining both and linking the Americas, the award reaches beyond geographic borders, as well as multicultural-international boundaries, focusing instead upon cultural heritages within the hemisphere. Sponsored by the national Consortium of Latin American Studies Programs (CLASP), the award/commended list was initiated in 1993.

The award winners and the other commended books are selected for their quality of story, cultural authenticity/sensitivity, and potential for classroom use. The winning books are honored at a ceremony held each summer at the Library of Congress, Washington, D.C.

The coordinator for the Americas Award is Julie Kline of the University of Wisconsin-Milwaukee. She can be reached at:

CLASP Committee on Teaching and Outreach
c/o The Center for Latin America
University of Wisconsin-Milwaukee
P.O. Box 413
Milwaukee, WI 53201
414–229–5986
414–229–2879 (fax)
e-mail: cla@csd.uwm.edu

The Center for Latin America's Web site has a complete annotated list of the awards that is updated annually as the award is presented. The URL is www.uwm.edu/Dept/CLA/outreach.html.

Annotated references to these books can be found in the bibliography. This list includes only books set in Spanish-speaking Carribean countries.

Americas Book Award Recipients

1997 Winner
Fiction

Jiménez, Francisco. *The Circuit: Stories from the Life of a Migrant Child*. Albuquerque: University of New Mexico Press, 1997.

1997 Honorable Mention

Ancona, George. *Mayeros: A Yucatec Maya Family*. New York: William Morrow, 1997.

1997 Commended List

Ada, Alma Flor. *Gathering the Sun: An Alphabet in Spanish and English*. Illus. Simón Silva. New York: Lothrop, 1997.

———. *The Lizard and the Sun/La largartija y el sol*. Illus. Felipe Dávalos. New York: Doubleday Dell, 1997.

Alarcón, Francisco X. *Laughing Tomatoes and Other Spring Poems/Jitomates risueños y otros poemas de primavera*. Illus. Maya Christina González. San Francisco: Children's Book Press, 1997.

Almada, Patricia. *From Father to Son*. Illus. Marianno de López. Crystal Lake, Ill.: Rigby, 1997.

Applebaum, Diana. *Cocoa Ice*. Illus. Holly Meade. New York: Orchard, 1997.

Capellinni, Mary. *The Story of Doña Chila*. Illus. Gershom Griffith. Crystal Lake, Ill.: Rigby, 1997.

Carden, Mary, and Mary Cappellini, ed. *I Am Of Two Places*. Illus. Christina González. Crystal Lake, Ill.: Rigby, 1997.

Corpi, Lucha. *Where Fireflies Dance/Ahi, donde bailan las luciernagas*. Illus. Mira Reisberg. San Francisco: Children's Book Press, 1997.

Ehlert, Lois. *Cuckoo/Cucu*. Trans. Gloria de Aragón Andújar. New York: Harcourt Brace, 1997.

Garay, Luis. *Pedrito's Day*. New York: Orchard, 1997.

González, Lucía M. *Señor Cat's Romance and Other Favorite Stories from Latin America*. Illus. Lulu Delacre. New York: Scholastic, 1997.

González-Jensen, Margarita. *Mexico's Marvelous Corn*. Crystal Lake, Ill.: Rigby, 1997.

Hernández, Jo Ann Yolanda. *White Bread Compe-*
tition. Houston: Piñata Books (Arte Público), 1997.

Hornstein, Henry. *Baseball in the Barrios*. New York: Gulliver (Harcourt Brace), 1997.

Johnston, Tony and Jeanette Winter. *Day of the Dead*. New York: Harcourt Brace, 1997.

Keane, Sofía Meza. *Dear Abuelita*. Illus. Enrique O. Sánchez. Crystal Lake, Ill.: Rigby, 1997.

Kroll, Virginia. *Butterfly Boy*. Illus. Gerado Suzán. Honesdale, Pa.: Boyds Mills, 1997.

Lopez, Loretta. *Birthday Swap/¡Que sorpresa de cumpleaños!* New York: Lee & Low, 1997.

Martinez, Floyd. *Spirits of the High Mesa*. Houston: Arte Público, 1997.

Mora, Pat. *Tomás and the Library Lady*. Illus. Raul Colón. New York: Knopf, 1997.

Moreton, Daniel. *La Cucaracha Martina: A Carribean Folktale/La cucaracha Martina: un cuento folklorico del Caribe*. New York: Turtle, 1997.

Orozco, Jose-Luis. *Diez deditos/Ten Little Fingers and Other Play Rhymes and Actions Songs from Latin America*. Illus. Elisa Kleven. New York: Dutton, 1997.

Sisnett, Ana. *Grannie Jus' Come*. Illus. Karen Lusebrink. San Francisco: Children's Book Press, 1997.

Sola, Michell. *Angela Weaves a Dream*. Illus. Jeffrey Jay Foxx. New York: Hyperion, 1997.

Soto, Gary. *Buried Onions*. New York: Harcourt Brace, 1997.

———. *Novio Boy*. New York: Harcourt Brace, 1997.

Stevens, Jan Romero. *Carlos and the Skunk/Carlos y el Zorillo*. Illus. Jeanne Arnold. Flagstaff, Ariz.: Rising Moon, 1997.

Viesti, Joe and Diane Hall. *Celebrate in Central America*. Illus. Joe Viesti. New York: Lothrop, Lee & Shepard, 1997.

1996 Winners
Picture Book

Garza, Carmen Lomas. *In My Family/En Mi Familia*. San Francisco: Children's Book Press, 1996.

Fiction

Martinez, Victor. *Parrot in the Oven: Mi Vida*. New York: HarperCollins, 1996.

1996 Honorable Mention
Picture Book

Hallworth, Grace, comp. *Down By the River: Afro-Carribean Rhymes, Games and Songs For Children*. Illus. Caroline Binch. New York: Scholastic, 1996.

Fiction

Becerra de Jenkins, Lyll. *So Loud a Silence*. New York: Lodestar, 1996.

1996 Commended List

Albert, Burton. *Journey of the Nightly Jaguar*. Illus. Robert Roth. New York: Atheneum, 1996.

Aldana, Patricia ed. *Jade and Iron: Latin American Tales from Two Cultures*. Trans. Hugh Hazelton. Illus. Luis Garay. Toronto: Groundwood/Douglas & McIntyre Ltd., 1996.

Alphin, Elaine Marie. *A Bear for Miguel*. Illus. Joan Sandin. New York: HarperCollins, 1996.

Anzaldua, Gloria. *Prietita and the Ghost Woman/ Prietita y La Llorona*. Illus. Christina González. San Francisco: Children's Book Press, 1996.

Belpré, Pura. *Firefly Summer*. Houston: Arte Público, 1996.

Bunting, Eve. *Going Home*. Illus. David Diaz. New York: HarperCollins, 1996.

Calhoun, Mary. *Tonio's Cat*. Illus. Edward Martínez. New York: Morrow, 1996.

Carlson, Lori Marie, ed. *Barrio Streets Carnival Dreams*. New York: Henry Holt, 1996.

Cooper, Martha and Ginger Gordon. *Anthony Reynoso: Born to Rope*. New York: Clarion, 1996.

Delacre, Lulu. *Golden Tales: Myths, Legends, and Folktales from Latin America /De oro y esmeraldas: mitos, leyendas y cuentos populares de Latino America*. (Separate English and Spanish editions.) New York: Scholastic, 1996.

Delgado, Maria Isable. *Chave's Memories/Los recuerdos de Chave*. Illus. Yvonne Symank. Houston: Arte Público, 1996.

Gage, Amy Glaser. *Pascual's Magic Pictures*. Illus. Karen Dugan. Minneapolis: Carolrhoda, 1996.

Geeslin, Campbell. *In Rosa's Mexico*. Illus. by Andrea Arroyo. New York: Knopf, 1996.

Gollub, Matthew. *Uncle Snake*. Illus. Leovigildo Martínez. New York: Tambourine, 1996.

Jaffe, Nina. *The Golden Flower: A Taino Myth from Puerto Rico*. Illus. Enrique O. Sánchez. New York: Simon & Schuster, 1996.

Johnston, Tony. *The Magic Maguey*. Illus. Elisa Kleven. San Diego: Harcourt Brace, 1996.

———. *My Mexico/México mío*. Illus. F. John Sierra. New York: G.P. Putnam's Sons, 1996.

Kleven, Elisa. *Hooray, a Piñata!* New York: Dutton, 1996.

Kurtz, Jane. *Miro in the Kingdom of the Sun*. Illus. David Frampton. Boston: Houghton Mifflin, 1996.

Machado, Ana Maria. *Nina Bonita*. Illus. Rosana Faría. Trans. Elena Iribarren. Brooklyn, N.Y.: Kane/Miller, 1996.

Mohr, Nicholasa. *Old Letivia and the Mountain of Sorrows*. Illus. Rudy Gutiérrez. New York: Viking, 1996.

Mora, Pat. *Confetti: Poems for Children*. Illus. Enrique O. Sánchez. New York: Lee & Low, 1996.

Schecter, Ellen. *The Big Idea*. Illus. Bob Dorsey. New York: Hyperion, 1996.

Silverman, Sarita Chavez. *Good News!* Illus. Melinda Levine. Carmel, Calif.: Hampton-Brown, 1996.

Soto, Gary. *The Old Man and His Door*. Illus. Joe Cepeda. New York: G.P. Putnam's Sons, 1996.

Stanley, Diane. *Elena*. New York: Hyperion, 1996.

Tamar, Erika. *Alphabet City Ballet*. New York: HarperCollins, 1996.

———. *The Garden of Happiness*. Illus.. Illustrated by Barbara Lambase. San Diego: Harcourt Brace, 1996.

Van Laan, Nancy. *La boda*. (The Wedding). Illus. Andrea Arroyo. Boston: Little, Brown, 1996.

Wing, Natasha. *Jalapeño Bagels*. Illus. Robert Casilla. New York: Atheneum, 1996.

Winter, Jeanette. *Josefina*. San Diego: Harcourt Brace, 1996.

Although beyond the criteria for the Américas Award, other notable 1996 publications include

Presilla, Maricel E., and Gloria Soto. *Life around the Lake: Embroideries by the Women of Lake Patzcuaro*. New York: Henry Holt, 1996.

Presilla, Maricel E. *Mola: Cuna Life Stories and Art*. New York: Henry Holt, 1996.

1995 Winner

Temple, Frances. *Tonight by Sea*. New York: Orchard Books, 1995.

1995 Honorable Mentions

Cofer, Judith Ortiz. *An Island Like You: Stories of the Barrio*. New York: Orchard Books, 1995.

Soto, Gary. *Chato's Kitchen*. Illus. Susan Guevara. New York: G.P. Putnam's Sons, 1995.

Talbert, Marc. *Heart of a Jaguar*. New York: Simon & Schuster, 1995.

1995 Commended List

Ada, Alma Flor. *Mediopollito/Half-Chicken*. Illus. Kim Howard. New York: Doubleday, 1995.

Anaya, Rudolfo. *The Farolitos of Christmas*. Illus. Edward Gonzales. New York: Hyperion, 1995.

Ancona, George. *Fiesta U.S.A.* (Spanish and English editions). New York: Lodestar, 1995.

Bertrand, Diane Gonzales. *Sweet Fifteen*. Houston: Arte Publico, 1995.

Brusca, Maria Cristina and Tona Wilson. *Pedro Fools the Gringo, and Other Tales*. Illus. Maria Cristina Brusca. New York: Henry Holt, 1995.

———. *When Jaguars Ate the Moon and Other Stories about Animals and Plants of the Americas*. Illus. Maria Cristina Brusca. New York: Holt, 1995.

Ciavonne, Jean. *Carlos, Light the Farolito*. Illus. Donna Clair. New York: Clarion, 1995.

Dorros, Arthur. *Isla/La isla*. (Separate English and Spanish editions.) Illus. Elisa Kleven. New York: Dutton, 1995.

Garland, Sherry. *Indio*. San Diego: Harcourt Brace, 1995.

Gerson, Mary-Joan. *People of Corn: A Mayan Story*. Illus. Carla Golembe. Boston: Little, Brown and Company, n.d.

González, Ralfka and Ana Ruiz. *My First Book of Proverbs/Mi primer libro de dichos*. Emeryville, Calif.: Children's Book Press, 1995.

Gregory, Kristiana. *The Stowaway: A Tale of California Pirates*. New York: Scholastic, 1995.

Hernandez, Irene Beltran. *The Secret of Two Brothers*. Houston: Piñata Books (Arte Publico Press), 1995.

Herrera, Juan Felipe. *Calling the Doves/ El canto de las palomas*. Illus. Elly Simmons. Emeryville, Calif.: Children's Book Press, 1995.

Keister, Douglas. *Fernando's Gift/El regalo de Fernando*. Illus. Douglas Keister. San Francisco: Sierra Club Books for Children, 1995.

Levy, Janice. *The Spirit of Tío Fernando: A Day of the Dead Story*. Illus. Morella Fuenmayor. Morton Grove, Ill.: Albert Whitman & Company, 1995.

Mike, Jan. *Juan Bobo and the Horse of Seven Colors: A Puerto Rican Legend*. Illus. Charles Reasoner. Mahwah, N.J.: Troll Associates, 1995.

Mohr, Nicholasa and Antonio Martorell. *The Song of El Coqui: And Other Tales of Puerto Rico*. New York: Viking, 1995.

Nye, Naomi Shihab, ed. *The Tree Is Older Than You Are: A Bilingual Gathering of Poems and Stories From Mexico With Paintings By Mexican Artists*. New York: Simon & Schuster, 1995.

Paulsen, Gary. *The Tortilla Factory/La tortilleria*. (Separate Spanish and English editions). Illus. Ruth Wright Paulsen. San Diego: Harcourt Brace, 1995.

Rossi, Joyce. *The Gullywasher*. Flagstaff: Northland, 1995.

Scott, Ann Herbert. *Hi*. Illus. Glo Coalson. New York: Philomel, 1994.

Shute, Linda. *Rabbit Wishes*. New York: Lothrop, Lee & Shepard, 1995.

Soto, Gary. *Canto Familiar*. Illus. Annika Nelson. San Diego: Harcourt Brace, 1995.

———. *Summer on Wheels*. New York: Scholastic, 1995.

Torres, Leyla. *Saturday Sancocho*. New York, Farrar, Straus and Giroux, 1995.

1994 Winner

Joseph, Lynn. *The Mermaid's Twin Sister: More Stories from Trinidad*. Illus. Donna Perrone. New York: Clarion, 1994.

1994 Commended List

Ada, Alma Flor. *Where the Flame Trees Bloom*. Illus. Antonio Martorell. New York: Atheneum, 1994.

Albert, Richard E. *Alejandro's Gift*. Illus. Sylvia Long. San Francisco: Chronicle Books, 1994.

Atkin, S. Beth. *Voices from the Fields: Children of Migrant Farmworkers Tell Their Stories*. Boston: Little, Brown, 1993.

Bernhard, Emery and Durga Bernhard. *The Tree That Rains: The Flood Myth of the Huichol Indians of Mexico*. New York: Holiday House, 1994.

Bernier-Grand., Carmen T. *Juan Bobo: Four Folktales from Puerto Rico*. Illus. Ernesto Ramos Nieves. New York: HarperCollins, 1994.

Blanco, Alberto. *Angel's Kite/La estrella de Angel*. Illus. Rodolfo Morales. Emeryville, Calif.: Children's Book Press, 1994.

Bunting, Eve. *A Day's Work*. Illus. Ronald Himler. New York: Clarion, 1994.

Carlson, Lori, ed. *Cool Salsa: Bilingual Poems on Growing Up Latino in the United States*. New York: Holt, 1994.

Castaneda, Omar S. *Imagining Isabel*. New York: Lodestar, 1994.

Czernecki, Stefan, and Timothy Rhodes. *The Hummingbird's Gift*. Straw weavings by Juliana Reyes de Silva and Juan Hilario Silva. New York: Hyperion, 1994.

Dawson, Mildred Leinweber. *Over Here It's Different: Carolina's Story*. Illus. Geroge Ancona. New York: Macmillan, 1993.

De Paola, Tomie. *The Legend of the Poinsettia*. New York: Putnam, 1994.

Franklin, Kristine L. *When the Monkeys Came Back*. Illus. Robert Roth. New York: Atheneum, 1994.

González, Lucía M. *The Bossy Gallito: A Traditional Cuban Folktale*. Illus. Lulu Delacre. New York: Scholastic, 1994.

Gordon, Ginger. *My Two Worlds*. Illus. Martha Cooper. New York: Clarion, 1993.

Grossman, Patricia. *Saturday Market*. Illus. Enrique O. Sanchez. New York: Lothrop, Lee & Shepard, 1994.

Jaramillo, Nelly Palacio. *Grandmother's Nursery Rhymes/Las nanas de Abuelita*. Illus. Elivia Savadier. New York: Holt, 1994.

Jimenez, Juan Ramon. *Platero y yo/Platero and I*. Selected, translated, and adapted from the Spanish by Myra Cohn Livingston and Joseph F. Dominguez. Illus. Antonio Frasconi. New York: Clarion, 1994.

Johnston, Tony. *The Tale of Rabbit and Coyote*. Illus. Tomie de Paola. New York: Putnam, 1994.

Kendall, Sarita. *Ransom for a River Dolphin*. Minneapolis: Lerner, 1993.

Mathews, Sally Schofer. *The Sad Night: The Story of an Aztec Victory and a Spanish Loss*. New York: Clarion Books, 1994.

Merino, José María. *Beyond the Ancient Cities*. Trans. Helen Lane. New York: Farrar, Straus and Giroux, 1994. (originally published in Spain in 1987).

Meyer, Carolyn. *Rio Grande Stories*. San Diego: Harcourt Brace, 1994.

Mora, Pat. *Pablo's Tree*. Illus. Cecily Lang. New York: Macmillan, 1994.

Ober, Hal. *How Music Came to the World: An Ancient Mexican Myth*. Illus. Carol. Ober. Boston: Houghton Mifflin, 1994.

Orozco, José-Luis. *De Colores and Other Latin-American Folk Songs for Children*. Illus. Elisa Kleven. New York: Dutton, 1994.

Pico, Fernando. *The Red Comb*. Illus. Maria Antonia Ordonez. (Originally published in Spanish by Ediciones Huracan, Puerto Rico and Ediciones Ekare, Venezuela) Mahwah, N.J.: BridgeWater Books, 1994.

Presilla, Maricel E. *Feliz nochebuena, Feliz navidad*. Illus. Ismael Espinosa Ferrer. New York: Holt, 1994.

Roybal, Laura. *Billy*. Boston: Houghton Mifflin, 1994.

Thomas, Jane Resh. *Lights on the River*. Illus. Michael Dooling. New York: Hyperion, 1994.

Villasenor, Victor. *Walking Stars: Stories of Magic and Power*. Houston: Arte Publico Press, 1994.

1993 Winner
Delacre, Lulu. *Vejigante Masquerader*. New York: Scholastic, 1993.

Commended List
Becerra de Jenkins, Lyll. *Celebrating the Hero*. New York: Lodestar, 1993.

Castaneda, Omar. *Abuela's Weave*. Illus. Enrique O. Sanchez. New York: Lee & Low, 1993.

Dorros, Arthur. *Radio Man: A Story in English and Spanish*. Trans. Sandra Marulanda Dorros. New York: HarperCollins. 1993.

Markun, Patricia Maloney. *The Little Painter of Sabana Grande*. Illus. Robert Casilla. New York: Bradbury, 1993.

PURA BELPRÉ AWARD

"Honors Latino writers and illustrators whose work best portrays, affirms, and celebrates the Latino cultural experience in a work of literature for children and youth. The award is named in honor of Pura Belpré, the first Latina librarian from the New York Public Library, who as a children's librarian, puppeteer, author, and storyteller enriched the lives of Puerto Rican children through her pioneer work in preserving and disseminating Puerto Rican folklore."

The first ALSC/REFORMA Pura Belpré awards were given at the first REFORMA National Conference held in Austin, Texas, in 1996. This biennial award has now taken its place along side all the other awards administered ALSC, and is announced together with the Newbery, Caldecott, and other awards at the American Library Association (ALA) Midwinter Meeting. The first award jury considered approximately 80 books for the period of 1990–1995 written or illustrated by Latino authors who were residents of the United States. (And, as with other ALA children's book awards, the recipients must be U.S. citizens or residents). The 1998 and all future awards were and will be given to books published only within the two-year time frame. It is important to note the stipulation that besides being written or illustrated by a Latino, the books must also exhibit cultural content. In other words, they must be relevant to and celebrate Latino culture.

Pura Belpré Award Recipients

1998 Awards for Writing

Victor Martinez for *Parrot in the Oven: Mi Vida*. Joanna Cotler Books (HarperCollins), 1996.

Honor Books for Writing

Floyd Martinez for *Spirits of the High Mesa*. Houston: Arte Público Press, 1997.

Francisco X. Alarcon for *Laughing Tomatoes and Other Poems*. Children's Book Press, 1997.

1998 Award for Illustration

Stephanie Garcia for *Snapshots from the Wedding* by Gary Soto. Putnam, 1997.

1998 Honor Books for Illustration

Enrique O. Sanchez for *The Golden Flower* by Nina Jaffe. Simon & Schuster, 1996.

Carmen Lomas Garza for *My Family/Mi Familia*. Children's Book Press, 1996.

Simon Silva for *Gathering the Sun: An Alphabet in Spanish and English* by Alma Flor Ada. Lothrop, 1997.

1996 Awards
1996 Award for Writing

Judith Ortiz Cofer for *An Island Like You: Stories of the Barrio*. Orchard Books, 1995.

1996 Honor Books for Writing

Lucía Gonzáles for *The Bossy Gallito/El gallo de bodas: A Traditional Cuban Folktale*. Scholastic, Inc. 1994.

Gary Soto for *Baseball in April and Other Stories*. Harcourt Brace, 1994.

1996 Award Winner for Illustration

Susan Guevara for *Chato's Kitchen* by Gary Soto. G. P. Putnam's Sons, 1995.

1996 Honor Books for Illustration

George Ancona for *Pablo Remembers: The Fiesta of the Day of the Dead/Pablo Recuerda: La Fiesta de el Día de los Muertos*. Lothrop, Lee & Shepard Books, 1993.

Lulu Delacre for *The Bossy Gallito/El Gallo de Bodas: A Traditional Cuban Folktale* by Lucía Gonzales. Scholastic, Inc., 1994.

Carmen Lomas Garza for *Family Pictures/Cuadros de familia*. Children's Book Press, 1990.

9 A SPANISH PRIMER JUST FOR CHILDREN'S LIBRARIANS

This primer is for readers of this book who do not speak Spanish but would like to do some programming and storytelling in that language. The good news is that, unlike English, Spanish is pronounced as it is written. There are few pesky anomalies like those that plague English. (This difference is the reason it is difficult for people to learn English when Spanish is their primary language.)

While it is beyond the scope of this book to provide a complete course in the Spanish language, I hope that the material provided here will give professionals the needed information to communicate basic phrases to children, to tell a passable story in Spanish, or to properly pronounce words in a bilingual story. Much of the material that follows is adapted from a course syllabus entitled "Speaking Spanish with Your Patrons" prepared by a committee of librarians at the Dallas Public Library and used as an in-house training document. Thanks to Lee Shuey, chair of that committee, for permission to adapt this material.

SPANISH PRONUNCIATION GUIDE

There are 30 letters in the Spanish alphabet. In addition to the letters of the English alphabet, Spanish treats ch, ll, ñ, and rr each as a letter. See Table 9.1 for the pronunciation of each letter. In Spanish, the letters k and w are used only in words of foreign origin.

Words ending in a vowel, n, or s are stressed on the second to last syllable. Other words are stressed on the last syllable. Any exception to this rule will have a written accent over the vowel of the stressed syllable.

Capitalization is used more often in English than in Spanish. Generally, in Spanish only the first word of a title is capitalized. The exception to this rule is proper nouns within a title, which are capitalized. Days of the week and months of the year are not capitalized. Names of countries are capitalized, but languages and nationalities are not.

You should be aware of some important differences in punctuation between English and Spanish. Instead of using quotation marks, conversation is indicated with the use of dashes (—) placed before what is being said. An inverted exclamation point or question mark is placed at the beginning of any exclamation or question. In working with numbers, be aware that commas and periods are used the opposite of the way they are used in English. In Spanish, a comma represents the decimal point and a period is used within a number to show thousands, millions, etc. ($5.674,84 vs. $5,674.84).

Table 9.1 Alphabet Pronunciation

Letter	Name	Sound	Notes
a	a	f<u>a</u>ther	
b	be	<u>b</u>oy	
c	ce	<u>s</u>in	before e or i
		<u>c</u>at	before other letters
ch	che	<u>ch</u>urch	
d	de	<u>d</u>ay	at beginning of word, or after n or l
		<u>th</u>is	in other positions
e	e	d<u>ay</u>	if syllable ends in a vowel
		p<u>e</u>t	if syllable ends in a consonant
f	efe	<u>f</u>ire	
g	ge	<u>h</u>a!	before e or i
		<u>g</u>oat	before other letters
h	hache		always silent
i	i	sk<u>i</u>	
j	jota	<u>h</u>a!	
k	ka	<u>k</u>ick	
l	ele	<u>l</u>et	
ll	elle	<u>y</u>es	pronounced like a soft English /j/ in some countries
m	eme	<u>m</u>an	
n	ene	<u>n</u>o	
ñ	eñe	can<u>y</u>on	
o	o	<u>o</u>pen	
p	pe	<u>p</u>ast	
q	cu	<u>k</u>ite	
r	ere	bu<u>tt</u>er	pronounce with a flap of the tongue
rr	erre		strongly trilled
s	ese	<u>s</u>ee	
t	te	<u>t</u>ip	
u	u	r<u>u</u>le	u after g or q is silent
v	ve	le<u>v</u>er	if v begins a word pronounce like <u>b</u>ib
w	doble u		pronounced as English v or w
x	equis	<u>h</u>at	before vowels
		<u>s</u>o	before consonants
y	i griega	<u>y</u>es	if y begins word or is between vowels
		sk<u>i</u>	as a word, or as last letter in word
z	zeta	<u>s</u>ee	

PHRASES

Spanish words in parentheses are synonyms for underlined words or the Spanish expression for the English word in parentheses.

GENERAL

Courtesy

Please.
Por favor.

Thank you.
Gracias.

You're welcome.
De nada.

I'm sorry.
Lo siento.

How may I help you?
¿Cómo puedo servirle?

You can get a library card at the circulation desk.
Puede obtener una tarjeta de <u>lector</u> (biblioteca) en el mostrador de circulación.

It will take at least ten minutes.
Tardará diez minutos a lo menos.

Return books here.
Devuelva los libros aquí.

The services of the library are free.
Los servicios de la biblioteca son gratis.

It is a pleasure to help you.
Es un placer ayudarle.

Did you find what you need?
¿Encontró lo que necesita?

Where is your mommy? (daddy, family)
¿Dónde está tu mamá? (papá, familia)

Is that your mother?
¿Es esa tu mamá?

Do you know where your child is?
¿Sabe usted donde está su hijo?

Please wait a moment.
Un momento, por favor.

Behavior
Don't yell.
No grite.

Don't cry. We will find your mother.
No llore. Encontraremos a tu mamá.

Walk. Don't run.
Camine. No corra.

Sit down.
Siéntese.

I am sorry, but eating (drinking) is not allowed in the library.
Lo siento, pero no se permite <u>comer</u> (beber) en la biblioteca.

Hours
We are closed on Sundays, but the central library is open.
Estamos cerrado los domingos, pero la biblioteca central esta abierta.

The library opens tomorrow at ten o'clock.
La biblioteca está abierta mañana a las diez.

The library closes today at eight o'clock.
La biblioteca cierra hoy a las ocho.

Language
Do you speak English?
¿Habla inglés?

I don't speak Spanish.
No hablo español.

I speak a little Spanish.
Hablo un poco de español.

Speak slowly.
Hable despacio.

Sorry, but I didn't understand you.
Perdon, pero no le entiendo.

I don't understand.
No entiendo.

Do you understand me?
¿Me entiende?

Now I understand.
Ahora entiendo.

Repeat the question.
Repita la pregunta.

I'll repeat it.
Voy a repetirlo.

Wait here while I find someone who speaks Spanish.
Espere aquí mientras encuentro alguien que habla español.

Location of Things

Where are the children's books? The books for children are on the second floor.
¿Dónde están los libros para los niños? Los libros para los niños están en el segundo piso.

Where is the bathroom? The bathroom is around the corner. Ask for the key at the information counter.
¿Dónde está <u>el baño</u>? (los servicios) <u>El baño está</u> a la vuelta de la esquina. Pida la llave en la mostrador de información. (los servicios estan)

Where is the water fountain? The water fountain is near the bathrooms.
¿Dónde está la fuente de agua? La fuente de agua está cerca <u>del baño</u>. (de los servicios)

Where is the card catalog? The catalog is on the computer.
¿Dónde está el catálogo? El catálogo está en la computadora.

Where is the telephone? The public telephone is near the entrance.
¿Donde esta el teléfono? El teléfono público está cerca de la entrada.

Is there a copy machine here?
¿Hay una <u>copiadora</u> aqui? (máquina de copias)

Machines

Do you have a telephone? May I use the phone?
¿Tiene usted un teléfono? ¿Puedo usar el teléfono?

I need your help with the copy machine.
Necesito su ayuda con la <u>copiadora</u>. (máquina de copias)

Can you show me how to use the copy machine?
¿Puede usted mostrarme como usar la copiadora? (máquina de copias)

The copy machine costs fifteen cents a page.
La <u>copiadora</u> cuesta quince centavos por cada página. (máquina de copias)

The machine is out of order.
La máquina no funciona.

CIRCULATION

Borrowing Materials

How can I check out books? You need to have a library card.
¿Cómo puedo <u>tomar</u> los libros prestados? (sacar) Necesita tener una tarjeta de <u>lector.</u> (la biblioteca)

How many books can I check out? You may borrow those you like.
¿Cuántos libros me permiten <u>tomar</u> prestados? (sacar) Puede <u>tomar</u> prestados los que usted quiera. (sacar)

Do I have to buy the books, or rent them? We lend them to you free of charge.
¿Tengo que comprar los libros, o <u>rentarlos</u>? (alquilarlos) Le prestamos los libros gratis.

How long can I borrow the books? The books may be checked out for three weeks.
¿Por cuánto tiempo puedo <u>tomar</u> los libros prestados? (sacar) Los libros se pueden <u>tomar</u> prestados por tres semanas. (sacar)

Do you want to check out this book? Please take it to the circulation counter. You need a library card to borrow the books.

¿Quiere <u>tomar</u> prestado este libro? (sacar) Por favor, traígalo al mostrador de circulación. Necesita una tarjeta de <u>lector</u> para <u>tomar</u> prestados los libros. (la biblioteca) (sacar)

The books may be checked out.

Se pueden <u>tomar</u> prestados los libros. (sacar)

The book may be checked out.

Se puede <u>tomar</u> prestado el libro. (sacar)

I am sorry, but the books you need are checked out.

Lo siento, pero los libros que necesita están prestados.

These magazines do not circulate.

Estas revistas no se pueden <u>tomar</u> prestadas. (sacar)

These magazines can be checked out.

Estas revistas se pueden <u>tomar</u> prestadas. (sacar)

This is a special loan, and you may check out the video for only one week.

Este es un <u>préstamo</u> especial y puede <u>tomar</u> prestado el video solamente por una semana. (servicio) (sacar)

This is a reference book. It may not be checked out, but you may use it here in the library.

Este es un libro de <u>consulta</u>. (referencia) No se puede <u>tomar</u> prestado, pero puede usarlo aqui en la biblioteca. (sacar)

I will need to hold some identification here at the desk. Do you have a driver's license or a library card?

Necesito retener alguna identificación aquí en el escritorio. ¿Tiene usted licencia para manejar o tarjeta de <u>lector</u>? (la biblioteca)

Courtesy

Please do not put the books back on the shelf. Leave them on the table/book truck/book bin when you finish. Thank you!

Por favor, no ponga los libros en el estante. Déjelos en la mesa/el carrito de libros/el depositorio cuando termine usted. ¡Muchas gracias!

Did the book help you?

¿Le ayudó el libro?

I am glad you are interested in this special service. Here is the schedule.
Me alegro que le interese en este servicio especial. Aquí está el horario.

What other kinds of services do you offer?
¿Qué otros tipos de servicios ofrecen ustedes?

Fines

If the books are late, you must pay a fine.
Si regresa los libros tarde, hay que pagar una multa.

How much is the fine? The fine is twenty cents per day per book.
¿Cuánto es la multa? La multa es veinte centavos por día por cada libro.

Library Card

Do you have a library card?
¿Tiene usted una tarjeta de <u>lector</u>? (la biblioteca)

May I see your identification?
¿Puedo ver su identificación?

What is your name? My name is . . .
¿Cómo se llama? Me llamo . . .

And your telephone number? My telephone number is . . .
¿Y su número de teléfono? Mi número de teléfono es . . .

How old are you? I am . . . years old.
¿Cúantos años tiene usted? Tengo . . . años.

Which school do you go to? I go to . . .
¿A qué escuela <u>atiende</u>? (asiste) Voy a . . .

What grade are you in? I am in . . . grade.
¿En qué grado está? Estoy en el grado . . .

If you do not have a library card, you may read books only in the library.
Si no tiene una tarjeta de <u>lector</u>, puede leer los libros solamente en la biblioteca. (la biblioteca)

Locate a Book

I need help in finding a book.
Necesito ayuda para encontrar un libro.

I don't know the author's name.
No sé el nombre del autor.

I don't know the title of the book.
No sé el título del libro.

I am looking for a book of/about (science projects, animals, biographies, sports, poetry).
Busco un libro de/acerca de (proyectos de ciencia, animales, biografías, deportes, poesía).

Here is the list of materials in Spanish.
Aquí está la lista de materias en español.

Follow me. I will show you the books in Spanish.
Sígame. Yo le indicaré los libros en español.

Fiction is arranged in alphabetical order by author's last name.
Libros de ficción están ordenados en orden alfabético por el apellido del autor.

Nonfiction books are arranged by numbers on the shelves. The numbers stand for subjects.
Los libros factuales están ordenados por números en los estantes. Los numeros representan los sujetos.

The classification number indicates the location of the book on the shelves.
El número de clasificación le indica donde se encuentra el libro en los estantes.

Where are the newspapers/magazines/videos/cassettes/CDs?
¿Dónde están los periódicos/las revistas/los videos/los casetes de música/los CDs?

DEWEY DECIMAL CLASSIFICATION

The chart on pages 216–218 shows the Dewey Decimal Classification in both English and Spanish. You can photocopy it for Spanish speaking patrons.

Table 9.2 Dewey Decimal Classification

Class	English	Spanish
000	Generalities	Generalidades
010	Bibliography	Bibliografías
020	Library & Information Sciences	Ciencia de biblioteca
030	Encyclopedias	Enciclopedias
040	[Not currently used]	—
050	Publications	Publicaciones
060	Museology	Museología
070	Periodicals	Periodismo
080	General Collections	Ensayos, disertaciones, etc.
090	Manuscripts	Manuscritos y libros de raros
100	Philosophy	Filosofía
110	Metaphysics	Metafísicos
120	Epistemology	Epistemología
130	Paranormal Phenomena	Parasicología
140	Specific Philosophical Schools & Viewpoints	Puntos de vista de filosóficos específicos
150	Psychology	Sicología
160	Logic	Lógica
170	Ethics	Éticos
180	Ancient Philosophy	Filosofía antigua
190	Modern and Western Philosophy	Filosofía occidental moderno
200	Religion	Religión
210	Religion Theory	Religión natural
220	Bible	Biblias
230	Christian Theology	Teologías cristianas
240	Christian Moral & Devotional Theology	Teologías cristianas morales y devocionales
250	Christian Religious Orders, local	Ordenes sagradas, locales
260	Christian Social & Ecclesiastical Theology	Teologías eclesiásticas y sociales
270	Christian Church History	Historia de iglesias cristianas
280	Denominations & Sects of Christian Church	Denominaciones y sectas de iglesias cristianas
290	Other Religions	Otras religiones
300	Social Sciences	Ciencias sociales
310	Collections of General Statistics	Estadísticas
320	Political Science	Ciencias políticas

Table 9.2 Dewey Decimal Classification (continued)

Class	English	Spanish
330	Economics	Ciencias económicas
340	Law	Ciencia jurídica
350	Public Administration	Administración pública
360	Social Problems & Services	Servicios sociales, asociaciones
370	Education	Educación
380	Commerce, Communications, Transportation	Comercio, comunicaciones, transportación
390	Customs, Etiquette, Folklore	Costumbres, etiqueta, tradiciones y leyendas
400	Language	Idioma
410	Linguistics	Linguísticos
420	English & Old English	Idiomas ingleses
430	Germanic	Idiomas alemanes
440	French	Idiomas franceses
450	Italian	Idiomas italianos
460	Spanish & Portuguese	Idiomas españoles y portugueses
470	Latin	Idiomas latinas
480	Classical Greek & Hellenic Languages	Idiomas griegos clásicos y helénicos
490	Other Languages	Otros idiomas
500	Natural Sciences	Ciencias puras
510	Mathematics	Matemáticas
520	Astronomy	Astronomía
530	Physics	Ciencias naturales (física)
540	Chemistry	Química
550	Earth Sciences	Ciencias del mundo y otros mundos
560	Paleontology; Paleozoology	Paleontología
570	Life Sciences; Biology	Ciencia de vida (existencia)
580	Plants	Ciencia botánica
590	Animals	Ciencia zoológico
600	Technology	Tecnología
610	Medicine	Ciencia de medicina
620	Engineering	Ingeniería
630	Agriculture	Agricultura, agronomía
640	Home Economics	Economía doméstica
650	Management & Auxiliary Services	Manejo y servicios auxiliares
660	Chemical Engineering	Tecnología química
670	Manufacturing	Manufactura (fabricación)

Table 9.2 Dewey Decimal Classification (continued)

Class	English	Spanish
680	Manufacturing Specific Products	Manufactura de productos específicos
690	Buildings	Edificios
700	The Arts	Los artes
710	Civic and Landscape Art	Artes cívicos y paisajes
720	Architecture	Arquitectura
730	Sculpture	Escultura
740	Drawing	Dibujo
750	Painting and Paintings	Pintura y cuadros
760	Graphic Arts	Dibujo lineal
770	Photography	Fotografía
780	Music	Música
790	Performing Arts	Arte amaestrado
800	Literature	Literatura
810	American Literature	Literatura americana
820	English and Old English Literature	Literatura de inglaterra y anglosajón
830	German Literature	Literatura alemana
840	French Literature	Literatura francasa
850	Italian Literature	Literatura italiana
860	Spanish & Portuguese Literature	Literatura española y portuguesa
870	Latin Literature	Literatura latina
880	Greek Literature	Literatura griega
890	Other Literature	Otras literaturas
900	Geography	Geografía
910	Travel	Viajar
920	Biography & Genealogy	Biografía y genealogía
930	History of Ancient World	Historia del mundo antiguo
940	History of Europe	Historia de europa
950	History of Asia	Historia de asia
960	History of Africa	Historia de áfrica
970	History of North America	Historia de norteamérica
980	History of South America	Historia de sudamérica
999	History of other Regions, Oceans, & Extraterrestrial	Historia de otras regiones, oceanas y extraterrestre

Table 9.3 Days of the Week

English	Spanish
Monday	lunes
Tuesday	martes
Wednesday	miércoles
Thursday	jueves
Friday	viernes
Saturday	sábado
Sunday	domingo

Table 9.4 Months of the Year

English	Spanish
January	enero
February	febrero
March	marzo
April	abril
May	mayo
June	junio
July	julio
August	agosto
September	septiembre
October	octubre
November	noviembre
December	diciembre

Table 9.5 Numbers		
Number	**English**	**Spanish**
1	one	uno
2	two	dos
3	three	tres
4	four	cuatro
5	five	cinco
6	six	seis
7	seven	siete
8	eight	ocho
9	nine	nueve
10	ten	diez
11	eleven	once
12	twelve	doce
13	thirteen	trece
14	fourteen	catorce
15	fifteen	quince
16	sixteen	diez y seis
17	seventeen	diez y siete
18	eighteen	diez y ocho
19	nineteen	diez y nueve
20	twenty	veinte
30	thirty	treinta
40	forty	cuarenta
50	fifty	cincuenta
60	sixty	sesenta
70	seventy	setenta
80	eighty	ochenta
90	ninety	noventa
100	one hundred	cien (ciento)
200	two hundred	doscientos
300	three hundred	trescientos
400	four hundred	cuatrocientos
500	five hundred	quinientos
600	six hundred	seiscientos
700	seven hundred	setecientos
800	eight hundred	ochocientos
900	nine hundred	novecientos
1000	one thousand	mil
1,000,000	one million	un millón

10 AN ANNOTATED BIBLIOGRAPHY OF LATINO CHILDREN'S LITERATURE

Note: This bibliography is divided into two simple sections: professional materials and literature. As elsewhere in the book I've distinguished between books in Spanish and bilingual books in the following way: If a book is available only in Spanish, I have translated the title and placed it in parentheses. If the book is bilingual, the Spanish and English titles are separated with a slash (/). If there is an English or Spanish translation of a book published separately, I've listed whichever came out first, with the translation noted in the annotation. With these Spanish translations I've only noted the publication information that is different from the original. If only the title is listed, then the translation has the same publisher and publication date as the original. Where the content of a book is made clear by the title (such as *Songs, Poems, and Rhymes for Children*), no annotation is included, unless there is something special about the book I've noted.

PROFESSIONAL RESOURCES

Ada, Alma Flor. *A Magical Encounter: Spanish-Language Children's Literature in the Classroom*. Mexico D.F.: Santillana, 1990.
A very useful book for classrooom teachers that pulls together books that relate to particular themes and provides activities to supplement their use in the curriculum.

Allen, Adela Artola. *Library Services for Hispanic Children: A Guide for Public and School Librarians*. Phoenix, Ariz.: Oryx, 1987.
Provides good background on the history of library services to Latino children, as well as lists of different resources. It also includes a chapter on materials selection.

Berdiales, Germán. *El alegre folklore de los niños* (The happy folklore of childhood). Buenos Aires, Argentina: Libreria Hachette, 1958.
A book directed at adults working with children. Includes rhymes,

riddles, stories to tell, and scenes to act out. Includes yet another version of Perez and Martina called "*La Hormiguita.*"

Bravo-Villasante, Carmen. *Adivina adivinanza* (Guess the riddle). Madrid: Ediciones Didascolia, 1978.
A collection of riddles for children to guess and try out on others.

———. *Antología de la literatura infantil en lengua española* (Anthology of children's literature in the Spanish language). Vol. I, II. Madrid: Editorial Doncel, 1973.
As Bravo-Villasante states in her introduction, this anthology goes beyond her anthology of children's literature from Spain to embrace that of all Hispanic countries. It is is arranged chronologically and includes biographical information about the authors. Here you can find a wealth of all kinds of literature, including riddles, stories, songs, poems, and plays.

———. *Antología de la literatura infantil española* (Anthology of Spanish children's literature). 9th ed. Vol. I, II. Madrid: Editorial Doncel, 1962, 1989.
The standard anthology of children's literature from Spain. It is organized historically.

———. *China, china, capuchina, en esta mano esta la china* (Nonsense rhyme). Illus. Carmen Andrada. Valladolid: Editorial Miñón, 1981.
Riddles, rhymes, and games with appealing illustrations.

———. *Colorín colorete* (Nonsense rhyme). Madrid: Ediciones Didascolia, 1983.
A book of riddles, rhymes, tongue twisters, lullabies, carols, and prayers.

———. *La hermosura del mundo y otros cuentos españoles* (The beauty of the world and other Spanish stories). Barcelona: Editorial Noguer, 1984, c. 1980.
A collection of retellings of popular Spanish stories. Includes versions of "The Rooster Who Went to His Uncle's Wedding" (El Gallo), and "Martina the Cockroach" (La cucarachita y el ratoncito).

———. *Historia de la literatura infantil española* (History of Spanish children's literature). Madrid: Editorial Doncel, 1983.
Chronicles the story of the children's literature of Spain beginning in medieval times up through the present day. Helpful features include a list of histories and other studies of children's literature in

addition to a catalog of Spanish children's books. It is indexed by author and title.

————. *Historia y antología de la literatura infantil iberoamericana* (History and anthology of Latin American children's literature) 3rd ed. Vol. I, II. Madrid: Editorial Doncel, 1965, 1988.
These books supply a history of children's literature in each Latin American country. They include folklore and samples of the works of the most important authors from each country as well as a brief description of their careers.

————. *El libro de las fabulas* (The Book of fables). Illus. Carmen Andrada. Valladolid: Editorial Miñón, 1982.
Fables in verse by Spanish as well as Latin American authors.

————. *Una, dola, tela, catola: el libro del folklore infantil* (The book of children's folklore). Valladolid: Editorial Miñon, 1976.
A collection that is filled with the diverse riches of Spanish of children's folklore. Includes such varied forms as prayers, riddles, Christmas songs, tongue twisters, *piñata* rhymes, and rhymes to begin and end stories.

Carrasquillo, Angela. *Hispanic Children and Youth in the United States: A Resource Guide*. New York: Garland, 1991.
A bibliographic reference with indexes for materials covering social issues facing Latino children.

Cordasco, Francesco. *Bilingual Education in American Schools: A Guide to Information Sources*. Detroit: Gale, 1979.
While this source is dated, it does provide some useful background on bilingual education issues, such as in tracing the origins of the Bilingual Education Act.

de Cortés, Oralia Garza, and Louise Yarian Zwick. "Hispanic Materials and Programs: Bibliography." *Venture into Cultures: A Resource Book of Multicultural Materials and Programs*, ed. Carla D. Hayden. Chicago: American Library Association, 1992, pp. 82–99.
The bibliography includes both fiction and nonfiction titles and divides them into English and Spanish. Includes grade levels and annotations.

DeSpain, Pleasant. *Thirty-Three Multicultural Tales to Tell*. Illus. Joe Shlichta. Little Rock, Ark.: August House, 1993.
Among the Latino folktales included in this collection are the following:

"Rabbit's Last Race," from Mexico. This is presented as a kind of sequel to "The Tortoise and the Hare." This time Rabbit competes with a frog, but it is actually Frog and a number of his friends who fool and beat the rabbit.

"Señor Rattlesnake Learns to Fly," from Mexico. Señor Rattlesnake tries flying when the birds get a stick that he can hold on to with his mouth while they carry it into the air. But the taunts of Señor Eagle cause him to fall to open his mouth, fall to the ground, and lose his desire to fly.

"The Chirimía," from Guatemala. The princess promises to marry a poor man when he can sing as sweetly as the songbirds. The Spirit of the Forest shows him how to make an instrument from a tree branch, and he returns able to play songs as beautiful as those of the birds.

"Juan's Maguey Plant," from Mexico. Juan has the largest maguey plant in all of Mexico. Coyote comes at night to drink the juice of the plant (which is used to make tequila). Juan tries to capture him and finally drives him away by giving him the scare of his life.

Duran, Daniel Flores. *Latino Materials: A Multimedia Guide for Children and Young Adults.* New York: Neal-Schuman, 1979.
Contains three bibliographies: books and films focusing on Mexican-Americans, those focusing on Puerto Ricans, and a general bibliography of materials that pertain to all Latino groups.

Ebinger, Virginia Nylander. *Spanish Songs, Games, and Stories of Childhood.* Santa Fe, N.M.: Sunstone, 1993.
Particularly notable for its explanations of how to play the various games. Includes the music for all the songs.

Ferré, Rosario. *Los cuentos de Juan Bobo* (The stories of Juan Bobo). Río Piedras, Puerto Rico: Ediciones Huracán, 1981.
Five Juan Bobo stories. They include a story about Juan and young ladies from Manto Prieto, Juan going to mass, Juan making a fool of himself dining in a wealthy home, and Juan journeying to the capital city.

Güereña, Salvador, ed. *Latino Librarianship: A Handbook for Professionals.* Jefferson, N.C.: McFarland, 1990.
A collection of articles on topics of interest to professionals giving library services to Latinos.

Jiménez, Emma Holgun, and Chonchita Morales Puncel. *Para chiquitines: cancionciats, versitos y juegos meñiques* (For little ones: songs, verses, and fingerplays). Illus. Gilbert T. Martinez. Glendale, Calif.: Bowmar, 1969.

A book of songs, poems, and fingerplays with colorful illustrations. Includes music and guitar chords for the songs. Some are traditional, others are new creations of the authors.

Llimona, Mercedes. *Juegos y canciones para los niños* (Stories and songs for children). Barcelona: Ediciones Hymnsa, 1984.
A selection of fingerplays with illustrations that suggest how to act them out. Includes "*Este niño tiene sueño*," "*Cinco lobitos*," "*Éste compró un huevito*," "*Que llueva*," "*La gallina ponicana*," "*Arroz con leche*," and many others.

Lubbock Public Schools. *Kindergarten Bilingual Resource Handbook*. Austin, Tex.: Dissemination and Assessment Center for Bilingual Education, 1973.
Includes a fairly large selection of nursery rhymes and fingerplays.

Medina, Arturo. *Pinto maraña: juegos populares infantiles* (Popular children's games). Illus. Carmen Andrada. Valladolid, Spain: Editorial Miñón, 1987.
Children's games, such as hopscotch, some with accompanying rhymes. Also some song lyrics at the end.

Miller-Lachman, Lyn. *Our Family, Our Friends, Our World: An Annotated Guide to Significant Multicultural Books for Children & Teenagers*. New Providence, N.J.: R. R. Bowker, 1991.
While this is a more general multicultural guide, it does contain some items of interest for those interested in materials for and about Latino children.

"Recommended and Not Recommended Books About Latinas/os for Young Readers." *Multicultural Review*, 2 (December 1994): 30–34.
This article shows in its discussion of recommended and not recommended titles that stereotyping is still a problem in literature for children.

Rochman, Hazel. "Latinos." *Against Borders: Promoting Books for a Multicultural World*. Chicago: American Library Association, 1993, 207–218.
Includes a section in the chapter on "Ethnic U.S.A." devoted to Latinos. Books listed are divided into nonfiction, fiction, and videos. The titles are annotated and grade levels are noted.

Sandoval, Rubén. *Games, Games, Games/Juegos, juegos, juegos: Chicano Children at Play—Games and Rhymes*. Illus. David Strick. New York: Doubleday, 1977.

Black-and-white photos of children illustrate this collection of traditional rhymes used in children's games such as jump rope.

Schon, Isabel. *Basic Collection of Children's Books in Spanish.* Lanham, Md.: Scarecrow, 1986.
A bibliography designed to provide a selector with a basis upon which to develop a collection of children's books in Spanish—the essential titles.

————. *The Best of the Latino Heritage: A Guide to the Best Juvenile Books about Latino People and Cultures.* Lanham, Md.: Scarecrow, 1997.
A good initial choice in that it combines some of the most outstanding titles from Ms. Schon's earlier books along with some new titles.

————. *A Bicultural Heritage: Themes for the Exploration of Mexican and Mexican-American Culture in Books for Children and Adolescents.* Metuchen, N.J.: Scarecrow, 1978.
This book is organized by grade level. Under each level, Schon discusses themes such as customs, lifestyles, heroes, folklore, and history. Each area is divided into three age levels from K-12. There are several types of activities mentioned within each grade level. Includes an extensive list of recommended as well as not recommended books.

————. *Books in Spanish for Children and Young Adults.* Lanham, Md.: Scarecrow, 1978.
This and the succeeding books in the series (listed below) are annotated bibliographies of children's books in Spanish. Schon covers both fiction and nonfiction, and arranges the titles by the nationality of the author. Helpfully, she includes books that are marginal or not recommended as well.

————. *Books in Spanish for Children and Young Adults.* Series II. Lanham, Md.: Scarecrow, 1983.

————. *Books in Spanish for Children and Young Adults.* Series III. Lanham, Md.: Scarecrow, 1985.

————. *Books in Spanish for Children and Young Adults.* Series IV. Lanham, Md.: Scarecrow, 1987.

————. *Books in Spanish for Children and Young Adults.* Series V. Lanham, Md.: Scarecrow, 1989.

———. *Books in Spanish for Children and Young Adults*. Series VI. Lanham, Md.: Scarecrow, 1993.

———. *Contemporary Spanish-Speaking Writers and Illustrators for Children and Young Adults: A Biographical Dictionary*. Westport, Conn.: Greenwood, 1994.
This book provides a wealth of data about of Spanish-speaking children's writers. Schon includes personal data, addresses, career information, membership in professional organizations, awards and honors received, a bibliography for each author, sidelights that include authors' thoughts on their work, and critical sources where one can find articles, books, and reviews of the authors' work.

———. *A Hispanic Heritage: A Guide to Juvenile Books about Hispanic People and Cultures*. Lanham, Md.: Scarecrow, 1980.
This bibliography and the succeeding ones in the series (listed below) are Schon's companion to her bibliographies of books in Spanish. These are comprehensive bibliographies of materials in English that related to Latino culture (note that the most recent book has replaced the word "Hispanic" with "Latino" in the title). The material is organized by country and includes author, title, and subject indices.

———. *A Hispanic Heritage: A Guide to Juvenile Books about Hispanic People and Cultures, Series II*. Lanham, Md.: Scarecrow, 1985.

———. *A Hispanic Heritage: A Guide to Juvenile Books about Hispanic People and Cultures*. Series III. Lanham, Md.: Scarecrow, 1988.

———. *A Hispanic Heritage: A Guide to Juvenile Books about Hispanic People and Cultures*. Series IV. Lanham, Md.: Scarecrow, 1991.

———. *Latino Heritage: A Guide to Juvenile Books about Latino People and Cultures*. Series V. Lanham, Md.: Scarecrow, 1995.

———. *Mexico and Its Literature for Children and Adolescents*. Arizona State University: Center for Latin American Studies, 1977.
An overview of Mexican literature for children and young adults in three sections. First, a history of Mexican children's literature with emphasis on the problems created by economics and the educational system. The second section focuses on the literature and specific nineteenth and twentieth century Mexican authors. The third section describes the prospects for the future. The book includes a bibliography, appendix, and a list of reference works for adults.

————. *Recommended Books in Spanish for Children and Young Adults, 1991–1995.* Lanham, Md.: Scarecrow, 1997.
Includes 1,055 titles that can be used as the basis for an excellent basic collection of books in Spanish for children. Schon provides an extensive annotation for each title. Nonfiction books are arranged by topic and fiction is divided into sections of easy picture books and more general fiction. An up-to-date essential resource.

Schon, Isabel, and S. Corona. *Introducción a la literatura infantil y juvenil* (Introduction to children's and young adult literature). Newark, Del.: International Reading Association, 1996.

Schon, Isabel, Fabio Restrepo, et al. *Spanish-Language Books for Public Libraries.* Chicago: American Library Association, 1986.
This annotated bibliography performs the function of the *Public Library Catalog* for selectors wishing either to build a basic collection of Spanish-language books, or as a standard upon which to evaluate their existing collection.

El silbo del aire: Antología lírica infantil—1 (A breath of air: anthology of children's songs). Barcelona: Editorica Vicens-Vivas, 1985.
A collection of songs in Spanish that caregivers, teachers, and librarians can use with children. Includes music.

Talbot, Jane Mitchell, and Gilbert R. Cruz. "Children's Literature." *A Comprehensive Chicano Bibliography, 1960–1972:* 285–298. Austin, Tex.: Jenkins, 1973.
Includes citations, albeit brief, for one hundred titles.

Tregenza, Elaine, and Joanne Millard. *Speaking Spanish in the Library: A Spanish and English Vocabulary for Library Users.* Yuma, Ariz.: Yuma City-County Library, 1984.

Velasquez Sanchez, José de Jesus. *Las enfermides nacionales y las commemoraciones en la escuela.* 1972.
Self-published. A source of information about Mexican heroes and holidays. Includes poems.

Vigil, Angel. ¡*Teatro! Hispanic Plays for Young People.* Englewood, Colo.: Teacher Ideas Press (Libraries Unlimited), 1996.
This book provides scripts for plays that are easy to produce. Especially nice are the scripts provided for holidays and *Cinco de Mayo.*

West, John O., ed. *Mexican-American Folklore: Legends, Songs, Festivals, Proverbs, Crafts, Tales of Saints, Revolutionaries, and More.* Little Rock, Ark.: August House, 1988.
Good source for folk rhymes, customs, stories, etc.

Zwick, Louise Yarian, and Oralia Garza de Cortés. "Library Programs for Hispanic Children." *Texas Libraries* (Spring 1989): 12–16.
Presents specific programs that these librarians found to be successful.

———. *Rimas y cancioncitas para niños* (Rhymes and songs for children). Houston Public Library, 1984.
A small pamphlet with rhymes and songs gathered by these librarians.

LITERATURE

The format and age level of each book is indicated in parentheses after each citation. The following are the designations used and a brief explanation:

Board Book
A storybook for children from birth to three years. Printed on heavy cardboard.

Picture Book
A storybook where the pictures are equally important as the text. Appropriate for ages 18 months to 7 years (preschool through second grade).

Picture Book Anthology
An anthology including different types of literature such as poetry and folk tales. Appropriate for ages 18 months through 7 years (preschool through second grade).

Picture Book Poetry ages 18 months–7 years
Poems for preschoolers and younger children.

Music
An illustrated book of songs that include both the music and lyrics. Appropriate for all ages.

Chapter Fiction ages 7–11
Shorter novels with content appropriate for ages 7–11 (grades 3–5).

Poetry ages 7–11
Poems for grade school children.

Short Story Collection ages 7–11
Short stories for ages 7–11 (grades 3–5).

Drama ages 7–11
Plays for grade schoolers.

Nonfiction ages 7–11
Nonfiction for younger grade-school children. Many of these books are heavily illustrated photo essays, with plenty of color pictures.

Novel ages 8–14
Novels (fiction) for slightly older grade-school children.

Poetry ages 8–14
Poetry with an appeal to slightly older grade-school children.

Short Story Collection ages 8–14
Short stories for older grade school children.

Nonfiction ages 8–14
Nonfiction books for older grade school children.

Young Adult
Fiction appropriate for ages 12 and up (grade 6 and up). Sometimes include mature content.

Young Adult Poetry
Poetry for young adults.

Young Adult Anthology
A collection of different types of literature for young adults.

Young Adult Short Story Collection
Short stories with young adult content.

Aardema, Verna. *Borreguita and the Coyote*. Illus. Petra Mathers. New York: Knopf, 1991. (picture book)
  Lamb has to use all of her wits to avoid being eaten by Coyote.

————. *Pedro and the Padre*. Illus. Friso Henstra. New York: Dial, 1991. (picture book)
A Pedro de Ordemalas tale in which lazy Pedro is sent out into the world by his father, gets in trouble with a priest for lying, tricks three men into thinking a toad under his hat is a magic bird, and makes off with their burro and their money.

————. *The Riddle of the Drum*. Illus. Tony Chen. New York: Macmillan/Four Winds, 1979. (picture book)
A prince gains the hand of a princess when he is able to solve the riddle of what leather a drum is made from.

Ada, Alma Flor. *El canto del mosquito* (The song of the mosquito). Illus. Vivi Escriva. Compton, Calif.: Santillana, 1989. (picture book)
Series: Libros para contar (Books to count).
A predictable story that illustrates the food chain. A frog eats a mosquito, etc. The top of the food chain is an alligator that gets a sick stomach from eating a bird with all of these other animals in it. Eventually all the animals get disgorged, and the mosquito is free to sing again.

————. *The Christmas Tree/El arbol de Navidad*. New York: Hyperion, 1997. (picture book)
A cumulative tale that describes the decoration of a Christmas tree.

————. *Gathering the Sun: An Alphabet in Spanish and English*. Illus. Simón Silva. New York: Lothrop, Lee & Shepard, 1997. (picture book)
A Pura Belpré Honor Book for illustration. Twenty-eight poems that celebrate the lives of migrant farmworkers.

————. *The Lizard and the Sun/La lagartija y el sol*. Illus. Felipe Dávalos. New York: Doubleday, 1997. (picture book)
When the sun disappears from the sky all the animals try to find it to wake it up. The lizard is the one who finds it after all the other animals have given up.

————. *Mediopollito/Half-Chicken: Cuento tradicional en español y ingles/A Folktale in Spanish and English*. Illus. Kim Howard. Trans. Rosalma Zubizaretta. New York: Doubleday, 1996. (picture book)
This cumulative tale explains how weather vanes came to be. Mediopollito, the one-legged chicken, helps the river, fire, and wind, among others, on his way to see the viceroy. When the viceroy wants his chef to use Mediopollito as the main ingredient in a soup, Mediopollito's friends come to his aid.

————. *My Name is María Isabel*. Illus. K. Dyble Thompson. Trans. Ana M. Cerro. New York: Atheneum, 1993. (chapter fiction ages 7–11)
Spanish translation: *Me llamo María Isabel*. New York: Atheneum/Libros Colibrí, 1994.
María Isabel wants her new teacher to call her by her own, real name, and not Mary Lopez. The teacher calls her this because there were so many María's in the class.

————. *Olmo y la mariposa azul* (Olmo and the blue butterfly). Illus. Vivi Escrivá. Torrance, Calif.: Laredo Publishing Company, 1992. (picture book)
Olmo follows the blue butterfly with every form of transportation.

————. *The Rooster Who Went to His Uncle's Wedding: A Latin American Folktale*. Illus. Kathleen Kuchera. New York: Whitebird (Putnam), 1993. (picture book)
Another version of "Gallo de Bodas."

————. *Where the Flame Trees Bloom*. Illus. Antonio Martorell. New York: Atheneum, 1994. (short story collection ages 7–11)
Ada recalls memories of her Cuban childhood.

Ada, Alma Flor and Maria del Pilar del Olave. *Aserrín aserrán: folklore infantíl* (Children's folklore). Mexico D.F.: Donar, 1979. (anthology ages 2–5)
A collection of nursery rhymes in Spanish.

Aguilera, Carmen. *Citlalli en las estrellas* (Citlalli in the stars). Spain: Editorial Novaro, 1982. (picture book)
Citlalli is made fun of because she doesn't have a mother, only her old ugly grandmother. The grandmother tells her that when she grows up she'll find out what happened to her mother. In an extraordinary adventure, Citlalli finds her answers in the stars. This is an Aztec folktale.

Alarcón, Francisco X. *From the Bellybutton of the Moon and Other Summer Poems/Del ombligo de la luna y otros poemas del verano*. Illus. Maya Christina Gonzalez. San Francisco, Calif.: Children's Book Press, 1998. (poetry ages 7–11)
This follow-up to *Laughing Tomatoes and Other Spring Poems* includes many short poems that vividly evoke the sights, sounds, and smells of summer.

————. *Laughing Tomatoes and Other Spring Poems/Jitomates risueños y otros poemas de primavera*. Illus. Maya Christina Gonzalez. San Francisco, Calif.: Children's Book Press, 1997. (poetry ages 7–11)
A Pura Belpré Honor Book. Excellent poems with cultural content. "*Tortilla*" and "*Chile*" would work with a food storytime. "*Cinco de mayo*" is perfect for a program about that holiday. "Words are Birds/*Las palabras son pájaros*" is great for an introductory library storytime.

Albert, Burton. *Journey of the Nightly Jaguar*. Illus. Robert Roth. New York: Atheneum, 1996. (picture book)
A retelling of a Mayan myth about how the sun becomes a jaguar during the night.

Albert, Richard E. *Alejandro's Gift*. Illus. Sylvia Long. San Francisco: Chronicle Books, 1994. (picture book)
Alejandro's gift is the water he is able to give to desert creatures who are attracted to the garden he has planted.

Alcántara, Ricardo. *El pirata valiente* (The brave pirate). Illus. Gusti. Madrid: SM, 1989. (picture book)
A board book in which a little boy plays at being a pirate until his mother calls him to dinner.

————. *Uña y carne* (One and the same). Illus. Gusti. Barcelona: Ediciones Destino 1990. (picture book)
Premio Apel les Mestres. Armando and Amando look exactly alike and do the same things together.

Aldana, Paricia ed. *Jade and Iron: Latin American Tales from Two Cultures*. Trans. Hugh Hazleton. Illus. Luis Garay. Toronto: Groundwood (Douglas & McIntyre), 1996. (anthology ages 7–11)
A selection of stories that represent a broad range of Latin American culture. Includes a Pedro story: "Pedro Rimales, the Healer."

Alegría, Ciro. *Fábulas y leyendas americanas* (American fables and legends). Illus. Horacio Elena. Madrid: Espasa-Calpe, 1982. (anthology ages 7–11)
Some of the excellent stories in this collection include "*El tigre negro y el vendado blanco*," in which a tiger and a deer who share a home both mistakenly think they want to eat each other. "*El barco fantasma*," (The Phantom boat) about a ghost ship that haunts the Amazon River. "*La madre de las enfermedades*," (The Mother of illness) is about a mysterious woman named Unguymamam, who

will talk to you, but you cannot answer or she will give you her sickness. The last two are great creepy stories for Halloween.

Alexander, Frances. *Mother Goose on the Rio Grande*. Illus. Charlotte Baker. Lincolnwood, Ill.: Passport (NTC), 1997. (picture book poetry)
Spanish versions of nursery rhymes from the Texas-Mexico border.

Almada, Patricia. *From Father to Son*. Illus. Marianno de López. Crystal Lake, Ill.: Rigby, 1997. (nonfiction ages 7–11)
Spanish edition: *De padre a hijo.*
A father and son carry on a family tradition that began in Mexico and is now established in Los Angeles. The photographs demonstrate the different steps in the preparation of dough and a variety of different kinds of breads. Includes a map and some riddles.

Almena, Fernando. *Un solo de clarinete* (A Clarinet solo). Madrid: Ediciones SM, 1984. (picture book)
At first Ramón is not excited about having to spend his summer with his grandparents in a rural Spanish village. He learns that there is a great deal to do, and that he can have a lot of fun exploring an old movie house, hiking, and watching his grandmother win a motorcycle race.

Alonso, Fernando. *Marco y los reyes* (Marco and the kings). Illus. Alberto Urdiales. Madrid: Altea, 1995. (novel ages 8–14)
Alonso tells the individual stories of each of the three kings: "Melchor and the Mountain of Gold," "Baltasar and Solomon's Ring," and "Gaspar and the Labyrinth of Mirrors."

Alonso, Manuel L. *Papá ya no vive con nosotros* (Father doesn't live with us anymore). Illus. Asun Balzoa. Madrid: Ediciones SM, 1993. (picture book)
Pablo has to adjust when his father, his best friend, leaves.

Alphin, Marie. *A Bear for Miguel*. Illus. Joan Sandin. New York: HarperCollins, 1996. (picture book)
An "I Can Read" book. María can't wait to go with her father to trade at the market in her village in El Salvador. They pass by guerrilla fighters on their way—an interesting touch of reality. She trades her stuffed bear to a couple who want it for their son.

Altman, Linda Jacobs. *Amelia's Road*. Illus. Enrique Sanchez. New York: Lee & Low, 1993. (picture book)
Amelia learns to cope with being the daughter of migrant farm work-

ers. When she is forced to leave, she leaves something personal behind.

Anaya, Rudolfo. *Bless Me, Ultima*. New York: Warner, 1994. (young adult)
Six-year-old Antonio becomes a friend and apprentice to the *curandera* or healer, named Ultima. Antonio's life is full of questions and doubts. Each chapter includes a dream sequence in which his worst fears are given a voice.

————. *The Farolitos of Christmas*. Illus. Edward Gonzales. New York: Hyperion, 1987, 1995. (picture book)
A Christmas story set in New Mexico in 1944. Luz wants to make *luminarias* with her grandfather. When he becomes ill, she makes *farolitos*, or little lanterns, instead using paper bags, candles, and sand.

Ancona, George. *Barrio: José's Neighborhood*. New York: Harcourt, 1998. (nonfiction ages 7–11)
José lives in San Francisco's mission district. Ancona photographs him engaging in his daily activities, as well as some significant cultural celebrations. In doing so he evokes what it is like to grow up Latino.

————. *Fiesta U.S.A.* New York: Lodestar (Dutton), 1995. (nonfiction ages 7–11)
Descriptions of the celebrations of various Latino holidays illustrated with photographs. Includes the Day of the Dead, *las posadas* (at Christmas), the *matachines* ritual on New Year's Day, which celebrates the arrival of Hernán Cortez and Christianity in the new world, and the Day of the Three Kings (January 6).

————. *Fiesta Fireworks*. New York: Lothrop, Lee and Shepherd, 1993. (nonfiction ages 7–11)
A family prepares fireworks in the Mexican town of Tultepec to celebrate the fiesta honoring the town's patron saint, San Juan de Dios.

————. *Mayeros: A Yucatec Maya Family*. New York: William Morrow, 1997. (nonfiction ages 7–11)
Armando and his family are descendants of the Mayas. The book follows Armando and his family through a week of preparations for the town's fiesta and gives some idea of their daily life as well. Ancona demonstrates connections between past and present Mayan culture in this photographic essay.

————. *Pablo Remembers: The Fiesta of the Day of the Dead.* New York: Lothrop, Lee & Shepherd, 1993. (nonfiction ages 7–11) Spanish translation: *Pablo recuerda: La fiesta de el día de los muertos.* Pura Belpré Honor Book for Illustration, 1996. Pablo and his family participate in Day of the Dead celebrations in Mexico.

————. *The Piñata Maker/El piñatero.* San Diego, Calif.: Harcourt, 1995. (nonfiction ages 7–11) Don Ricardo makes piñatas for all the village events.

Anderson, Joan. *Spanish Pioneers of the Southwest.* Illus. George Ancona. New York: Lodestar (Dutton), 1989. (nonfiction ages 7–11) Ancona's photos portray a re-enactment of family and village life in New Mexico in the 1700s.

Antoniorobles. *Cuentos de las cosas que hablan* (Stories of things that speak). Illus. Juan R. Alonso. Madrid: Epasa-Calpe, 1981. (short story collection ages 7–11) A collection of animal short stories.

Anzaldúa, Gloria. *Prietita and the Ghost Woman/Prietita y la llorona.* Illus. Christina Gonzalez. San Francisco, Calif.: Children's Book Press, 1996. (picture book) La Llorona helps Prietita find an herb that the *curandera* needs to heal Prietita's mother.

————. *Friends from the Other Side/Amigos del otro lado.* Illus. Consuelo Méndez. San Francisco, Calif.: Children's Press, 1993. (picture book) Prietita meets Joaquin, who has just come across the great river to America.

Aparicio, Frances R. (ed). *Latino Voices.* Brookfield, Conn.: Millbrook Press, 1994. (young adult anthology) A collection of writings by Latino authors geared toward young adult readers. They are grouped under seven themes: immigration, homes, family, religious faith, work, language, and race and racial discrimination.

Applebaum, Diana. *Cocoa Ice.* Illus. Holly Meade. New York: Orchard, 1997. (chapter fiction ages 7–11) Two young girls, one who lives in Santo Domingo, Dominican Republic, and the other who lives in Maine, each dream of the other's place. The stories are linked together through the cocoa ice trade of schooners in the late nineteenth century.

Araujo, Orlando. *Miguel Vicente, pata caliente* (Miguel Vincente, hot-foot). Illus. Morelle Fuenmayor. Caracas, Venezuela: Ediciones Ekaré/Banco del Libro, 1992. (picture book)
Miguel Vincente, the shoe-shine boy, dreams of being able to travel places and see things. He knows that he will probably never be able to make his dreams a reality. It especially bothers him at Christmastime that his family is so poor that all he receives is a used shoe-shine brush and cream. At the end of the story his mother becomes ill, and his older brother picks him up and he begins a new adventure.

Argueta, Manlio. *Magic Dogs of the Volcanoes/Los perros mágicos de los volcanes*. Illus. Elly Simmons. San Francisco, Calif.: Children's Book Press, 1990. (picture book)
Set in El Salvador, this is an original story about the mythic characters, the *cadejos*, or magic volcano dogs. The *cadejos* function like guardian angels, except for Don Tonio and his 13 brothers who do not like them and sic the lead soldiers on them. But the soldiers begin to melt when they get too near the volcanoes.

Armella de Aspe, Virginia. *La lana* (Wool). Illus. Noé Katz. Mexico D.F.: Editorial Patria, 1983. (picture book)
Colleción Piñata. Series: *Las materias primas* (The primary materials).
Hilario is a shepherd. This is the story of how wool is made from his sheep.

Armijo, Consuelo. *Bam, bim, bom, arriba el telon* (Up goes the curtain). Valladolid: Editorial Miñón, 1984. (drama ages 7–11)

Plays for kids to put on:
"*Gorros y botas*" (Caps and boots)
"*Cumpleaños de verano*" (A summer birthday)
"*Una historia de sacos*" (A history of sacks)
"*Pájaros de invierno*" (Birds in winter)
"*Un duende en palacio*" (A goblin in the palace)
"*Disimulando*" (Hiding)

———. *Moné*. Valladolid: Editorial Miñón, 1982. (picture book)
Moné is a teddy bear who gets in all sorts of trouble. He drives a car, falls off the balcony, gets his clothes dirty when drinking hot

chocolate, learns to swim in the bathtub, and ends up in a tree branch.

————. *El mono imatamonos* (The imitating monkey). Illus. Alfonso Ruano. Madrid: Ediciones SM, 1984. (chapter fiction ages 7–11)
A monkey gets lost and finds his way to the city where he variously frightens and entertains people until he is taken in by Tere and Pepito. He amuses their family a great deal. In the end, the monkey's mother arrives and takes him home.

Arnold, Sandra. *Child of the Sun: A Cuban Legend.* Illus. Dave Albers. Troll, 1995. (picture book)
Sun refuses to share the sky with the moon. This myth explains why we have eclipses.

Ashabranner, Brent. *Children of the Maya: A Guatemalan Indian Odyssey.* Illus. Paul Conklin. New York: Dodd Mead, 1986. (nonfiction ages 8–14)
Describes the struggles of Guatemalan Indians who have relocated to Florida to escape political oppression. Illustrated with black-and-white photographs.

————. *Dark Harvest: Migrant Farmworkers in America.* Illus. Paul Conklin. New York: Shoe String, 1993. (nonfiction ages 8–14)
Discusses the very real social problems encountered by migrant farmworkers.

————. *Our Beckoning Borders: Illegal Immigration to America.* New York: Cobblehill, 1996. (nonfiction ages 8–14)
This book offers both sides of the immigration argument. While it focuses on the Mexican border and Latino immigrants, it covers the whole spectrum of immigration from all nations.

————. *Still a Nation of Immigrants.* New York: Cobblehill, 1993. (nonfiction ages 8–14)
Presents a historical overview as well as success stories of individual immigrants.

Atkin, S. Beth. *Voices from the Fields: Children of Migrant Farmworkers Tell Their Stories.* Boston: Little Brown, 1993. (young adult nonfiction)
The author interviewed children ages 9–18, and they candidly tell what life is like for migrant farmworkers—the heat in the fields and other issues such as gangs and constantly having to move to different schools.

Avila, Alfred. *Mexican Ghost Tales of the Southwest*. Comp. Kat Avila. Houston: Piñata (Arte Publico), 1994. (young adult short story collection)
Gruesome tales that young adults will devour. Collected by the author's daughter, they include stories about La Llorona, as well as stories about unburied bodies getting vengeance, abandoned ashes becoming a giant human-eating cat, and vampires.

Baden, Robert. *Y domingo, siete* (And Sunday makes seven). Trans. Alma Flor Ada. Illus. Michelle Edwards. Niles, Ill.: Albert Whitman, 1990. (picture book)
A folktale from Costa Rica. Two cousins are exact opposites of each other. One is rich and selfish; the other lives in poverty and is very kind. They encounter witches who sing the traditional rhyme about the days of the week. When the poor brother adds a verse to their song, he is rewarded with gold.

Balcells, Jacqueline. *The Enchanted Raisin*. Pittsburgh, Penn.: Latin American Literary Review Press, 1988. (young adult short story collection)
Magically realistic stories by a Chilean writer that resemble fairy tales.

Balzoa, Asun. *Guillermo, un raton de biblioteca* (Guillermo, a library rat). Editorial Miñón, 1982. (picture book)
A rat named Shakespeare tries to escape from his library. A cat provides danger.

———. *Munia y el crocolilo naraja* (Munia and the orange crocodile). Barcelona: Ediciones Destino, 1984. (picture book)
Munia's two front teeth have fallen out, and she is scared of crocodiles because they have teeth. Then one night she meets the *crocolilo*, an orange crocodile without teeth. Munia is no longer scared, and she learns from the *crocolilo* that teeth grow back. The *crocolilo* returns to Egypt and writes her from there.

Other Munia books are:

Munia y la luna (Munia and the moon). 1982. Munia lives at the top of a mountain. She has to go down to the river one night to fetch water. She fills up her bottle with some water that had the moon's reflection in it. She dreams that the moon asks her to return the piece of him she has taken.

Los zapatos de Munia (Munia's shoes). Munia worries because her shoes are too tight. She is concerned that they might have shrunk. When she gets the chance to go into town she asks the shoemaker, and learns that her feet are growing bigger, along with the rest of her.

Munia y la señora piltronera (Munia and the grumpy girl). Munia gets up on the wrong side of the bed in this story. She has a rotten day during which she refuses to do school work, kicks her sister, fights with a classmate, and even allows cows into the garden. By the end Munia manages to atone for these misdeeds.

Munia y los hallazgos (Munia and the finds). In this story Munia has a little museum of things she has found. A toy pistol becomes in her mind a weapon used in the Napoleonic wars. "*Si no invento, me aburro*" ("If I don't imagine, I get bored), she says. Munia also encounters a thief.

————. *Pablito*. Madrid: Ediciones SM, 1989. (board book)

A poetic evocation of Pablito's day at the seashore.

Barberis. *¿De quien es este rabo?* (Who does this tail belong to?). Valladolid: Editorial Miñón, 1974. (picture book)
Shows tails, and the reader has to guess to whom they belong. Good for preschoolers.

Barbot, Daniel. *Un diente se mueve* (A tooth moves). Illus. Gian Calvi. Caracas, Venezuela: Ediciones Ekaré, 1981. (picture book)
Clarissa meets a rat who takes children's teeth to make jewelry.

————. *Rosaura en bicicleta* (Rosaura on a bicycle). Illus. Morella Fuenmayor. Caracas, Venezuela: Ediciones Ekaré, 1990. (picture book)
Rosaura, a chicken, asks for a bicycle for her birthday. A man comes to town and makes one for her. It doesn't have brakes.

Beatty, Patricia. *Lupita Mañana*. New York: William Morrow, 1993. (chapter fiction ages 7–11)
Lupita Torres and her older brother leave their home in Mexico, where they expect to have a happy life with a rich Aunt. Instead they find themselves as field workers trying to evade the immigration authorities.

Becerra de Jenkins, Lyll. *Celebrating the Hero*. New York: Lodestar (Dutton), 1993. (young adult)
Camila Draper travels back to Columbia after her mother dies to attend a ceremony honoring her grandfather. She discovers some disturbing things as she attempts to learn more about her mother's family.

————. *The Honorable Prison*. New York: Lodestar (Dutton), 1988. (young adult)
Marta and her family find themselves prisoners of the government because of the stand that Marta's father has taken as a newspaper editor attacking the country's dictator.

————. *So Loud a Silence*. New York: Lodestar (Dutton), 1996. (young adult)
Juan Guillermo doesn't feel like he fits in with his family. Then he spends some time in Columbia with his grandmother and gets involved in guerilla warfare, and comes to appreciate his family life.

Beherens, June. *¡Fiesta! cinco de mayo* (Party! May 5th). Illus. Scott Taylor. Trans. Lada Josefa Kratky. Chicago: Children's Press, 1985, 1978. (nonfiction ages 7–11)
Describes typical celebrations that commemorate the victory of the Mexican army over the French on May 5, 1862. Lots of color pictures.

Belpré, Pura. *Firefly Summer*. Houston: Piñata (Arte Público), 1996. (young adult)
Series: *Recovering the U.S. Hispanic Literary Heritage*.
    Teresa returns to the Puerto Rican countryside at the turn of the century.

————. *Oté: A Puerto Rican Folktale*. Illus. Paul Galdone. New York: Pantheon, 1969. (picture book)
Oté brings the nearsighted devil home with him after sharing his food. The devil eats all the family's food, leaving them only scraps until Oté consults the wise woman, who gives him magic words to say just before they eat. Only he may eat nothing on the way home. He does not heed this advice, so after more hunger he goes again to the wise woman, this time followed by his son, Chiquitín. The little one saves the day.

————. *Perez and Martina*. New York: Viking, 1991, 1960. (picture book)
The classic folktale about the lovely cockroach Martina who rejects all her suitors except the noble *ratoncito* Perez.

―――. *The Rainbow-Colored Horse*. Illus. Antonio Martorell. New York: Warne, 1978. (picture book)
A father sends his sons to discover who or what has been eating their crops and ruining their fields. The youngest son discovers that it is a rainbow-colored horse. The horse offers the boy three favors if he will let him go.

―――. *Santiago*. Illus. Symeon Shimin. Warne, 1969. (picture book)
Spanish translation 1971. Santiago lives in two worlds at once: Puerto Rico and New York. His Grandmother Seline has sent him a stereoscope with pictures of Puerto Rico. He wants to take it to school, but ends up bringing his class home to look at it.

Beltrán Hernández, Irene. *Across the Great River*. Houston: Piñata (Arte Público), 1989. (novel ages 8–14)
The story of a family's illegal entry into the United States as seen through the eyes of a young girl.

―――. *Heartbeat, Drumbeat*. Houston: Piñata (Arte Público), 1992. (young adult)
Morgana Cruz struggles with her dual Latina and Native American heritage.

―――. *The Secret of Two Brothers*. Houston, Tex.: Piñata Books (Arte Público), 1995. (young adult)
Beaver comes back to West Dallas after being released from three years in prison for robbing a Jack-in-the-Box. He discovers that his artistic younger brother, Cande, is being abused by their alcoholic father. The book is marred by some incredibly unbelievable dialogue and a too sweet, pat resolution to everyone's problems.

Berenguer, Carmen. *El rey mocho* (The king without an ear). Illus. Luz Maria Hevia. Adap Verónica Uribe. Caracas, Venezuela: Ediciones Ekaré/Banco Del Libro, 1981. (picture book)
There once was a king who lacked an ear, but he covered this fact up by his long, curly black wig. The only person who knew the secret was his barber. When his barber got sick and died, the king searched for a new barber. The new barber couldn't keep the secret and told it to a hole. Later a shepherd boy made a flute from cane that grew there, and it began to sing: "*El rey es mocho.*" Now the whole country knew, and the king decided that wigs were too hot.
Note: Includes the music for a brief song.

Bernhard, Emery, and Durga Bernhard. *The Tree that Rains: The Flood Myth of the Huichol Indians of Mexico*. New York: Holiday House, 1994. (picture book)
Watakame is able to begin a new life after surviving a flood with the help of the earth, characterized as "Great-Grandmother."

Bernier-Grand, Carmen T. *Juan Bobo: Four Folktales from Puerto Rico*. Illus. Ernesto Ramos Nieves. New York: HarperCollins, 1994 (picture book)
An "I Can Read" book that contains the following stories:
"The Best Way to Carry Water." Juan Bobo brings home water in baskets. They mysteriously keep getting lighter.
"A Pig in Sunday Clothes." Juan Bobo dresses a pig to go to church. Pig falls in the mud. Mom finds it on the way home. Juan Bobo thinks you can play with mud in church.
"Do Not Sneeze, Do Not Scratch . . . Do Not Eat!" Juan Bobo has a hard time following Mama's instructions.
"A Dime a Jug." Juan Bobo is accidentally successful in selling syrup.

Bertrand, Diane Gonzales. *Alicia's Treasure*. Houston: Piñata (Arte Público), 1996. (chapter fiction ages 7–11)
This book tells the story of Alicia's journey to the seashore at Port Aransas, Texas.

————. *Sip, Slurp, Soup, Soup/Caldo, caldo, caldo*. Illus. Alex Pardo DeLange. Houston: Piñata (Arte Público), 1997. (picture book)
This book captures a warm family ritual. Mama pulls out the large soup pot, and the children know it's *caldo* day. Everyone helps Mama make the soup, then they go to buy tortillas to make the soup complete. Includes a recipe.

————. *Sweet Fifteen*. Houston: Piñata (Arte Público), 1995. (young adult)
Stephanie prepares for her *quinceñera* after her father passes away. The seamstress who makes her dress, Rita Navarro, also becomes involved with the family.

Bierhorst, John. trans. *Spirit Child: The Story of the Nativity*. Illus. Barbara Cooney. New York: William Morrow, 1984. (picture book)
An Aztec version of the birth of Christ.

Blanco, Alberto. *Angel's Kite/La estrella de Angel*. Illus. Rodolfo Morales. Trans. Dan Bellim. Emeryville, Calif.: Children's Book Press, 1994. (picture book)

Angel makes a remarkable kite that miraculously restores the long-missing church bell of his village.

Brenner, Anita. *The Boy Who Could Do Anything and Other Mexican Folktales.* Illus. Jean Charlot. New York: William R. Scott, 1970. (short story collection ages 7–11)
The "boy who could do anything" is Tepozton, who is the son of a god who wants him dead. This collection includes the story "Dumb Juan and the Bandits."

Brusca, María Cristina, and Tona Wilson. *The Blacksmith and the Devils.* Illus. María Cristina Brusca. New York: Holt, 1992. (picture book)
Spanish translation: *El herrero y el diablo.* A version of the Pedro de Ordimalas story. Juan Pobreza lives in the Argentine pampas.

———. *Pedro Fools the Gringo, and Other Tales of a Latin American Trickster.* Illus. María Cristina Brusca. New York: Redfeather (Holt), 1995. (chapter fiction ages 7–11)
Pedro de Ordimalas stories including "Clever Little Pedro," "Painted Horses," "Golden Partridge," "Magic Pot," "Money Tree," "Pig Tails in the Swamp," "Helper Rabbit," "Burro Gold," "Pedro and the Devil," "Pedro Fools the Gringo," "Good-bye to Your Machetes," and "Pedro Goes to Heaven."

———. *Three Friends/Tres amigos: A Counting Book/Un cuento para contar.* Illus. María Cristina Brusca. New York: Henry Holt, 1995. (picture books)
A counting book with cowboy characters.

———. *When Jaguars Ate the Moon and Other Stories about Animals and Plants of the Americas.* Illus. María Cristina Brusca. New York: Henry Holt, 1995. (picture book)
An alphabet of "How" and "Why" tales from the Americas.

Bunting, Eve. *A Day's Work.* Illus. Ronald Himler. New York: Clarion, 1994. (picture book)
Francisco tries to help his grandfather obtain work. His grandfather doesn't speak English, but despite this barrier, he is able to teach Francisco some valuable lessons.

———. *Going Home.* Illus. David Diaz. New York: HarperCollins, 1996. (picture book)
A Mexican family comes to work as migrant laborers in the United States. In their hearts, Mexico remains their home.

Caballero, Fernan. *El picaro pajarillo* (The mischievious bird). Chrysalis Books, 1980. (picture book)
A mischievous bird steals clothing from his employers then sings outside the king's house. The king gets mad and has the bird cooked. He eats it but it's still alive in his stomach. He vomits it up (in a very graphic illustration), and then the bird sings outside the king's house again. To escape the king's wrath, the bird flys up to the moon.

Calders, Pere. *Cepillo*. Illus. Carme Solé Vendrell. Barcelona: Ediciones Hymsa, 1981. (picture book)
English edition: *Brush*. Brooklyn, New York: Kane Miller, 1986. Trans. Marguerite Feitlowitz.
When Little Sala's dog Turco is banished for bad behavior, he searches for a new companion. He tries a bird, " . . . but the number of really fun things he could do with a bird were so few, he immediately knew they could never be close friends." He tries to create lasting friendships with a ball of string and an American-made top, without success. He finally finds a brush in the attic. It becomes his companion and begins acting like a dog.

Calhoun, Mary. *Tonio's Cat*. Illus. Edward Martinez. New York: Morrow, 1996. (picture book)
Tonio feels empty after not only leaving Mexico, but also his dog behind. A cat named Toughy begins to fill that place in his heart.

Cameron, Ann. *The Most Beautiful Place in the World*. Illus. Thomas B. Allen. New York: Knopf, 1988. (chapter fiction ages 7–11)
Seven-year-old Juan grows up with his grandmother in a small Guatemalan village. He enjoys the beauty of his surroundings, but is afraid to communicate to her his desire to go to school.

Capellinni, Mary. *The Story of Doña Chila*. Illus. Gershom Griffith. Crystal Lake, Ill.: Rigby, 1997. (picture book)
Spanish edition: *El cuento de doña Chila*.
Oscar's mother has to decide whether to have him treated by a doctor or by the local *curandera* after he is bitten by a scorpion. The conflict between two cultures is realistically shown in this engaging story set in Honduras.

Carden, Mary, and Mary Cappellini, eds. *I Am of Two Places*. Illus. Christina González. Crystal Lake, Ill.: Rigby, 1997. (picture book poetry 18 months–7 years)
Spanish edition: *Soy de dos lugares*.
A collection of poetry written by five children, ages eight to eleven,

that deal with the issues they must face in speaking two languages and feeling love for the people and places of two cultures.

Cárdenas, Magolo. *La zona de silencio* (The silent zone). Mexico D.F.: Editorial Patria, 1984. (picture book)
Colleción Piñata. Series: *Nuestro país* (Our country).
The silent zone is the Mexican desert. This rhyming story takes a girl, Jorge Lauro, and a dinosaur named Tomás to visit it.

Carlin, Joi. *La cama de mamá*. Illus. Morella Fuenmayor. Caracas, Venezuela: Ediciones Ekaré/Volcano Press, 1984, 1994. (picture book)
English translation: *Mommy's Bed Is Best*.
Mommy's bed can be a football field, an explorer's tent, an Olympic trampoline, and a space station.

Carlson, Lori M., ed. *Barrio Streets, Carnival Dreams: Three Generations of Latino Artistry*. New York: Holt, 1996. (young adult anthology)
A collection of poetry, literature, artwork, and essays that celebrate Latino contributions.

———. *Cool Salsa: Bilingual Poems on Growing Up Latino in the United States*. New York: Holt, 1994. Intro. by Oscar Hijuelos. (young adult poetry)
A book that celebrates the challenges of growing up Latino in the United States with two languages and two cultures. "Speaking more than one language, I have found, enriches life, broadens perspective, extends horizons of opportunity, and makes us more sensitive to nuance, difference, contrast" xiv.

———. *Sol a sol: Bilingual Poems Written and Selected by Lori Marie Carlson*. Illus. Emily Lisker. New York: Holt, 1998. (poetry ages 7–11)
A selection of original and selected poems.

Carlson, Lori M., and Cynthia L. Ventura, eds. *Where Angels Glide at Dawn: New Stories from Latin America*. Illus. José Ortega. New York: HarperCollins, 1990. (young adult short story collection)
Exciting new stories by contemporary Latino authors.

Carvajal, Víctor. *Cuentatrapos*. Madrid: Ediciones SM, 1984. (young adult)
Eight short stories that treat the common theme of the life of the poorest, and the social dilemmas they encounter.

Castellanos, Diana (Illus.). *Casa que Juan construyo: tradición oral* (The house that Jack built: oral tradition). Bogotá Columbia: Editorial Norma, 1987. (picture book)
A Latin take on the rhyme "The House that Jack Built."

Castelló, Beatriz de Maria Y Campos. *Tres colorantes prehispanicos* (Three prehispanic coloring agents). Illus. Pascuala Corona. Mexico D.F.: Editorial Patria, 1985. (nonfiction ages 7–11)
Colleción Piñata. Series: *Las materias primas* (The primary materials).
    Three methods the Indians used for coloring fabric: cactus, shells, and plants.

Casteneda, Omar S. *Abuela's Weave*. Illus. Enrique O. Sanchez. New York: Lee & Low, 1993. (picture book)
Spanish translation: *El tapiz de abuela*. Trans. Aida E. Marcuse.
    Esperanza and her grandmother sell traditional woven items. Because her grandmother's birthmark discourages people from buying, they pretend not to know each other. Esperanza finds buyers while grandmother stays in the background.

———. *Among the Volcanoes*. New York: Lodestar, 1991. (young adult)
Isabel, a Mayan girl living in present day Columbia, must care for her mother when she becomes ill.

———. *Imagining Isabel*. New York: Lodestar, 1994. (young adult)
Sequel to: *Among the Volcanoes*. Isabel is now fifteen years old and married. She joins a government-sponsored teacher training program and must deal with Columbia's harsh political realities.

Chumba la cachumba. A traditional song illustrated by Carlos Cotte. Caracas, Venezuela: Ediciones Ekaré, 1995. (picture book)
Colleción Clave del Sol.
    Canciones tradicionales para cantar y contar (Traditional songs to sing and tell). What the skeletons do at each hour of the night.

Ciavonne, Jean. *Carlos, Light the Farolito*. Illus. Donna Clair. New York: Clarion, 1995. (picture book)
Carlos has to take his grandfather's role in the traditional Mexican celebration of *las posadas* when his grandfather and parents are late.

Cisneros, Sandra. *Hairs/Pelitos*. Illus. Terry Ybáñez. Trans. Liliana Valenzuela. New York: Apple Soup (Alfred A. Knopf), 1984, 1994. (picture book)
Adapted from the book *The House on Mango Street*. Cisneros describes how the hair of each person in the family looks.

Claret, Maria. *La ratita blasa* (The little mouse). Barcelona: Editoria Juventud, 1983. (picture book)
The adventures of "*la ratita*" in each month of the year.

Clark, Ann Nolan. *Secret of the Andes*. Illus. Jean Charlot. New York: Viking, 1952. (novel ages 8–14)
A young boy tends llamas in a hidden valley in the Andes mountains. He learns his purpose for being there and the secrets of his Incan ancestors.

Climo, Shirley, reteller. *The Little Red Ant and the Great Big Crumb: A Mexican Fable*. Illus. Francisco X. Mora. New York: Clarion, 1995. (picture book)
English with Spanish words. The little red ant tries to find someone strong to help her carry home a crumb, and realizes that she is the strongest of all.

Cockroft, James D. *Latinos in the Making of the United States*. The Hispanic Experience in the Americas Series. New York: Watts, 1995. (nonfiction ages 8–14)
Cockroft shows the the many contributions Latinos have made to our country.

Colón-Vilá, Lilian. *Salsa/Salsa*. Illus. Roberta Collier-Morales. Houston: Piñata (Arte Público), 1998. (picture book)
Rita dreams of someday becoming a salsa band director. Her family gives her a great deal of advice, and this book gives young children a sense of what salsa music is all about—including the dance steps and the musical instruments used to make the unique sounds.

Como surgieron los seres y las cosas (How people and things came to be). Lima, Peru: PIESA Coedicíon Latinoamericana, 1986. (short story collection ages 7–11)
A collection of Latin "porquoi" tales. A Puerto Rican tale describes the origin of the island itself. A Nicaraguan tale tells how mosquitoes came to a great river.

Cooper, Martha, and Ginger Gordon. *Anthony Reynoso: Born to Rope*. New York: Clarion, 1996. (nonfiction ages 7–11)

Anthony is a nine-year-old whose father is teaching him how to become a rodeo performer in the Mexican tradition.

Corona, Sarah. *El misterio del tiempo robado* (The mystery of robbed time). Illus. Martha Avilés. Amecameca, Mexico: C.E.L.T.A. (Consejo National para la Cultura y las Artes), 1991. (picture book) Someone robs the only watch in the narrator's small village, and suddenly no one knows what time it is. It turns out that the watch was stolen by the old watchmaker, who despaired that there was no longer any work for him.

Corpi, Lucha. *Where Fireflies Dance/Ahí donde bailan las luciérnagas*. San Francisco: Children's Book Press, 1997. (picture book) An autobiographical tale. Lucha and Victor sneak into a house that is supposed to be haunted by the ghost of the Mexican revolutionary Juan Sebastián. Later, their grandmother tells them Sebastián's story, and it inspires Lucha to fulfill her own destiny.

Cuentos de animales fantasticos para niños (Stories of fantasic animals for children). São Paulo, Brazil: Editorial Atica. Coedición Latinoamericana: 1984. (short story collection ages 7–11) Includes the stories *"El caballito de siete colores"* (The Seven-colored horse) from Guatemala and *"El murciélago"* (The Bat) from Mexico.

Cuentos de enredos y travesuras (Stories of tangled-up mischief). Stories of Bolivia : Centro Pedagogico y Cultural de Portales, Coedición Latinoamericana, ages 1986. (short story collection ages 7–11) Stories about playing tricks from many Latin American countries. Brief notes regarding cultural background preface each story. Glossaries also explain the meaning of any unusual words.

Cuentos de espantos y aparecidos (Stories of ghosts and apparitions). Editorial Veronica Uribe. São Paulo, Brazil: Editorial Atica, Coedición Latinoamericana, 1984. (short story collection ages 7–11) A great place to find scary stories for Halloween like *"El barco negro"* (The black boat) from Nicaragua; *"María Angula"* from Ecuador; and *"Abad Alfau y la calavera"* (Abad Alfau and the skeleton) from the Dominican Republic.

Cuentos, mitos y leyendas para niños de américa latina (Stories, myths, and legends for Latin American children). Buenos Aires, Argentina: Editorial Plus Ultra, Coedicíon Latinoamericana, 1981. (short story collection ages 7–11)

Includes a version of "La leyenda del Dorado" (The legend of El Dorado or the Golden One) from Columbia.

Cuentos picarescos para niños de america latina (Adventure stories for Latin American children). Buenos Aires, Argentina: Editorial Plus Ultra Coedicíon Latinoamericana, 1983. (short story collection ages 7–11)
Includes the following stories:
"Domingo siete" (. . . And Sunday makes seven) from Columbia; "Tío Conejo y Tío Lobo" (Uncle Rabbit and Uncle Wolf) from Ecuador; "Pedro Urdemalas" from Guatemala; "Juan Bobo y el secreto de la Princesa" (Juan Bobo and the Princess's secret) from Dominican Republic; and "Pedro Rimales, curandero" (Pedro Rimales, healer) from Venezuela.

Cuentos y leyendas de amor para ninos (Stories and legends of love for children). Buenos Aires, Argentina: Editorial Plus Ultra, Coedicíon Latinoamericana, 1984. (short story collection ages 7–11)
Love stories from all over Latin America.

Couvalt, Ruth M. *Pablo and Pimienta/Pablo y Pimienta*. Trans. Patricia Hinton Davison. Illus. Francisco Mora. Flagstaff, Ariz.: Northland, 1994. (picture book)
Pablo gets thrown out of the bed of his father's truck and has to make his way across the border with a coyote pup he encounters and names Pimienta. Father is going to work as a migrant farmworker in watermelon patches near Phoenix.

Culla, Rita. *Marta y sus amigos* (Marta and her friends). Barcelona: Editorial Juventud, 1975. (picture book)
Marta has many friends, including animals. Children can make the animal sounds.

Culla, Rita. ¿*Sabes por que*? (Do you know why?). Barcelona: Editorial Juventud, 1975. (picture book)
A child is sad not to have glasses when everyone else has them.

Czernecki, Stefan, and Timothy Rhodes. *The Hummingbird's Gift*. Straw weavings by Juliana Reyes de Silva and Juan Hilario Silva. New York: Hyperion, 1994. (picture book)
Consuelo saves the hummingbirds' lives. In return, they are able to help her save her family from a drought.

Da Coll, Ivar. *Hamamelis y el secreto* (Hamamelis and the secret).
Caracas, Venezuela: Ediciones Ekaré/Banco del Libro, 1991. (picture book)
"*Un secreto es un secreto.*" (A secret is a secret). Hamamelis gets a secret from friend Mistosis. He puts it in his toybox and sits on it. It plays with the toys in the box. Hamamelis wants to play, but he doesn't want to let the secret out.

————. *Tengo miedo* (I'm afraid). Columbia: Carlos Valencia Editores, 1989. (picture book)
Shows how Eusebio deals with his fear of terrible monsters. He learns that they like to do some of the same things he does.

Dario, Ruben. *Margarita*. Illus. Monika Doppert. Caracas, Venezuela: Ediciones Ekaré/Banco del Libro, 1979. (picture book)
An illustrated version of the mystical poem about a princess.

Dawson, Mildred Leinweber. *Over Here It's Different: Carolina's Story*. Illus. George Ancona. New York: Macmillan, 1993. (nonfiction ages 7–11)
Black-and-white photographs tell the story of Carolina, who immigrates from the Dominican Republic.

de Posadas, Carmen. *Kiwi*. Illus. Antonio Tello. Madrid: Ediciones SM, 1984. (picture book)
A package arrives at the farm—everyone wonders what it is. When it's opened, they discover it's an egg. The farm animals try to find someone to care for it. A kiwi bird hatches from it.

DePaola, Tomie. *The Legend of the Poinsettia*. New York: Putnam, 1994. (picture book)
Spanish translation: *La leyenda de la flor de nochebuena*. Lucinda is unable to finish her gift for the baby Jesus on time, but receives a miracle and is able to offer the poinsettia as her gift.

————. *The Lady of Guadelupe*. New York: Holiday House, 1980. (picture book)
Spanish Translation: *Nuestra Señora de Guadelupe*. Trans. Pura Belpré.
This retelling of the story of the appearance of the Virgin Mary to the peasant Juan Diego is enhanced by DePaola's simple and respectful illustrations.

de Terán, Rocío. *Los mifenses* (The people from the planet MIF). Madrid: Ediciones SM, 1984.

A squadron of spaceships from the planet MIF inspect our earth. X2, a very friendly alien, falls asleep at the wheel of his spaceship and crashes into earth, where he befriends a farmer and his family.

de Treviño, Elizabeth Borton. *I, Juan de Pareja*. New York: Farrar, Straus & Giroux, 1965. (novel ages 8–14)
The story of the great Spanish painter, Velásquez, and his black slave, Juan de Pareja.

del Amo, Montserrat. *Rastro de Dios y otros cuentos* (The face of God and other stories). Madrid: Ediciones SM, 1981. (short story collection ages 7–11)
Three stories about angels. The title story won several prizes.

del Cañizo, Jose A. *El maestro y el robot* (The teacher and the robot). Madrid: Ediciones SM, 1983. (chapter fiction ages 7–11)
In a small village hidden in the mountains strange things happen when a new super-modern school is built and the old teacher is replaced by a robot.

Delacre, Lulu. *Arroz con leche: Popular Songs and Rhymes from Latin America* (Rice with milk). New York: Scholastic, 1984. (music)
The Spanish and English lyrics to these songs are enhanced by Delacre's lovely illustrations. The music is included at the back of the book. Includes: "*Aserrín, asserán.*"

———. *Golden Tales: Myths, Legends, and Folktales from Latin America*. New York: Scholastic, 1996. (short story collection ages 7–11)
Spanish translation: *De oro y esmeraldas: Mitos, leyendas y cuentos populares de Latinoamérica.*
   These stories are from 13 Latin American countries as well as indigenous cultures. Delacre demonstrates the breadth of her research by including maps as well as source and background notes.

———. *Las Navidades: Popular Christmas Songs from Latin America*. New York: Scholastic, 1990. (music)
Selected and illustrated by Lulu Delacre. English lyrics by Elena Paz. Musical arrangements by Ana-María Rosado.

———. *Vejigante masquerader*. New York: Scholastic, 1993. (picture book)
This story is set during carnival time in Puerto Rico. Ramon encounters difficulties in finding an appropriate costume and mask for the festivities. Look for the 28 lizards hidden in the illustrations.

Delgado, María Isabel. *Chave's Memories/Los recuerdos de Chave.* Houston: Piñata (Arte Público), 1996. (picture book)
Chave leaves the city behind to visit his grandparents in Mexico. His experiences on his grandparent's rural ranch become a magical time for him.

Denou, Violeta. *Llueve Teo* (It's raining, Teo). Barcelona: Editorial Timun Mas, 1983. (board book)
Series: *Tus Primeros Libros Teo* (Your first books, Teo).
   This wordless book shows what happens when it rains and what children wear.
   This series is perfect for sharing with toddlers. Parents, teachers, and caregivers can describe these books to children regardless of whether they or the children speak Spanish, English, or both. They are universal. Other books in this series are (publication dates provided when available):
Los animales de Teo (Teo's animals)
Teo juega (Teo plays)
Teo come (Teo eats)
Teo en el parvulario (Teo in preschool) 1983
Teo se lava (Teo washes)
Así es Teo (That's how Teo is)
La granja de Teo (Teo's farm) 1984
Es Navidad Teo (It's Christmastime, Teo)
Teo, vamos al parque (Teo, let's go to the park) 1987
Teo, vamos a la playa (Teo, let's go to the beach)
Teo, vamos al circo (Teo, let's go to the circus)
La familia de Teo (Teo's family) 1991
Vamos al zoo Teo (Let's go to the zoo, Teo) 1993
Teo se viste (Teo gets dressed)
Teo en el cumpleaños de Cleta (Teo at Cleta's birthday party) 1993
Vamos de paseo Teo (Let's go for a walk, Teo) 1993
Teo en la cocina (Teo in the kitchen) 1993
Mira las flores, Teo (Look at the flowers, Teo) 1994
Teo, hace frío (Teo, it's cold)
Hace calor, Teo (Teo, it's hot) 1996
Caen las hojas, Teo (The leaves are falling, Teo) 1996
Los disfraces de Teo (Teo's disguises) 1997

———. *Nico y Ana pescadores* (Nico and Ana, fishermen). Barcelona: Timun Mas, n.d. (picture book)
Nico and Ana spend a day with fishermen.

———. *Teo está enfermo* (Teo is sick). Barcelona: Editorial Timun Mas, 1983. (picture book)
Series: Teo descubre el mundo (Teo discovers the world).

Teo gets sick and doesn't like it too well. This series is perfect for preschoolers and storytimes because it covers very simple events and has simple text and appealing illustrations. It is also very popular with Latino parents. Other books in the series are (publication dates are given where available):

Teo en tren (Teo on a train) 1977
Teo en barco (Teo on a boat)
Teo en avión (Teo on a plane) 1977
Teo en el zoo (Teo at the zoo) 1978
Teo en la granja (Teo at the farm) 1978
Teo en el circo (Teo at the circus)
Teo en la escuela (Teo at school) 1978
Teo y su familia (Teo and his family) 1978
Teo en la nieve (Teo in the snow) 1979
Teo va de camping (Teo goes camping) 1981
Teo va de compras (Teo goes shopping) 1981
Teo y su perro (Teo and his dog) 1981
Teo va de vacaciones (Teo goes on vacation) 1982
Teo y su cumpleaños (Teo's birthday) 1982
Teo en la feria (Teo at the fair) 1983
Teo se disfraza (Teo puts on a disguise) 1984
Teo va al mercado (Teo goes to the market) 1984
Teo y sus amigos (Teo and his friends) 1985
Teo y su hermana (Teo and his sister) 1985
Teo en la piscina (Teo in the swimming pool) 1986
Teo en un día de fiesta (Teo in a holiday) 1987
Teo va de pesca (Teo goes fishing) 1989
Teo y los deportes (Teo and sports) 1989
Teo juega en casa (Teo plays at home) 1990
Teo y sus abuelos (Teo and his grandparents) 1992
Teo en el hipermercado (Teo at the hypermart) 1992
Teo va de campamento (Teo goes to camp) 1983
Teo hace travesuras (Teo makes mischief) 1994
Teo va a casa de una amiga (Teo goes to his girlfriend's house) 1995

Devetach, Laura. *Barril sin fondo* (Bottomless barrel). Buenos Aires: Colihue, 1992. (young adult anthology)
An anthology of ballads and riddles.

Díaz, Gloria Cecelia. *El sol de los venados* (The deer's sun). Madrid: Ediciones SM: 1993. (young adult)
Jana narrates the story of the first ten years of her life and talks

about the love in her family, the political violence they experience, and the death of her mother.

————. *El valle de los Cocuyos* (The valley of the fireflies). Madrid: Ediciones SM, 1986. (chapter fiction ages 7–11)
Cocuyos are insects like fireflies. Jerónimo goes on an adventure through this valley.

Dorros, Arthur. *Abuela* (Grandmother). Illus. Elisa Kleven. New York: Dutton, 1991. (picture book)
Spanish translation: *Abuela*. Trans. Sandra Marulandra Dorros.
     Rosalba and her grandmother fly high above the city streets.

————. *Isla*. Illus. Elisa Kleven. New York: Dutton, 1991. (picture book)
Spanish translation: *La isla*. Trans. Sandra Marulandra Dorros. In this sequel to *Abuela*, Rosalba and Abuela fly to the Carribean island where Abuela grew up.

————. *Radio Man: A Story in English and Spanish*. Trans. Sandra Marulanda Dorros. New York: HarperCollins, 1996. (picture book)
Diego relies on the radio to keep him connected as he travels from place to place with his family of migrant farm workers.

————. *Tonight Is Carnival*. Illustrated with *arpilleras* made by the Mothers Club Virgin del Carmen, of Lima, Perú. New York: Dutton, 1991. (picture book)
Spanish Translation: *Por fin es carnaval*. Trans. Sandra Marulanda Dorros.
     A boy prepares for the carnival celebration in the Andean countryside of Peru. He will play his wooden flute in a band with his father. This story is strikingly illustrated with *arpilleras*, or pieces of cloth sewn together and decorated with applique, embroidery, and needlework. These illustrations were done by a Mother's Club in Lima, Peru. The book includes a brief description of their craft.

Ehlert, Lois. *Cuckoo/Cucú*. Trans. Gloria de Aragón Andújar. San Diego, Calif.: Harcourt, 1997. (picture book)
Cuckoo is lazy until a fire threatens the seed crop and she is the only one who can save it.

————. *Moon Rope/Un lazo a la luna: A Peruvian Tale/Una leyenda peruana*. Trans. Amy Prince. San Diego, Calif.: Harcourt, 1992. (picture book)
Fox and Mole try to climb up to the moon on a rope woven of stars.

Elya, Susan Middleton. *Say Hola to Spanish*. Illus. Loretta Lopez. New York: Lee & Low, 1996. (picture book)
Teaches children simple Spanish words. A sequel is *Say Hola to Spanish, Otra vez* (Again) published by Lee & Low in 1997.

Emberly, Rebecca. *Let's Go/Vamos: A Book in Two Languages/Un libro en dos lenguas*. Trans. Alicia Marquis. Boston: Little Brown, 1993 (picture book).
This book gives the Spanish and English words for everyday objects. Other books by Emberly include:
My Day/Mi Dia.
My House/Mi Casa.
Taking a Walk/Caminando.

Estaba el Señor Don Gato (There was Mr. Cat). Illus. Carmen Salvador. Caracas, Venezuela: Ediciones Ekaré, 1993. (picture book)
Colleción clave del sol.
Song about the death and resurrection of Señor Don Gato, who wakes up with the stench of sardines after everyone thinks he's dead.

Ets, Marie Hall. *Gilberto and the Wind*. New York: Viking, 1963. (picture book)
Gilberto plays alone and imagines the wind to be his playmate.

———. *Nine Days to Christmas*. New York: Viking, 1959. (picture book)
Caldecott Medal. Five-year-old Ceci is permitted to choose her own piñata and stay up for *las posadas*.

Fern, Eugene. *Pepito's Story*. New York: Ariel, 1960. (picture book)
All the children want to give gifts to make the Lord Mayor's daughter well. Pepito has only one special gift.

Fernández, Laura. *De tin marín: cantos y rondas infantiles* (Children's songs and rhymes). Mexico D.F.: Editorial Trillas, 1983. (picture book)
Nursery rhymes and songs enhanced by Fernández's delicate illustrations.

———. *Luis y su genio* (Luis and his genie). Mexico D.F.: Editorial Trillas, n.d. (picture book)
One day Luis' genie magically appears in his room. He's a bread genie—they ask *you* to grant *their* wishes. He wants first to play ball, and second, to go to school as Luis. Everyone loves him when he makes three goals in the soccer game. His final wish is to go a

bakery, where he disappears. Luis knows it really happened because he got a "300" on his math test. Luis' parents tell him that genies only get "10s."

————. *Mariposa* (Butterfly). Mexico D.F.: Trillas, 1983. (picture book)
Butterfly wings around bragging to her friends that she can fly like the clouds and play with the wind. The other butterflies decide to put her boasts to the test. She has to ask for help when she becomes afraid she will fall. A little boy sends up a long string and butterfly becomes a kite.

————. *Pajaros en la cabeza* (Birds in your head). Mexico D.F.: Trillas, n.d. (picture book)
Premio Antoniorrobles. Based on a popular folk expression usually referring to big hair, this is the story of a girl who wakes up with real bluebirds dancing in her head. They stay with her during the day, but at night they go to their tree house to sleep. The girl is consoled by the knowledge that they are just outside her window.

Finger, Charles J. *Tales from Silver Lands*. New York: Doubleday, 1924. (short story collection ages 7–11)
Newbery Medal winner. A collection of tales from South America.

Fortun, Elena. *Celia en el colegio* (Celia in school). Madrid, Spain: Aguilar, 1973. (chapter fiction ages 7–11)
Celia's adventures in a Catholic boarding school.

Francia, Sylvia. *Las vacaciones de Roberta*. Caracas, Venezuela: Ediciones Ekaré, 1994, 1998. (picture book)
Originally published in French, but too good to pass up. Roberta, a dog, goes on vacation to her grandparent's house. Bored while her grandparents are napping, she goes to the beach and on the way meets a ferocious dog, Grorex. Delightfully, she ends up saving Grorex's life and they become friends.

Franklin, Kristine L. *When the Monkeys Came Back*. Illus. Robert Roth. New York: Atheneum, 1994. (picture book)
Marta goes back to her Costa Rican village and plants more trees to bring back the monkeys who used to play in them before they were cut down.

Gage, Amy Glaser. *Pascual's Magic Pictures*. Illus. Karen Dugan. Minneapolis: Carolrhoda, 1996. (picture book)
After he has saved the money he needs to purchase a disposable camera, Pascual takes pictures of the howler monkeys in the Guate-

malan rainforest of Tikal with unexpected results. The borders of the illustrations are Guatemalan weaving.

Galarza, Ernesto. *Poemas parvulos* (Poems for infants). Illus. Vincent P. Rascón. Editorial Almadén, 1971. (picture book poetry)
Sequel is: *Mas poemas parvulos* (More poems for infants). 1972. Simple rhymes.

———. *Rimas tontas* (Silly rhymes). Illus. Arthur J. Schneida. Editorial Almadén, 1971. (picture book poetry)

Garay, Luis. *Pedrito's Day*. New York: Orchard, 1997. (picture book)
Pedrito has to stay behind with his mother and grandmother and work every day as a shoeshine boy to help earn money for his family after his father goes North to find work. His wise-for-his years response in a time of crisis convinces his mother that he is finally old enough for the thing he most wants: his own bicycle.

Garcia, Guy. *Spirit of the Maya: A Boy Explores His People's Mysterious Past*. Illus. Ted Wood. New York: Walker & Co., 1995. (nonfiction ages 7–11)
Kin is a direct descendent of the Maya. He learns to appreciate his heritage through his father's traditional artwork and through a visit to the ancient ruins of temples and pyramids.

García, María. *The Adventures of Connie and Diego/Las aventuras del Connie y Diego*. Illus. Malaquias Montoya. San Francisco: Children's Book Press, 1987. (picture book)
The twins Connie and Diego run away because everyone makes fun of them. They meet various animals and try to live with them. Eventually they discover they are humans, that they belong with people.

García, Richard. *My Aunt Otilia's Spirits/Los espiritus de me Tía Otilia*. San Francisco: Children's Book Press, 1987. (picture book)
Aunt Otilia from Puerto Rico is the quintessential weird aunt who visits her family in San Francisco each year. When Aunt Otilia tries to contact the spirit world one evening, she precipitates a funny series of events that end up with her going away, never to return.

García Dominquez, Ramón. *Un grillo del año dos mil y pico* (A Cricket of the year 2000 and something). Illus. Javier González Solas. Valladolid: Editorial Miñón, 1981. (chapter fiction ages 7–11)
A group of children in the future leave their school for the country and discover a cricket.

García Lorca, Federico. *Canciones y poemas para niños* (Songs and poems for children). Illus. Daniel Zarza. Barcelona: Editorial Labor, 1990. (poetry ages 7–11)
A volume that collects all of García Lorca's children's poetry, some humorous, others lyrical.

Garland, Sherry. *Indio*. New York: Harcourt, 1995. (young adult)
Historical fiction in the time that the Spanish are setting their sights on the conquest of native peoples along the Texas border. Ipa survives this time, but she also returns to her village with Spanish language and religion.

Geeslin, Campbell. *In Rosa's Mexico*. Illus. Andrea Arroyo. New York: Knopf, 1997. (picture book)
Three stories about a small girl named Rosa. In "Rosa and El Gallo" her rooster's magical crow saves the day. In "Rosa's Estrella" she saves the day herself, and does something magical with a star. "In Rosa and El Lobo" she saves a wolf and gets a magic pillow.

Gershator, David and Phyllis. *Bread Is for Eating*. Illus. Emma Shaw-Smith. New York: Holt, 1995. (picture book)
Original song with lyrics in Spanish and English.

Gerson, Mary-Joan. *People of Corn: A Mayan Story*. Illus. Carla Golembe. Boston: Little Brown, n.d. (picture book)
A story taken from the Popol Vuh, the sacred book of the Maya. The Mayan gods attempt to fashion people who will express gratitude. They are eventually able to create people from their sacred corn.

Gerson, Sara. *El hada Delia* (Delia the witch). Illus. Alejandro Walls. Mexico, D.F.: Editorial Trillas, 1986. (picture book)
Delia is different from all the other fairies. She shows the other fairies that children still believe in them and love them.

Girón, Nicole. *El barro* (Clay). Illus. Abraham Mauricio Salazar. Mexico D.F.: Editorial Patria, 1983. (picture book)
Collección Piñata. Series: *Las materias primas* (Primary materials).
Making pottery and other objects from clay.

———. *El azúcar* (Sugar). Illus. Ana Villaseñor. Mexico D.F.: Editorial Patria, 1985. (picture book)
Collección Piñata. Series: *Las materias primas* (Primary materials).
A little boy narrates the story of how his father makes cane sugar.

Gisbert, Juan Manuel. *El guardián del olvido* (The guardian of forgetfulness). Illus. Alfonso Ruano. Madrid: Ediciones SM, 1990. (chapter fiction ages 7–11)
Gabriel loses his toy top one day, and a strange girl in his class, Analisa, shows him a house where he can find it. It is in a large house with rooms in which all lost things can be found. Gabriel returns to find some things his mother had lost, and is told to tell no one of the secret. Analisa does not return to school, but Gabriel finds the mirror that she always carried and takes it back to the house of lost things, hoping that she would come there to find it.

Goldsmith, Patrick. *Espejo de obsidiana* (The obsidian mirror). Illus. Felipe Ehrenberg. Editorial Navaro, 1982. (chapter fiction ages 7–11)
In the year 1561 Pablito goes to school in the only place where Indian children can study side by side with Spanish children. He makes friends with Pablo, who has a very important secret: he knows the location of a mirror in which one can see more that just reflections. Through the mirror they watch events in the history of Mexico.

Gollub, Matthew. *The Moon Was at a Fiesta*. Illus. Leovigildo Martinez. New York : Tambourine Books, 1994. (picture book)
The moon is jealous of the sun, and decides to have her own party, but she ends up partying a bit too much.

———. *Uncle Snake*. Illus. Leovigildo Martinez. New York: Tambourine Books, 1996. (picture book)
A folktale from Oaxaca, Mexico. A young boy is forced to wear a mask for twenty years after he takes on a snake's face while exploring a cave that was forbidden. He finally is taken up into the sky and becomes lightning.

González, Lucía M. *The Bossy Gallito/El gallo de bodas: A Traditional Cuban Folktale*. New York: Scholastic, 1997. (picture book)
Pura Belpré Honor Book for Writing and Illustration, 1996. The Gallito dirties his beak on the way to the wedding of his Uncle Parrot, but no one will help him clean it until he calls on his friend, the sun. The illustrations set the tale in Miami's "Little Havana."

———. *Señor Cat's Romance: And Other Stories from Latin America*. Illus. Lulu Delacre. New York: Scholastic, 1997. (short story collection ages 7–11)
Includes the following stories:
"Little Half-Chicken"
"Juan Bobo and the Three-Legged Pot"

"Martina, the Little Cockroach"
"The Billy Goat and the Vegetable Garden"
"How Uncle Rabbit Tricked Uncle Tiger"
"Señor Cat's Romance"

Gonzalez, Ralfka, and Ana Ruiz. *Mi primer libro de dichos/My First Book of Proverbs*. Emeryville, Calif.: Children's Book Press, 1995. (picture book)
Contains familiar proverbs and others not so familiar:
"Pig out while you have the chance/Atáscate ahora que hay lodo."
"If you hang out with wolves you will learn how to howl/El que anda con lobos a aullar se enseña."

González-Jensen, Margarita. *Mexico's Marvelous Corn*. Crystal Lake, Ill.: Rigby, 1997. (nonfiction ages 7–11)
Spanish edition: *El maravilloso maiz de México*.
Corn is described in all its variety and flavors in this book, with brief, descriptions of various ancient and modern methods of preparation.

Gordon, Ginger. *My Two Worlds*. Illus. Martha Cooper. New York: Clarion, 1993. (nonfiction ages 7–11)
Kirsey Rodriguez has two homes: New York City and the Dominican Republic. She does not have to choose one or the other, and is able to travel between these two homes on a regular basis.

Gregory, Kristiana. *The Stowaway: A Tale of California Pirates*. New York: Scholastic, 1995. (young adult)
Historical fiction set on the Monterey, California, coast of 1818. An eleven-year-old boy named Carlito has his world disrupted when the Argentine pirate Hippolyted de Bouchard attacks.

Griego y Maestas, José, and Rudolfo A. Anaya. *Cuentos: Tales from the Hispanic Southwest*. Bilingual Stories in Spanish and English. Illus. Jaime Valdez. Santa Fe: The Museum of New Mexico Press, 1980. (young adult short story collection)
Based on stories originally collected by Juan B. Rael.

Griego, Margot C. and Betsy L. Bucks, Sharon S. Gilbert, and Laurel H. Kimball. (select. and trans.). *Tortillitas para mama and Other Nursery Rhymes/Spanish and English*. Illus. Barbara Cooney. New York: Holt, 1981. (picture book)
This classic should be in the collection of any librarian or teacher working with Latino children. Includes some of the most common rhymes.

Grossman, Patricia. *Saturday Market*. Illus. Enrique O. Sanchez. New York: Lothrop, Lee & Shepard, 1994. (picture book)
Tells some of the stories of the individual vendors at a Saturday Mexican market.

Gutierrez, Douglas. *La noche de las estrellas* (The night of stars). Illus. María Fernanda Oliver. Caracas, Venezuela: Ediciones Ekaré/Banco del Libro, 1987. (picture book)
A beautifully illustrated book that tells how the stars and the moon came to be. A man who lives in a village that is not near and yet not far does not like the night. One night he climbs his mountain and punches holes in the night, creating the moon and stars.

Guy, Ginger Foglesong. ¡*Fiesta*! (Party!). Illus. René King. New York: Greenwillow, 1996. (picture book)
A bilingual counting book about kids on the way to a party.

Hall, Nancy Abraham and Jilly Syverson-Stork. *Los pollitos dicen/ The Baby Chicks Sing: Juegos, rimas y canciones infantiles de paises de habla hispana/Traditional Games, Nursery Rhymes, and Songs from Spanish-Speaking Countries*. Illus. Kay Chorao. Boston: Little Brown, 1994. (picture book anthology)
Traditional songs, rhymes, and games presented in a bilingual format. Includes "*A la víbora de la mar.*"

Haskins, Jim. *Count Your Way through Mexico*. Illus. Helen Byers. Minneapolis, Minn.: Carolrhoda, 1989. (picture book)
Through the device of a counting book, Haskins relays some basic information about Mexico and its culture, such as food and holidays.

Hayes, Joe. *La llorona/The Weeping Woman*. El Paso, Tex.: Cinco Puntos Press, n.d. (picture book)
This is a written rendition of the version that Joy Hayes tells, which makes the best version of this classic tale to be told or read aloud.

————. *Mariposa, mariposa*. (Butterfly, butterfly). Illus. Lucy Jelinek. Santa Fe, N.M.: Trails West, 1988. (picture book)
Note: This book is bilingual—the title is just not translated. A variation on "Perez and Martina." Mariposa finds some money and gets a beautiful dress (her wings). She asks various animals who want to marry her how they will talk to her when they are married. She likes the mouse. Mouse gets eaten by cat. Friends bring flowers, and she likes them so much that she flys from flower to flower to this day.

————. *Monday, Tuesday, Wednesday, Oh!/Lunes, martes, miercoles, ¡Oh!* Illus. Lucy Jelinek. Santa Fe, N.M.: Trails West, 1987. (picture book)
A poor woman is forced to work for a rich, snobby woman for pay that consists of stale tortillas. The poor woman finds some little men whom she hears singing. She inadvertantly adds to their day-of-the-week song. (They only knew the first three verses). They give her gold in thanks. The rich woman tries, messes up, and gets a present.

————. *No Way, José/¡De ninguna manera José!* Illus. Lucy Jelinek. Santa Fe, N.M.: Trails West, 1986. (picture book)
A rooster named José goes to the wedding of his Uncle Perico. Jose gets his beak dirty through eating, but no one will help him clean it so he can be presentable.

————. *The Terrible Tragadabas/El terrible tragadabas.* Illus. Lucy Jelinek. Santa Fe, N.M.: Trails West, 1987. (picture book)
Great monster story/cumulative tale. Three sisters, one by one, get scared up into a tree by the Tragadabas. The Tragadabas gets stung by a bee and the girls return home safely to their grandmother.

————. *Watch Out for Clever Women!/¡Cuidado con las mujeres astutas!.* Illus. Vicky Trego Hill. El Paso, Texas: Cinco Puntos Press, 1994. (short story collection ages 7–11)
Texas Bluebonnet Award Nominee. Stories that celebrate the strength of Latina women. Includes "The Day It Snowed Tortillas."

Heide, Florence Parry, and Roxanne Heide Pierce. *Tío Armando.* Illus. Ann Grifalconi. New York: Lothrop, Lee & Shepard, 1998. (picture book)
After he dies Tío Armando's influence lives on in the life of his niece, Lucitita.

Hernández, Jo Ann Yolanda. *White Bread Competition.* Houston: Piñata Books (Arte Público), 1997. (novel ages 8–14)
The story revolves around the reactions of friends, family, and community when one of their own, Luz, wins a spelling competition. Set in San Antonio, Texas.

Herrera, Juan Felipe. *Calling the Doves/El canto de las palomas.* Illus. Elly Simmons. Emeryville, Calif.: Children's Book Press, 1995. (picture book)
The author recalls his farmworker parents who inspired him through singing.

————. *Laughing Out Loud, I Fly: Poems in English and Spanish.* Illus. Karen Barbour. New York: HarperCollins, 1998. (poetry ages 7–11)
A book of whimsical poetry from this award-winning writer.

Herrmann, Marjorie E. *Perez and Martina/Perez y Martina: Fables in English and Spanish/Fábulas Bilingües.* Lincolnwood, Ill.: National Textbook Company, 1988. (picture book)
A controlled vocabulary version of the story for children to read on their own.

Hewett, Joan. *Hector Lives in the United States Now: The Story of a Mexican-American Child.* Illus. Richard R. Hewett. New York: HarperCollins, 1990. (nonfiction ages 7–11)
Hector Almaraz is ten years old. This book shows some of the everyday events in his life, from playing sports to attending first holy communion.

Hinojosa, Francisco. *A golpe de calcetin* (By means of a sock). Illus. Carmen Parra. Mexico D.F.: Editorial Novaro, 1982. (chapter fiction ages 7–11)
Manuel has to take care of his family in 1930s Mexico City while his father is on strike. Then a strange man buys all his papers and asks him to deliver a letter to a man in the hospital. Manuel finds himself in the middle of a bank heist, and becomes a hero.

Hispanic, Female and Young: An Anthology. Ed. Phyllis Tashlik. Houston: Piñata (Arte Publico), 1994. (young adult anthology)
Writings by a group of Latina High School students are placed along side those of established Latina authors. It also includes interviews with Latina role models.

Horenstein, Henry. *Baseball in the Barrios.* San Diego, Calif.: Harcourt, 1997. (nonfiction ages 7–11)
Spanish translation, *Béisbol en los barrios.* Trans. Alma Flor Ada and F. Isabel Campoy.
Young boys playing baseball in Venezuela hope to break into the big leagues.

Hoyt-Goldsmith, Diane. *Day of the Dead: A Mexican-American Celebration.* Illus. Lawrence Migdale. New York: Holiday House, 1994. (nonfiction ages 7–11)
Shows how two children from Sacramento, California celebrate this holiday.

Hughes, Monica. *A Handful of Seeds*. Illus. Luis Garay. New York: Orchard, 1993. (picture book)
Spanish translation: *Un puñado de semillas*. Caracas, Venezuela: Ediciones Ekaré, 1996.
A story that could take place in any number of Central or South American countries. Concepción lives with her grandmother in a little house on a hill. They have a beautiful garden of corn and beans and chiles. When Grandmother dies, the landlord kicks Concepción out. She goes to the barrio in the city and lives with other street children in a slum. She thought the city would be beautiful. She grows a garden there, and teaches the other barrio children to do the same. Could be used with *La calle es libre*.

Jaffe, Nina. *The Golden Flower: A Taino Myth from Puerto Rico*. Illus. Enrique O. Sanchez. New York: Simon and Schuster, 1996. (picture book)
A Pura Belpré Honor Book for illustration. A Puerto Rican myth about the origin of the sea, the forest, and the island of Puerto Rico itself. A helpful afterword gives the background of the Taino people.

Jacob, Esther. *Las tortugas de mar* (The sea turtles). Illus. Felipe Dávalos. Mexico D.F.: CONAFE (Consejo Nacional de Fomento Educativo), 1984. (picture book)
A science book about turtles that also includes Mexican legends concerning the turtle. This book brought illustrator Felipe Dávalos to wider attention and earned him the Ezra Jack Keats award.

Jagendorf, M. A., and R. S. Boggs. *The King of the Mountains: A Treasury of Latin American Folk Stories*. Illus. Carybé. New York: Vanguard, 1960. (short story collection ages 8–14)
Includes stories about Tío Conejo, Juan Bobo, and Our Lady of Guadelupe. "Uncle Rabbit Flies to Heaven" tells why Tío Conejo has long ears and why the buzzard's neck is featherless.

Jaramillo, Nelly Palacio. *Grandmother's Nursery Rhymes/ Las nanas de abuelita: Lullabies, Tounge Twisters, and Riddles from South America*. Illus. Elivia Savadier. New York: Henry Holt, 1994. (picture book)
The author, who hails from Columbia collected these to share after the birth of a grandchild. This book provides English versions of the rhymes, which non-Spanish speakers will find helpful. Includes "Aserrín Asserán" with an explanation of the wordplay.

Jiménez, Juan Ramón. *Canta pájaro lejano* (Sing faraway bird). Illus. Luis de Horna. Madrid: Espasa-Calpe, S. A., 1981. (poetry ages 8–14)
Children's poems by one of Spain's greatest poets.

———. *Platero y yo/Platero and I*. Trans. Myra Cohn Livingston. Illus. Antonio Frasconi New York: Clarion, 1957, 1994. (novel ages 8–14)
Bilingual selections from the children's classic from Spain about a boy and his beloved donkey who wander through the landscape of southern Spain.

———. *Poesia en prosa y verso* (Poetry in prose and verse). Illus. Rafael Munoa. Madrid: Aguilar, 1960. (poetry ages 8–14)
Selected for children by Zenobia Camprubi Aymar.

Jiménez, Francisco. *The Circuit: Stories for the Life of a Migrant Child*. Albuquerque, University of New Mexico Press, 1997. (short story collection ages 8–14)
Poignant short stories about the life of a child of migrant farmworkers in California. These simple stories are realistic and don't shrink from portraying the unpleasant aspects of Jiménez's life.

———. *La Mariposa*. Illus. Simon Silva. Boston: Houghton Mifflin, 1998. (picture book)
Spanish edition: *La mariposa*. A young Spanish-speaking boy is unable to understand his new teacher and classmates. His observation of the metamorphosis of a caterpillar into a butterfly in his classroom becomes a metaphor for his struggle to understand English.

Johnston, Tony. *Day of the Dead*. Illus. Jeanette Winter. New York: Harcourt, 1997. (picture book)
A small format picture book that details Day of the Dead celebrations.

———. *The Iguana Brothers: A Tale of Two Lizards*. Illus. Mark Teague. New York: Blue Sky (Scholastic), 1995. (picture book)
Dom likes who he is, but his brother Tom does not. This is a story of friendship set in Mexico.

———. *Lorenzo, the Naughty Parrot*. Illus. Leo Politi. San Diego, Calif.: Harcourt, 1992. (picture book)
Lorenzo loves cookies. He tries to help his human family but ends up getting into trouble.

———. *The Magic Maguey*. Illus. Elisa Kleven. San Diego, Calif.: Harcourt, 1996. (picture book)
Miguel and his friends try to save the giant maguey plant from being destroyed by an evil landowner. Tale takes place around the Christmas holiday.

———. *My Mexico/México mío*. Illus. F. John Sierra. New York: Putnam, 1996. (picture book)
Poems about Mexico that are filled with a love of the country that developed over the 15 years the author lived there.

———. *The Old Lady and the Birds*. Illus. Stephanie García. San Diego, Calif.: Harcourt, 1994. (picture book)
An old lady enjoys her garden in Mexico.

———. *The Tale of Rabbit and Coyote*. Illus. Tomie DePaola. New York: Putnam, 1994. (picture book)
Rabbit stays one step ahead of both Coyote and the farmer who wants to eat him. The tale explains why Coyote howls at the moon—that this is where Rabbit went to hide.

Jordan, Tanis. *Angel Falls: A South American Journey*. Illus. Martin Jordan. New York: Kingfisher, 1995. (nonfiction ages 7–11)
The fauna of the Angel Falls region of southeast Venezuela is portrayed with beautiful illustrations. Includes a glossary of all the animals discussed.

Juegos y diversiones Mexicanos: un libro para divertirse y aprender algo (Mexican games and diversion: A book to have fun with and learn something from). Illus. Maribel Suárez. Mexico D.F.: Sitesa, 1988. (nonfiction ages 7–11)
Information on Mexican sweets, geography, dichos, games, Day of the Dead, puzzles, tongue twisters, and riddles.

Keane, Sofía Meza. *Dear Abuelita*. Illus. Enrique O. Sánchez. Crystal Lake, Ill.: Rigby, 1997. (picture book)
Spanish edition: *Querida Abuelita*.
Marco writes to his grandmother after he moves from Mexico to California to tell her all about his new surroundings, as well as how much he misses the things he left behind. He misses Grandma's stories most.

Keister, Douglas. *Fernando's Gift/El regalo de Fernando*. San Francisco, Calif.: Sierra Club, 1995. (picture book)
Fernando, who lives in Costa Rica, goes to his favorite climbing tree one day only to find that it has been cut down.

Kendall, Sarita. *Ransom for a River Dolphin*. Minneapolis: Lerner, 1993. (young adult)
Carmenza nurses a dolphin back to health. She finds the dolphin near her village, and suspects it may have been wounded by her stepfather.

King, Elizabeth. *Chile Fever: A Celebration of Peppers*. New York: Dutton, 1995. (nonfiction ages 7–11)
Color photos demonstrate the history and cultivation of chile peppers.

————. *Quinceñera: Celebrating Fifteen*. New York: Dutton, 1998. (nonfiction ages 7–11)
Spanish edition: *Quinceñera: celebrando los quince*.
King traces the history of this tradition and recounts the real-life *quiceañera* of Cindy Chávez.

Kleven, Elisa. *Hooray, A Piñata*! New York: Dutton, 1996. (picture book)
Clara pretends her new dog-shaped *piñata* is a pet so that it won't get broken.

Kouzel, Daisy, and Earl Thollander. *The Cuckoo's Reward/El premio del cuco*. New York: Doubleday, 1977. (picture book)
The cuckoo is considered a trouble-maker until she performs an act of heroism.

Kroll, Virginia. *Butterfly Boy*. Illus. Gerado Suzán. Honesdale, Penn.: Boyds Mills, 1997. (picture book)
This book describes the a young boy's relationship with his disabled grandfather. Every day they watch butterflies in their backyard, attracted by the white garage door. This relationship is challenged when the boy's father paints the garage door.

Krull, Kathleen. *Maria Molina and the Day of the Dead*. Illus. Enrique O. Sanchez. New York: Macmillan, 1994. (nonfiction ages 7–11)
Describes how Maria and her family celebrate the Day of the Dead in Mexico. Includes a recipe for "*Pan de los muertos*." (Bread of the dead).

————. *The Other Side: How Kids Live in a California Latino Neighborhood*. Illus. David Hautzig. New York: Lodestar (Dutton), 1994. (nonfiction ages 7–11)
Kids tell why they left Mexico with their families and what is different about their lives in California.

Krumgold, Joseph. *. . . and now Miguel*. Illus. Jean Charlot. New York: HarperCollins, 1953. (novel ages 8–14)
Miguel wants to be a man and go with his father and brothers to herd the sheep in the mountains of New Mexico.

Kurtz, Jane. *Miro in the Kingdom of the Sun*. Illus. David Frampton. Boston: Houghton Mifflin, 1996. (picture book)
Woodcut illustrations decorate this tale of an Inca girl who is able to heal the king's son after others, including her brothers, have failed.

Kurusa. *La calle es libre*. Illus. Monika Doppert. Caracas, Venezuela: Ediciones Ekaré/Banco del Libro, 1981. (picture book)
English translation: *The Streets are Free*. Trans. Karen Englander. Toronto: Annick Press, 1985.
   The true story of a group of kids who, with support from the neighborhood librarian, take matters into their own hands when the government won't supply them with a park to play in instead of the streets.

————. *El cocuyo y la more* (The firebug and the berry bush). Illus. Veronica Uribe. Caracas, Venezuela: Ediciones Ekaré/Banco del Libro, 1983. (picture book)
A Venezuelan legend about how the firebug got the light on its tail.

Lachtman, Ofelia Dumas. *Big Enough/Bastante grande*. Illus. Enrique O. Sánchez. Houston: Piñata (Arte Publico), 1998. (picture book)
Lupita's mother tells her that she is too little to help out in the restaurant that her mother owns. She is able to show that she is big enough to be able to do some things when she apprehends a thief.

————. *Call Me Consuelo*. Houston: Piñata (Arte Publico), 1997. (novel ages 8–14)
A farm girl, Consuelo, must adjust to city life after being orphaned. Consuelo is drawn into a mystery when houses in her neighborhood are burglarized.

————. *The Girl from Playa Blanca*. Houston: Piñata (Arte Público), 1995. (novel ages 8–14)
Elena and her brother Carlos leave their seaside village in Mexico and travel to the United States to find their father, who has disappeared. Elena obtains employment with a wealthy family, and becomes involved in mystery and intrigue she searches for her father.

————. *Leticia's Secret*. Houston: Piñata (Arte Público), 1997. (novel ages 7–11)
Rosario fumes over the special treatment her cousin Leticia receives until she discovers that Leticia's secret is that she is dying. Leticia ends up making a big impact on the lives of Rosario and some of her friends.

————. *Pepita Talks Twice/Pepita habla does veces*. Illus. Alex Pardo DeLange. Houston: Piñata (Arte Público), 1995. (picture book)
Pepita is frustrated that she is bilingual and has to translate for everyone. She decides to stop speaking Spanish, but the problems she then encounters lead her to realize the value of both languages.

————. *Pepita Thinks Pink/Pepita y el color rosado*. Illus. Alex Pardo DeLange. Houston: Piñata (Arte Público), 1998. (picture book)
In this sequel to *Pepita Talks Twice*, Pepita can't stand the new neighbor girl Sonya, who dresses entirely in pink, even though her family and her friend Mr. Hobbs urge her to make friends.

Lankford, Mary. *Quinceñera: A Latina's Journey toward Womanhood*. Illus. Jesse Herrera. New York: Millbrook Press, 1994. (nonfiction ages 7–11)
Describes the rituals associated with this very important coming-of-age ceremony for young Latinas.

Lasky, Kathryn. *Days of the Dead*. Illus. Christoper G. Knight. New York: Hyperion, 1994. (nonfiction ages 7–11)
Personalizes the story of the Day of the Dead holiday through the story of the child Gamalier.

Leclercq, Jean Paul and Vendrell, Carme Solé. *Peluso y la cometa* (Peluso and the kite). Valladolid: Editorial Miñón, 1979. (picture book)
Peluso is a small, gray bird, not very exciting. When he sees a colorful kite, he wants to be like it. He meets a little boy who tries to help him.

Lee, Héctor Viveros. *Yo tenía un hipopótamo* (I had a hippopatamus). New York: Lee & Low, 1996, 1997. (picture book)
In this preditcable tale, the narrator tells the fate of each of his pets, until he finally comes to the cat, which he keeps. A natural for storytime.

Levert, Claude, and Vendrell, Carme Solé. *Pedro y su roble* (Pedro and his tree). Valladolid: Editorial Miñón, 1979. (picture book)
A boy cares for his tree through the four seasons. In autumn, he mistakenly thinks that it's dying. He wraps a blanket around it during winter, and in spring experiences the miracle of new life.

Levy, Janice. *The Spirit of Tío Fernando/El espíritu de Tío Fernando*. Illus. Morella Fuenmayor. Morton Grove, Ill.: Albert Whitman, 1995. (picture book)
A young boy remembers his uncle as he and his mother prepare to celebrate the uncle's memory on the Day of the Dead.

Lewis, Thomas P. *Hill of Fire*. Illus. Joan Sandin. New York: HarperCollins, 1971. (picture book)
An "I Can Read" book. A farmer plowing his field accidentally finds a volcano that erupts and ruins homes and schools.

Lionni, Leo. *Suimi*. New York: Pantheon (Random House), 1963. (picture book)
Translation of *Swimmy*. A new translation, *Nadarin*, appeared in 1986. (Trans. Ana María Matute. Barcelona: Editorial Lumen).
I include this title because I have found that Latino children relate well to the theme of the story. This book works particularly well when told aloud, and it is one of my favorites.

Llorente, Pilar Molina. *El mensaje de Maese Zamaor* (Maese Zamaor's message). Madrid: Ediciones SM, 1981. (chapter fiction ages 7–11)
The King of Fartuel is in trouble if he can't find the money to pay his debts, because then his daughter will have to marry a tyrant by the name of Dresion. The King's court painter, Maese Zamaor, saves the situation.

———. *Patatita*. Illus. Marina Seoane. Madrid: Ediciones SM, 1983. (chapter fiction ages 7–11)
Patatita, a gypsy boy, wants to explore a village with his dog, Caldero. But then Caldero gets lost. A novel told in free verse poetry.

Lomas Garza, Carmen. *Family Pictures/Cuadros de familia.* Stories by Carmen Lomas Garza as told to Harriet Rohmer. Trans. by Rosalma Zubizaretta. San Francisco, Calif.: Children's Book Press, 1990. (picture book)
Pictures of growing up Latino in Kingsville, Texas. This book feels like a family album with its folk art illustrations. The accompanying text is equally descriptive and conversational.

————. *In My Family/En mi familia.* Paintings and Stories by/*Cuadros y relatos de* Carmen Lomas Garza As told to/*Contados a* Harriet Rohmer. Edited by/*Editado por* David Schecter. Spanish translation by/*Traducido al español* por Francisco X. Alarcón. San Francisco, Calif.: Children's Book Press, 1996. (picture book)
A Pura Belpré Honor Book for illustration. This follow up to *Family Pictures* is another bilingual picture book that celebrates Mexican-American culture. Some of the memories Lomas Garza shares about her childhood in Kingsville, Texas, include an encounter with horned toads, eating cactus and *empanadas*, and having a birthday barbecue.

López de Almeida, Fernando. *La margarita friolenta* (Margarita is cold). Illus. Laura Liberatore. Caracas, Venezuela: Ediciones Ekaré, 1979, 1988. (picture book)
Margarita, a flower, is cold. A butterfly tells the girl Ana María. She discovers that it's the kind of cold that a jacket can't help.

López de Mariscal, Blanca. *The Harvest Birds/Los pájaros de la cosecha.* Illus. Enrique Flores. Emeryville, Calif.: Children's Book Press, 1995. (picture book)
After his father's land is divided between his two older brothers, Juan Zanate is left with nothing but his dream of owning his own farm. His constant companions, the Zanate, or harvest birds, teach him the secret of sucess.

Lopez, Loretta. *The Birthday Swap.* New York: Lee & Low, 1991. (picture book)
Spanish translation ¡*Que sorpresa de cumpleaños*! 1997.
Lori lives near the Texas-Mexico border. In this book she tells the story of her best birthday ever—when her sister swaps birthdays with her so she won't have to wait until December.

Luenn, Nancy. *A Gift for Abuelita: Celebrating the Day of the Dead/ Un regalo para Abuelita: En celebración del Día de los Muertos.* Illus. Robert Chapman. Flagstaff, Ariz.: Rising Moon, 1998. (picture book)

In this moving tale, Rosita prepares a gift to place on the grave of her recently deceased grandmother during the Day of the Dead celebrations. After much thought, she is able to make a gift which contains all the memories she has of her relationship with this special woman.

Lyons, Grant. *Tales the People Tell in Mexico*. New York: Messner, 1972. (short story collection ages 7–11)
This collection includes a version of "La Llorona" as well as some *dichos* and a couple of riddles.

Lyra, Carmen. *Los Cuentos de mi Tía Panchita* (The stories of my aunt Panchita). Educa, 1984. (short story collection ages 7–11)
The classic collection of Costa Rican stories. The second half of the book is composed entirely of stories about Tío Conejo.

McDermott, Gerald. *Musicians of the Sun*. New York: Simon and Schuster, 1997. (picture book)
McDermott retells the Mexican story of the Lord of the Night, who restores color and music to a dreary world.

Machado, Ana Maria. *El perro del cerro y la rana de la sabana* (The dog from the hill and the frog from the plains). Caracas, Venezuela: Ediciones Ekaré/Banco del Libro, 1981, 1986. (picture book)
Frog and Dog argue that each is braver than the other. A Lion scares them both.

Madrigal, Antonio Hernández. *The Eagle and the Rainbow: Timeless Tales from Mexico*. Illus. Tomie DePaola. Golden, Colorado: Fulcrum Kids, 1997. (short story collection ages 7–11)
Includes "The Eagle and the Rainbow"; "Tahui," about a young boy who overcomes illness and runs in the Great Race; "The Boy Who Cried Tears of Jade"; "Tribe of the Deer," in which a deer saves his people from drought and famine when he brings them a rainbow; and "Legend of the Feathered Serpent."

Markun, Patricia Maloney. *The Little Painter of Sabana Grande*. Illus. Robert Casilla. New York: Bradbury, 1993. (picture book)
Fernando paints the outside of his adobe house, since he doesn't have any paper.

Mariño, Carlos. *El mar preferido de los piratas* (The pirate's favorite sea). Illus. Carlos Nine. Buenos Aires, Argentina: Colleción Pan Flauta, 1988. (chapter fiction ages 7–11)
Episodic story about an old man who builds a sea in front of his

house. All sorts of interesting creatures come, and it becomes the preferred sea of a pirate band.

Marrin, Albert. *Empires Lost and Won: The Spanish Heritage in the Southwest*. New York: Atheneum, 1997. (nonfiction ages 8–14)
Details the influence of Spanish explorers and *conquistadores* on what is now the southwestern United States.

Martel, Cruz. *Yagua Days*. Illus. Jerry Pinkney. New York: Dial, 1976. (picture book)
Adan experiences Puerto Rico for the first time when his family takes him to visit his uncle's plantation.

Martí, José. *La edad de oro* (The age of gold). Río Piedras, Puerto Rico: Editorial San Juan, 1976. (short story collection ages 8–14)
A collection of all the articles that appeared in the four issues of the magazine *Le edad de oro*, which José Martí published in New York between July and October 1889.

Martínez, Alejandro Cruz. *The Woman Who Outshone the Sun/La mujer que brillaba aún mas que el sol*. Illus. Fernando Olivera. San Francisco: Children's Book Press, 1991. (picture book)
Story by Rosalma Zubizaretta, Harriet Rohmer, and David Schecter. The river falls in love with Lucia and comes into her hair. When she is treated badly by the villagers, she takes the river with her.

Martínez, Floyd. *Spirits of the High Mesa*. Houston: Piñata Books (Arte Público Press), 1997. (chapter fiction ages 7–11)
Pura Belpré Honor Book. A historical novel about life in a village in New Mexico that intertwines the story of the boy, Flavio, coming of age with the coming of technology and the end of an era.

Martínez i Vendrell, Maria. *Hablemos de . . . como duele* (Let's talk about . . . how it hurts). Illus. Roger Capdevila. Barcelona: Ediciones Destino, 1987. (picture book)
Martin bangs his head on a tree playing soccer and has to go to the hospital. There are funny scenes of an imaginary operation, with the doctors using a saw and a large needle. Martin sees himself as a toy. Others in the series include
El agua inquieta. (The restless water). 1989. Eloy is afraid to swim. But he gets goggles so he can see in the water. "¡Esto funciona!," he says, "Jamás habia visto mis propios pies con tanta nitidez." ("This works! I've never seen my own feet with such clarity before.")

Hola y adios (Hello and goodbye). 1987. Juan doesn't want to go to camp.

Los conflictos de Ana (Ana's conflicts). 1988. Ana deals with divorce.

Cambios y distancias (Changes and distances). 1988. Blas moves with his family to a farm.

Martinez, Victor. *Parrot in the Oven: Mi vida.* New York: Harper Collins, 1996. (young adult)
This series of vignettes shows Manuel Hernandez trying to find his way in the world and in his family. Winner of the National Book Award and the Pura Belpré Award.

Mateos, Pilar. *La bruja Mon* (Mon, the witch). Illus. Viví Escrivá. Madrid: Ediciones SM, 1985. (chapter fiction ages 7–11)
La Bruja Mon no longer changes children into frogs after she finds she can't travel anywhere with a frog. In the final story she gets angry at an echo and turns herself into a fish.

———. *Capitanes de plástico* (Plastic captains). Madrid: Ediciones SM, 1982. (novel ages 8–14)
Premio Lazarillo. Capitan Ernest solves his problems, especially his conflicts with his brother Miguel, by taking refuge in fantasy. Also includes the story "¿Chico o chica?" (Boy or girl?) In this story mysterious smells appear from a mysterious visitor.

———. *Historias de ninguno* (Stories of nobody). Madrid: Ediciones SM, 1981. (novel ages 8–14)
Stories about a child named Nobody. He's very small and refuses to grow. He has to put stones in his pocket so he won't blow away on a windy day. His classmates don't pay much attention to him.

———. *Jeruso quiere ser gente* (Jeruso wants to be a person). Madrid: Ediciones SM, 1982. (novel ages 8–14)
Jeruso delivers for the shopkeeper, Julian, but one day his box of things for the Señora de Rodríguez is stolen. He has to solve the mystery before he gets into trouble.

———. *Molinete.* Madrid: Ediciones SM, 1984. (novel ages 8–14)
Everyone thinks Molinete is stupid; he's afraid of everything. He finds courage, and the ability to write verse, when he becomes his alter ego, Monli Límon.

Mathews, Sally Schofer. *The Sad Night: The Story of an Aztec Victory and a Spanish Loss.* New York: Clarion, 1994. (picture book)

Shows how the Aztecs created their empire and then what happened when they were found by the Spanish Conquistadores led by Cortés.

Maury, Inez. *Mi Mamá la cartera/My Mother the Mail Carrier*. Illus. Lady McCrady. Trans. Norah E. Alemany. Feminist Press, 1991. (picture book)
Short vignettes about Lupita's relationship with her single mother, who works as a mail carrier.

Medero, Marines. *Al otro lado de la puerta* (On the other side of the door). Illus. Claudio Isaac. Mexico D.F.: Editorial Novaro, 1982. (chapter fiction ages 7–11)
Ana is a very rebellious child living in Mexico in the eighteenth century, the Century of Lights. She is most curious about the inaccessible door behind which her father works, and dearly wishes to know what he and his friends discuss there. Ana begins to see the contrast between her life and that of those who live in poverty. She begins to become involved in her father's struggle for human rights.

Meltzer, Milton. *The Hispanic Americans*. New York: HarperCollins, 1982. (nonfiction ages 8–14)
Meltzer profiles ordinary people and shows the problems they faced immigrating to this country.

Méndez, Leticia. *El mercado* (The market). Illus. Felipe Ugalde. Mexico: Editorial Patria, 1989. (picture book)
Colleción Piñata. Series: *La vida social* (Social life).
Flor goes to the marketplace in the village.

———. *La piñata*. Illus. Felipe Morales. Mexico: Editorial Patria, 1987. (picture book)
Colleción Piñata series: *Cuentos y leyendas* (Stories and legends).
A piñata itself tells children the story behind piñatas.

Menéndez, Margarita. *Un abrigo crecedero* (The overcoat that got bigger). Madrid: Ediciones SM, 1989. (picture book)
Rita has a slightly-too-big-for-her overcoat that grows. She uses it to create shadows that make her look like an elephant or a ghost. She can hide all her toys in it. When it rains she doesn't need an umbrella. She can hide in it when she doesn't want to see anybody. And she can jump without a parachute. This board book is told in rhyme.

Merino, José María. *Beyond the Ancient Cities*. Trans. Helen Lane. New York: Farrar, Straus, and Giroux, 1994. (young adult)

The *mestizo* son of a lost Spanish conquistador accompanies his godfather to Panama, where the godfather is to assume a royal appointment.

Meyer, Carolyn. *Rio Grande Stories*. New York: Harcourt, 1994. (young adult)
A seventh-grade class in Albuquerque, New Mexico, discovers a wealth of information about their city as they prepare a book about the culture and traditions of their city.

Mike, Jan M. *La zarigüeya y el gran creador de fuego* (Opossum and the great firemaker). Illus. Charles Reasoner. Troll, 1993. (picture book)
Opossum outwits the larger and more powerful iguana and returns fire to the world.

————. *Juan Bobo and the Horse of Seven Colors: A Puerto Rican Legend*. Illus. Charles Reasoner. Troll, 1995. (picture book)
Juan Bobo wastes six of the wishes he is granted by a magical horse on his journey to make the king's daughter laugh.

Mistral, Gabriela. *Crickets and Frogs: A Fable*. Trans. Doris Dana. Illus. Antonio Frasconi. New York: Atheneum, 1972. (picture book)
The crickets and the frogs battle each other to determine which of them can sing the loudest.

————. *Ternura* (Tenderness). Santiago, Chile: Universitaria, 1989. (poetry ages 7–11)
A selection of children's poetry that includes nursery rhymes, games, school poems, stories in rhyme, and Mistral's own personal favorite poem, "La Pajita."

Moguel, Margarita Robleda. *Trabalenguas, colmos, tantanes, refranes, y un pilón de Margarita Robleda Moguel* (Tongue twisters, wordplays, nursery rhymes, verses, and something extra from Margarita Robleda Moguel). Illus. Laura Fernández. Mexico, D.F.: Sitesa, 1989. (anthology ages 7–11)
Cartoon-like drawings illustrate wordgames, tongue twisters, questions and answers, all calculated to make children laugh.

————. *Y va de nuez (Adivinanzas, colmos, juegos y pilónes de Margarita Robleda Miguel.)* (And it goes nuts: riddles, wordplays, games and something more from Margarita Robleda Miguel). Illus. Laura Fernández. Mexico, D.F.: Sitesa, 1989. (anthology ages 7–11)

A book full of jokes, riddles, and wordplay that has immense kid appeal. Includes simple line drawings.

Mohedano, Victor. *Viajando con Otrébor: descubriendo el maíz* (Traveling with Otrébor: discovering corn). Puebla, México: Fundación Amparo. Museo Amparo, 1994. (picture book)
Otrébor the dinosaur tells a group of children the story of corn.

———. *Viajando con Otrébor: A través de la pintura rupestre* (Traveling with Otrébor: through the cave paintings). Puebla, México: Fundación Amparo. Museo Amparo, 1994. (picture book)
Otrébor the dinosaur takes children visiting the museum on a journey to see cave paintings.

Mohr, Nicolasa. *All for the Better: A Story of El Barrio*. Illus. Rudy Gutierrez. New York: Steck-Vaughn, 1993. (young adult nonfiction)
Series: Stories of America.
The biography of Evelina Lopez Antonetty, who became a Latina activist after seeing how so many people in New York's Spanish Harlem were too ashamed to apply for the food packages that were made available. An immigrant from Puerto Rico, she is an example of finding solutions to social problems.

———. *El Bronx Remembered*. New York: HarperTrophy, 1993. (short story collection ages 8–14)
Twelve short stories about life in the Bronx. These stories are often sad, but tell the truth of the constant struggle for life in the barrio.

———. *Felita*. New York: Dial, 1979. (chapter fiction ages 7–11)
Felita loves her neighborhood, the Puerto Rican barrio in New York. She knows everyone and plays street games with her friends. When her parents want to move to a better neighborhood, she can't understand it.

———. *Going Home*. Houston: Arte Público, 1988. (novel 8–14)
In this sequel to *Felita*, our heroine turns twelve and finally gets her dream of spending two months in Puerto Rico. But when the time comes to go, Felita realizes how difficult it is to leave her friends in New York. And in Puerto Rico, she becomes homesick, and is not accepted by some of the girls her age.

———. *In Nueva York*. Houston: Arte Público, 1988. (chapter fiction ages 7–11)
Seven connected short stories set in tenements in a Puerto Rican barrio focus on individual lives.

————. *The Magic Shell*. Illus. Rudy Gutierrez. Scholastic, 1995. (chapter fiction ages 7–11)
Spanish translation: *El regalo mágico*. Jamie Ramos has to leave the Dominican Republic when his dad gets a good job in New York City. He doesn't like the cold, and he can't speak English. He has a shell that takes him back to his island in his imagination.

————. *Nilda*. Harper, 1973. Arte Público, 1986. (chapter fiction ages 7–11)
Set during World War II, this novel tells the story of a young Puerto Rican girl growing up in New York's Spanish Harlem amidst racial prejudice and poverty.

————. *Old Letivia and the Mountain of Sorrows*. Illus. Rudy Gutierrez. Viking, 1996. (picture book)
Spanish translation *La Vieja Letivia y el monte de los pesares*.
Old Letivia is a *curandera* (healer) who goes on a quest with her whistling turtle Cervantes and a tiny boy named Simon, whom she found floating in a river. Together they save a village that is besieged by a terrible wind. After undergoing many adventures, the group finds the wind and learn that it is stuck in the mountain by mistake and wants to be free. They assist the wind, and Old Letivia gets four wishes in return. An original folktale from Puerto Rico.

————. *The Song of El Coqui and Other Tales of Puerto Rico*. New York: Viking, 1995. (picture book)
Three animal stories from Puerto Rican folklore. One story is about a mule who comes from Spain to an awful work camp. He escapes with a slave to the mountains.

Montes, Graciela. *Mas chiquito que una arveja, mas grande que una ballena* (Smaller than a pea, bigger than a whale). llus. Sergio Kern. Buenos Aires: Editorial Sudamericana, 1989. (picture book)
A great little story about a small cat and a large cat. The large cat thinks he's pretty tough, but the small cat eventually triumphs, as he should.

Mora, Pat. *A Birthday Basket for Tía*. Illus. Cecily Lang. New York: Macmillan, 1992. (picture book)
Cecelia searches for the perfect present for her great aunt's ninetieth birthday, and ends up putting together a memory basket—items representing their favorite activities together.

————. *Confetti*. Illus. Enrique O. Sanchez. New York: Lee & Low, 1996. (picture book)

Poems that mix English and Spanish and touch on familiar things in Latino life. Mora's best book to date.

————. *Delicious Hullabaloo/Pachanga deliciosa*. Illus. Francisco X. Mora. Trans. Alba Nora Martínez and Pat Mora. Houston: Piñata (Arte Público), 1998. (picture book)
Birds, armadillos, and an assortment of other creatures cavort at night in a kitchen to the music of a lizard *mariachi* band. They are all very hungry and will eat anything.

————. *The Desert is My Mother/El desierto es mi madre*. Illus. Daniel Lechon. Houston: Piñata (Arte Público), 1994. (picture book)
A simple text narrated by a girl with long, dark hair evokes the power of the desert.

————. *Listen to the Desert/Oye al desierto*. Illus. Daniel Lechon. New York: Clarion, 1994. (picture book)
A bilingual chant depicting the sounds of the desert.

————. *Pablo's Tree*. Illus. Cecily Lange. New York: Macmillan, 1994. (picture book)
Every year on his birthday, Pablo goes to his grandfather Lito's house. Lito decorates a special tree in Pablo's honor that was planted when he was adopted. Each year Lito uses something different to decorate—chimes, balloons, paper lanterns, tiny birdcages.

————. *The Race of Toad and Deer*. Illus. Maya Itzna Brooks. New York: Orchard, 1995. (picture book)
This Guatemalan folktale is a version of the tortoise and the hare. In this case it's Tío Sapo, or Uncle Toad, whose friends trick Venado, the Deer into running himself out before the end of the race.

————. *Tomás and the Library Lady*. Illus. Raul Colón. New York: Knopf, 1997. (picture book)
Spanish Translation: *Tomás y la señora de la biblioteca*.
This is based on the true story of Tomás Rivera, who grew up to be the first chancellor of the University of California system. Tomás hears stories from his grandfather, who then takes him to the library for more. The "Library Lady" becomes an important influence in his life.

————. *Uno, dos, tres: One, Two, Three*. Illus. Barbara Lavalee. New York: Clarion, 1996. (picture book)
A bilingual rhyme with girls going to the market to buy birthday presents for their mother.

Mora, Pat, and Charles Ramírez Berg. *The Gift of the Poinsettia/El regalo de la flor de nochebuena.* Illus. Daniel Lechón. Houston: Piñata (Arte Público), 1995. (picture book)
Takes place in the Mexican town of San Bernando. Carlos worries about what gifts he'll have for *las posadas.* He has songs. He gives a plant by a favorite rock—it turns into a poinsettia. Use with Tomie DePaola's *The Legend of the Poinsettia.*

Moreton, Daniel. *La cucaracha Martina: A Carribean Folktale.* New York: Turtle Books, 1997. (picture book)
A hip version of the "Perez and Martina" story. In this version, Martina marries a cricket instead of the *ratoncito* Perez.

Morey, Janet Nomura, and Wendy Dunn. *Famous Hispanic Americans.* New York: Cobblehill, 1996. (nonfiction ages 8–14)
A collective biography of fourteen notable Hispanic Americans including math teacher Jaime Escalante, astronaut Ellen Ochoa, singer Gloria Estefan, and actor Andy Garcia.

Muria, Anna. *El maravilloso viaje de Nico Huehuetl a través de México* (The marvelous voyage of Nico Huehuetl across Mexico). Illus. Felipe Dávalos. Amecameca, Mexico: Editorial Amaquemecan, 1986. (novel ages 8–14)
Nico wants to discover the marvels of his country like the Scandinavian children's book hero, Nils Holgerson. He gets his wish and is able to take magical journey through Mexico's past.

Naranjo, Carmen. *Nunca hubo alguna vez* (There was never a time . . .). Amecameca, Mexico: Editorial Amaquemecan, 1986. (young adult short story collection)
A book of short stories for adolescents about the mysteries of life and death and the contradictions of the teenage world.

Nizri, Vicki. *Un asalto mayusculo* (A capital assault). Illus. Felipe Dávalos. Mexico, 1985. (picture book)
The letters want to attack the numbers—which they think are useless. But then, to discover which of the letters is missing they are forced to use numbers. The missing letter is "Z," the sleepiest letter of the alphabet. Z discovers many things he has in common with 29, and they get married. Letters and numbers live together in harmony. Better than it sounds. Weird, award-winning pictures.

Núñez, Pablo. *¿A que tú no sabes . . . ?* (Didn't you know that. . . . ?) Illus. Moises Ruano. Madrid: Ediciones SM, 1989. (picture book)
A board book with a series of offbeat questions. For example: "And

you don't know where elephants keep their books?" "And you don't know where the moon is before it goes to bed?" The pictures give amusing answers.

Nye, Naomi Shihab. *The Tree is Older Than You Are: A Bilingual Gathering of Poems and Stories from Mexico with Paintings by Mexican Artists*. New York: Simon and Schuster, 1995. (poetry ages 8–14)
A bilingual collection that includes works of varying lengths and difficulty making it possible to find something appropriate for all ages.

Ober, Hal. *How Music Came to the World: An Ancient Mexican Myth*. Illus. Carol Ober. Boston: Houghton Mifflin, 1994. (picture book)
The sky god and the wind god bring music from the sun's house down to earth.

Ocampo, Carlos. *Si ves pasar un condor* (If you see a condor pass by). Amecameca, Mexico: Editorial Amaquemecan, 1986. (novel ages 8–14)
A novel about developing a sincere and human love for animals, and looking at our companions in nature with more natural eyes.

Olaizola, José Luis. *Bibiana y su mundo* (Bibiana and her world). Madrid: Ediciones SM, 1985. (novel ages 8–14)
Bibiana's mother has died, and she grows up quickly as she struggles to keep the house running while living with her father, Rogelio, who is an alcoholic.

———. *Cucho*. Madrid: Ediciones SM, 1983. (chapter fiction ages 7–11)
Premio Planeta. Premio Barco de Vapor. Cucho lives with his grandmother. He wants to help out by earning some money, and he gets involved in all sorts of schemes.

Orozco, José-Luis. *De colores and Other Latin-American Folk Songs for Children*. Illus. Elisa Kleven. New York: Dutton, 1994. (music)
Selected, arranged, and translated by José Luis Orozco. Orozco includes background on the origins of the songs as well as some related games.
Includes "*El chocolate*," "*La araña pequeñita*/The Eensy, Weensy Spider," and "*Los pollitos*."

———. *Diez deditos and Other Play Rhymes and Action Songs from Latin America*. Illus. Elisa Kleven. New York: Dutton, 1997. (picture book)

The book that teachers and librarians have been waiting for forever. Includes the rhymes in Spanish and English, with line drawings that show how to do the actions. Includes *"Este compró un huevito,"* and many others.

Ortiz Cofer, Judith. *An Island Like You: Stories of the Barrio.* New York: Orchard, 1996. (young adult)
Pura Belpré award. Twelve stories about young people in a New Jersey *barrio* struggling to reconcile their Puerto Rican heritage with their American life.

Osorio, Marta. *El caballito que queria volar* (The horse who wanted to fly). Illus. Maite Miralles. Valladolid: Editoria Editorial Miñón, 1982. chapter (fiction 7–11)
A beautiful story about a wooden carousel horse who wants to become a bird so that he can fly. He finally gets his wish. He is a different sort of horse from the beginning—he is the only horse on the carousel who is different. When he was made, he came from the carpenter's last piece of tree trunk, which had a large open gash. Two church bells overhear his wish and dispatch an owl to work some magic.
"Yo quiero volar—dijo más arriba aún de donde pueden ver mis ojos, cantar libremente y vivir en los jardines y en los parques, aunque existen el frío y el hambre, el calor y la sed . . . " ("I want to fly. I want to fly higher than even my eyes can see, sing freely and live in the gardens and in the parks, even though I may be cold and hungry, or hot and thirsty . . . ")

————. *La mariposa dorada* (The golden butterfly). Spain: Editorial Editorial Miñón, 1978. (picture book)
Literatura Infantil. 2nd Premio a la Mejor Labor de Creación 1978. A caterpillar turns into a butterfly. A particularly well-written book: "¿Que habrá más allá de las hojas? . . . —seguía pensando—. El mundo no puede ser sólo esto . . . tiene que haber muchas cosas mas, aunque yo no alcanzo a verlas . . . tengo que llegar a discubrirlo . . . Pero el camino era trabajoso y difícil". ("'What is out there beyond the leaves?' he continued thinking. 'The world can't be just this . . . there have to be many more things, even though I haven't seen them . . . I have to discover it . . . But the path was tiring and difficult.")

Otero, Clara Rose. *La cena de Tío Tigre y otras de teatro para niños* (Uncle Tiger's dinner and other theater pieces for children). Caracas, Venezuela: Ediciones Ekaré, 1993.
This useful book includes four easy-to-produce plays based on Uncle

Lion and Uncle Rabbit folktales. In the title play, Rabbit helps Turtle when Uncle Lion comes into Turtle's house and takes over his bed. The book includes delightful illustrations that provide costume and set ideas for productions by young people.

Palacios, Argentina. *The Hummingbird King: A Guatemalan Legend.* Illus. Felipe Davalos. Troll, 1993. (picture book)
A legend that tells the origin of the Quetzal bird. Kukul is a boy king protected by a hummingbird feather. His jealous uncle steals the talisman and Kukul is killed, but the uncle, Chirumá, gets his due when he is kidnapped by the enemy. Kukul turns into a symbol of freedom.

Parish, Helen Rand. *Our Lady of Guadelupe.* Illus. Jean Charlot. New York: Viking, 1955. (picture book)
This older version of the story is most appropriate for providing material for the storyteller who is going to tell the tale of Juan Diego and the Virgin Mary.

Pas Ipuana, Ramón. Adapted by Verónica Uribe. *Conejo y el mapurite: cuento guajiro* (Rabbit and the skunk: peasant story). Illus. Vicky Sempere. Caracas, Venezuela: Ediciones Ekaré/Banco del Libro, 1985. (picture book)
Delightful Venezuelan folktale about a skunk who is tricked by a rabbit into giving away all his cigarettes. (Rabbit appears in various guises). Skunk gets revenge by spiking some cigarettes.

Paulsen, Gary. *The Crossing.* New York: Orchard, 1987. (young adult)
Manny is a street kid in a Mexican border town. He befriends a soldier who agrees to help him cross over to the other side.

———. *Sisters/Hermanas.* Trans. Gloria de Aragón Andújar. San Diego, Calif.: Harcourt, 1993. (young adult)
Two young women, one Anglo, one Latino, encounter each other very briefly. Paulsen explores the fact that despite the differences in culture, they are very much the same.

———. *The Tortilla Factory.* Illus. Ruth Wright Paulsen. San Diego, Calif.: Harcourt, 1995. (picture book)
Spanish translation: *La tortillería.* Trans. Gloria Aragón.
A simple, lyrical story of how tortillas are made, beginning with the planting of a seed.

Paz, Marcela. *Papelucho.* Santiago, Chile: Universitaria, 1983. (novel ages 8–14)

This is one of the most beloved classics of Chilean children's literature. Papelucho's diaries give insight into the world and mind of a school-age child. The other "Papelucho" books are *Papelucho casi húerfano* (Papelucho almost an orphan); *Papelucho en la clínica* (Papelucho in the clinic); *Papelucho, misionero* (Papelucho, missionary); and *Papelucho y el marciano* (Papelucho and the martian).

Pellicer Lopez, Carlos. *Juan y sus zapatos* (Juan and his shoes). Mexico: Promexa, 1982. (picture book)
A terrific little book about Juan, who gets sick and has to stay in bed. His shoes begin to walk and talk. They take him on an adventure. He goes to a bell tower and sees the night creatures. The shoes allow him always to hear the voices of nature that speak of dreams and stories.

———. *Julieta y su caja de colores* (Julieta and her box of paints). Mexico, D. F.: Fondo de Cultura Económica. (picture book)
Awarded the Antonniorobles prize in 1983. A reprint of a book originally published by Editorial Patria in 1984. Julieta opens up her box of paints and discovers that through her imagination and her paintings, cities, animals, fruits, and even dreams can magically appear.

Perales, Alonso M. *La lechuza: cuentos de mi barrio* (The owl witch: stories of my neighborhood). Illus. Barbara Brigham. San Antonio, Tex.: Naylor, 1972. (short story collection 8–14)
Stories include the following:
"*La lechuza y el buho*" (The owl witch and the owl). Owls carry off a son, then a father.
"*Violeta y las lechuzas*" (Vioileta and the owl witches). A young girl sells her soul for beauty and intelligence to an owl in the shape of a young woman.
"*¿Que Resolló?*" A play on words. A man and wife go out to dig for treasure. The husband bolts when his wife says, "*¿Que rezo yo?*" (What prayer should I recite?) and he thinks she said, "*¿Que resolló?*" (What was that breathing hard?).
"*Doña Victoria: la curandera*" (Doña Victoria: the healer). A boy has a nightmare about a woman trying to take him to the land of the dead while he lies on his sick bed.

Perera, Hilda. *Cuentos para chicos y grandes* (Stories for young and old). Illus. Ana Bermejo. Valladolid: Editorial Miñón, 1985. (short story collection ages 8–14)
Premio Lazarillo. Stories include the following:
"*Los burritos*" (The burros). Burros wreak havoc in a small village.

Bumbling politicians say they'll do something about it. Children save the burros from death by sending them away; then everybody misses them. An amusing read-aloud.

"*Chichi la osita panda*" (Chichi the panda bear). Chichi is a small panda bear. None of the animals will play with Chichi. They all marry. When An An is brought from China to be Chichis's mate at first he will have nothing to do with her because he think's he's the only one of his kind.

"*Pedrin y la garza*" (Pedrin and the crane). This story is about a poor boy who finds a crane and tries to keep it like a toy. The crane discovers that it is a bird, and needs to fly free. The boy follows it to the sea and goes into the ocean as the crane flies out. The boy nearly drowns. The crane sees this and gives up its freedom to rescue the boy.

Other stories are "Tatica," about a dog, and "Quintin," about a gnome who invents sleep.

—————. *Kike*. Madrid: Ediciones SM, 1984. (novel ages 8–14)
English translation: *Kiki: A Cuban Boy's Adventures in America*. Trans. Warren Hampton and Hilda Gonzalez. S. Miami, Fla.: Pickering Press, 1982.
Based on the true stories of over 14,000 unaccompanied Cuban children who came secretly to the United States in the 60s, this book personalizes the experience in the boy Jesus Gonzalez, nicknamed Kike. (Pronounced Kee-kay). Kike becomes entranced by the Anglo-American culture, which makes it difficult when his parents arrive in Miami four years later.

—————. *La pata Pita : libro primero de lectura* (The duck Pita: My first reader). Mana F. Fraga. Illus. Olivia Robain. New York: Minerva Books, 1979. (picture book)
The landmark Spanish reader, the "Dick and Jane" of Latino children. The sequel is: *La pata Pita vuelve: libro segundo de lectura*. 1984.

—————. *Podría ser que una vez* . . . (It could be that once . . .). Madrid: Editorial Everest, 1981. (short story collection ages 8–14)
Six contemporary stories. A particularly notable one is "Kilo," which concerns a young boy who desires a pet.

Perl, Lila. *Piñatas and Paper Flowers: Holidays of the Americas in English and Spanish/Piñatas y flores de papel: Fiestas de las Américas en inglés y español*. Trans. Alma Flor Ada. New York: Clarion, 1983. (nonfiction ages 7–11)
Describes the Latino holidays celebrated in the United States, as well as those observed in Latin America.

Pico, Fernando. *The Red Comb*. Illus. Maria Antonia Ordonez. Mahwah, N.J.: BridgeWater Books, 1994. (picture book)
A young girl and her elderly neighbor help a runaway slave. Based on actual historical events from nineteenth century Puerto Rico.

Pierini, Fabio. *El niño que queria volar*. (The boy who wanted to fly). Illus. Carme Solé Vendrell. Valladolid: Editorial Miñón, 1979. (picture book)
A little boy wants to fly, and he looks for someone to teach him how. He looks in important books; he looks everywhere. He asks animals, and finally realizes that he wasn't made to fly.

Pijoan, Teresa. *La cuentista: Traditional Tales in Spanish and English/ Cuentos tradicionales en español e ingles*. Trans. Nancy Zimmerman. Santa Fe: Red Crane, 1994. (short story collection ages 7–11)
Includes notes on the origin of each the tales. Stories include: "Rain Clouds" in which Mother Frog and Mother Grasshopper sing for rain. "The Kernel of Corn" is a variant on "the cat ate the rat . . . "

Pitre, Felix. *Juan Bobo and the Pig: A Puerto Rican Folktale*. Illus. Christy Hale. New York: Lodestar (Dutton), 1993. (picture book)
Juan cares for a pig while his mother goes to church, and of course it turns out disastrously.

———. *Paco and the Witch*. Illus. Christy Hale. New York: Lodestar (Dutton), 1995. (picture book)
Spanish Translation: *Paco y la bruja*. Trans. Osvaldo Blanco. A young boy is trapped by a witch who will not set him free unless he guesses her name. A Puerto Rican version of "Rumpelstiltskin."

Pomerantz, Charlotte. *The Outside Dog*. Illus. Jennifer Plecas. New York: HarperCollins, 1993. (picture book)
Set in Puerto Rico, this is the story of Marisol, who has always wanted a dog. Her grandfather has always objected because they have fleas. Marisol tries to convince her grandfather to allow them to keep a skinny brown mutt who appears outside their house. A rare example of a reader geared toward Latino children. Includes a glossary of Spanish words.

Posadas Mañé, Carmen De. *Señor Viento Norte* (Mr. North Wind). Illus. Alfonso Ruano. Madrid: Ediciones SM, 1984. (picture book)
The animals tell Arthur that they are suffering because Mr. North Wind is not letting spring come. He sets out go to the north wind's house, but finds his friend, María, went before him so he wouldn't

have to go. Together they convince Mr. North Wind to blow south so that spring can come.

Presilla, Maricel E., and Gloria Soto. *Life around the Lake: Embroideries by the Women of Lake Patzcuaro*. New York: Holt, 1996. (nonfiction ages 7–11)
The book relates how the traditional embroidery of the women of the Lake Patzcuaro region of Mexico continues and adapts to changing times.

Presilla, Maricel E. *Feliz Nochebuena, Feliz Navidad* (Happy Christmas, Merry Christmas). Illus. Ismael Espinosa Ferrer. New York: Holt, 1994. (picture book)
This book takes the reader on a culinary trip to the Caribbean, but most particularly to Cuba at Christmastime. The author combines history with her memories, and shows how food connects peoples.

———. *Mola: Cuna Life Stories and Art*. New York: Holt, 1996. (nonfiction ages 7–11).
Mola art is created by women who live in the San Blas Islands off Panama. The text describes the method through which these colorful fabric designs are created as well as history, customs, and even songs that relate to this art form.

Puncel, María. *Un duende a rayas* (The striped elf). Madrid: Ediciones SM, 1982. (chapter fiction ages 7–11)
There are many different types of elves, but has anyone ever heard of a striped elf? This is the story of just such an elf, who is mischievous, but finally decides to change his ways.

Quiroga, Horacio. *Cuentos de la selva* (Tales of the jungle). Mexico: Editores Mexicanos Unidos, 1975. (short story collection ages 8–14)
Short stories about jungle animals.

Ramírez, Elisa. *Adivinanzas indigenas* (Indigeneous riddles). Illus. Máximo Javier. Mexico: Editorial Patria, 1983. (picture book)
Collección Piñata. Series: *Cuentos y Leyendas*.
Riddles, with the picture showing the answer. The culture from which the riddle originates is also noted.

Ramirez, Michelle Rose. *The Little Ant/La hormiga chiquita*. Illus. Dalal Sawaya. New York: Rizzolli, 1995. (picture book)
The subtitle says this is based on a Mexican folktale. It is actually a Mexican variant of the Chinese cumulative tale "The Greatest of All."

Reid, Alastair, trans. *Mother Goose in Spanish*. Illus. Barbara Cooney. New York: Crowell, 1968. (picture book poetry)
Translations of English Mother Goose rhymes into Spanish. Many are very literal, and have references to Spain. For instance, the "Guardia Civil" couldn't put Humpty Dumpty together again. Some of the rhymes are cleverly translated.

Reiser, Lynn. *Margaret and Margarita/Margarita y Margaret*. New York: Greenwillow, 1993. (picture book)
Perfect for bilingual storytime. Margaret speaks only English; Margarita speaks only Spanish. They meet in a park.

————. *Tortillas and Lullabies/Tortillas y cancioncitas*. Illus. "*Corazones Valientes*." New York: Greenwillow, 1998. (picture book)
Depicts four everyday activities of Central American life: making tortillas, gathering flowers, washing clothes, and singing a lullaby. The illustrations are folk art by a group of Costa Rican women.

Reviejo, Carlos, and Eduardo Soler. *Canto y cuento: Antología poetica para niños* (Song and story: A poetry anthology for children) Madrid: Editiones SM, 1997. (poetry ages 7–11)
An excellent poetry anthology that is a must for all collections.

Riehecky, Janet. *Cinco de Mayo* (Fifth of May). Illus. Krystyna Stasiak. Chicago: Children's Press, 1993. (nonfiction ages 7–11)
María has a talent for breaking things. On Cinco de Mayo no one wants her to help after she causes minor disasters. Then she enters an art contest at the library and after she wins the others decide she is not half bad.

————. *Barranco el rebelde* (Barranco the rebel). León, Spain: Editorial Everest, 1985. (picture book)
"Una escoba es una escoba y se pone a barrer, pero hay escobas differentes . . . ¡No me van a creer!" (A broom is a broom and they are used for sweeping. But there are different sorts of brooms . . . You won't believe me!)
A story about an unusual broom the moves on its own and causes complications until it is discovered that it is actually a horse. A broom can also be a horse in the imagination of a child.

————. *Cajon de los tiliches*. (The box of junk). León, Spain: Editorial Everest, 1985. (picture book)
"Lo que no sirve o estroba lo metemos a un cajón. A eso le llaman tiliches y viven en un rincón." ("Whatever is of no use any more we put in a box. We call them junk, and they live in a corner"). A story

about a special box, like all houses have. One day a boy opened it and marbles, a string, and an electric plug came out along with other miscellaneous objects. These objects talk to the boy, and one of them, a top, helps him when they stop talking.

————. *Carlota es una pelota* (Carlota is a ball). León, Spain: Editorial Everest, 1985. (picture book)
"Carlota es una pelota de teni de campeonato y desertó, ¡vaya broma! a causa de un raquetazo" (Carlota is a championship tennis ball, who left, what a joke, all because of a racquet).
A story about a super ball that broke things and caused problems. It follows the storyteller and gets caught up in a game of tennis, which it doesn't like. It spends the rest of its days on the storyteller's shelf with his books.

————. *Chispa de luz* (A spark of light). Illus. Gloria Calderas Lim. Mexico D.F.: Editorial Trillas, 1984. (picture book)
A spark of light leaves its lightbulb in its desire to be free. It finds its place sparkling in a child's eyes.

————. *Los cuentos de Tío Patota* (The stories of Uncle Bigfoot). Mexico D.F.: Patria, 1980. (short story collection ages 7–11)
Six stories illustrated by children.

————. *La Computadora K-J* (K-J the Computer). Mexico D.F.: Editorial Trillas, 1984. (picture book)
Santiago helps a computer packing box realize its dreams and become a computer itself.

————. *La Cosquilla* (The tickle). Mexico D.F.: Editorial Trillas, 1985. (picture book)
Erika tries to find out where tickles come from.

————. *Cuatro letras se escaparon* (Four letters escaped). Illus. Rebeca Cerda. Mexico D.F.: Editorial Trillas, 1986. (picture book)
Four letters escape from a page and try to form a word.

————. *En la maleta vivia un poeta* (In the suitcase lived a poet). León, Spain: Editorial Everest, 1985. (picture book)
"Un lápiz desconchinflado que tiene muchos problemas, pero vive illusionado." ("A pencil who has a lot of problems, but who is a dreamer").
A letter from Tío Patota. He describes his cabin in the mountains. One day he finds a briefcase there that contains things from his childhood. Among them is a pencil that wants to be a poet.

————. *Ha nacido un libro* (A book has been born). León, Spain: Editorial Everest, 1985. (picture book)
The story of how a book comes from the imagination of an author.

————. *Las increíbles peripecias de una hoja de papel* (The incredible viccissitudes of a piece of paper). Léon, Spain: Editorial Everest, 1985. (picture book)
A piece of paper gets thrown away, then goes on a journey, blown by the wind, carried by a stream, and finally found by a little girl who draws a heart on it.

————. *Las letras de mi maquina de escribir* (The letters on my typewriter). Léon, Spain: Editorial Everest, 1985. (picture book)
An author talks with the letters on his typewriter.

————. *Mi amigo dice mentiras* (My friend lies). Illus. Roberto López. Mexico D.F.: Editorial Grijalbo, 1989. (picture book)
Series: *Los problemas de me amigo* (My friend's problems). Didactic story about lying.

————. *Mi amigo tiene miedo* (My friend is afraid). Mexico D.F.: Editorial Grijalbo, 1989. (picture book)
Series: *Los problemas de mi amigo* (My friend's problems).
Kind of like a Spanish version of *There's A Nightmare in My Closet*, only more didactic.

————. *Rollito*. Mexico D.F.: Editorial Trillas, 1985. (picture book)
Rollito is a caterpillar who eats alot. The little girl, Xóchitl who takes him to school doesn't realize he'll turn into a butterfly.

————. *Una noche en la escuela* (One night in school). Léon, Spain: Editorial Everest, 1985. (picture book)
Two friends spend the night in their school, where the school supplies appear to have come to life.

————. *Vida secreta de una maceta* (The secret life of a flowerpot). Léon, Spain: Editorial Everest, 1985. (picture book)
The secret life of a flowerpot helps a tree grow until it is time to be transplanted.

Rockwell, Ann. *El toro pinto and Other Songs in Spanish*. New York: Macmillan, 1971. (music)
Music and guitar chords are included for songs from all over Latin America. The country of origin of each song is noted, and English

translations are included. Includes *"Señor Don Gato"* and *"Cielito Lindo."*

Roe, Eileen. *Con mi hermano/With My Brother.* Illus. Robert Casilla. Trans. Jo Mintzer. New York: Macmillan, 1991. (picture book) A young Latino boy can only watch as his older brother goes to school.

Rohmer, Harriet, and Mary Anchondo adaptation. *Cuna Song/Canción de los cunas.* Illus. Irene Perez. San Francisco: Children's Book Press, 1976. (picture book) A legend of people who live under the sea.

———. *The Headless Pirate/El pirata sin cabeza.* Illus. Ray Rios. San Francisco: Children's Book Press, 1976. (picture book) A tale of pirates, gold, and the devil.

———. *How We Came to the Fifth World/Como vinimos al quinto mundo.* San Francisco: Children's Book Press, 1987. (picture book) This is a retelling of an Aztec myth. Four gods who represent each of the basic elements create, then destroy the earth.

———. *The Legend of Food Mountain/La leyenda de la montaña de alimento.* Illus. Graciela Carrillo. Trans. Alma Flor Ada and Rosalma Zubizaretta. San Francisco: Children's Book Press, 1982. (picture book) This Aztec legend explains why the people pray to the rain god for food.

———. *The Little Horse of Seven Colors/El caballito de siete colores.* Illus. Roger I. Reyes. San Francisco: Children's Book Press, 1976. (picture book) This folktale from Nicaragua tells the story of a magical horse who takes a boy on a journey. He gets a princess for a bride.

———. *The Magic Boys/Los niños mágicos.* Illus. Patricia Rodriguez. San Francisco: Children's Book Press, 1975. (picture book) The older brothers who are mean are turned into monkeys, but the magic boys get to come live with their grandmother.

———. *Uncle Nacho's Hat/El sombrero del Tío Nacho.* Illus. Veg Reisberg. San Francisco: Children's Book Press, 1989. (picture book) A Nicaraguan folktale about a little girl who teaches her uncle to overcome an old habit.

Rondón, Javier. *El sapo distraído* (The distracted frog). Illus. Marcela Cabrera. Caracas, Venezuela: Ediciones Ekaré, 1988. (picture book) Sapo goes out to shop, gets distracted, and comes home with nothing.

Rosenberg, Joe ed. *¡Aplauso!* Hispanic Children's Theater. Houston: Piñata (Arte Público), 1995. (drama ages 8–14) An anthology of plays by Latino authors.

Rossi, Joyce. *The Gullywasher.* Flagstaff: Northland Publishing, 1995. (picture book) Once upon a time, Leticia's grandfather was a *vaquero*, a cowboy. In this story he tells her a tall tale which explains, among other things, why he now has white hair, a protruding belly, and wrinkles.

Roybal, Laura. *Billy.* Boston: Houghton Mifflin, 1994. (young adult) Billy is reunited with his family after having been kidnapped six years earlier by his natural father.

Ruano, Moises. *El caballo fantastico* (The fantastic horse). Illus. Alfonso Ruano. Madrid: Ediciones S.M., 1985. (picture book) Juan believes that he has seen a unicorn, driven by a man with a beard and a turban, as he goes to school. No one believes him until the next morning.

Sánchez, Isidro. Series: *Un día en la escuela* (One day at school). Illus. Irene Borday. Barcelona: Parramón, 1992. (picture book) Titles in this series include *Mi primer día de colegio* (My first day at school); *La clase* (The Class); *El recreo* (Recess); *Salimos de la escuela* (We leave school).

———. Series: *Mis plantas* (My plants). Illus. Carme Peris. Barcelona: Parramón, 1991. (picture book) Titles in this series include *El bosque* (The forest); *El jardín* (The garden); *El huerto* (The vegetable garden); *Los aborles frutales* (Fruit trees).

———. Series: *Mis animales preferidos* (My favorite animals). Illus. María Rius. Barcelona: Parramón, 1992. (picture book) *Mi perro* (My dog); *Mi gato* (My cat); *Mi pájaro* (My bird); and *Mi hámster* (My hamster).

Sanchez Silva, José María. *Marcelino, pan y vino* (Marcelino, bread and wine). Editorial Miñón, 1982. (chapter fiction ages 7–11) An orphan appears at the door of a monastery. Named Marcelino, he is raised and cared for by the friars. A beloved story known throughout the Spanish-speaking world.

Sanromán, Susana. *Señora Regañona: A Mexican Bedtime Story* (Old grouch). Illus. Domi. Toronto: Groundwood (Douglas & McIntyre), 1997, 98. (picture book)
A frightened child keeps a light under the covers to scare away the night. In a dream the night becomes a friendly playmate.

Santiago, Danny. *Famous All Over Town*. New York: Simon & Schuster, 1983. (young adult)
Tells the story of Rudy Medina, better known as Chato, who lives on Shamrock Street in East L. A. The story begins on Rudy's 14th birthday. To prove his manhood, his father asks him to kill a chicken. Rudy can't manage to slit its throat, so he gets a gun and shoots it instead. Of course, Rudy's father is furious. The neighborhood is abuzz. When asked what all the confusion is about, people reply: "Medina's kid just shot a chicken."

Schecter, Ellen. *The Big Idea*. Illus. Bob Dorsey. New York: Hyperion, 1996. (chapter fiction ages 7–11)
Luz Mendez is eight years old and wants to create a garden just like her grandfather's in Puerto Rico. All she has is a vacant lot, so she has to obtain help from the neighbors.

Schon, Isabel. *Tito, tito: Rimas, adivinanzas y juegos infantiles* (Tito, tito: Rhymes, riddles, and children's games). Illus. Victoria Monreal. Léon, Spain: Editorial Everest, 1995. (poetry 7–11)
Isabel Schon collects the rhymes games she loved the best as a child. The book is complimented by beautiful watercolor illustrations.

Schrade, Arlene. *Gabriel el fantasmita simpatico* (Gabriel the friendly ghost). Skokie, Ill.: National Textbook, 1979. (picture book)
A bilingual story about celebrating the Day of the Dead in Mexico.

Scott, Ann Herbert. *Hi*. Illus. Glo Coalson. New York: Philomel, 1994. (picture book)
Margarita greets all the people who come into the post office while she is waiting in line with her mother. She hopes someone will greet her.

Shute, Linda. *Rabbit Wishes*. New York: Lothrop, Lee & Shepard, 1995. (picture book)
An Afro-Cuban *porquoi* tale that provides an explanation for Rabbit's long ears.

Sierra i Fabra, Jordi. *Los mayores están locos, locos, locos* (The Adults are crazy, crazy, crazy). Illus. Federico Delicado. Madrid: Ediciones SM, 1994. (young adult)
Series: *Los libros de Víctor y Cía.*
Victor doesn't understand. His father is shouting, his mother is preoccupied and is considering giving him socks, underpants, and undershirts for his birthday when what he really wants is a John Lennon t-shirt, a chemistry set, and skates. His sister won't speak, and his brother won't stop complaining. They all blame him for what happened, but he's convinced they're all crazy.
Others in series include:
Noticias frescas (Fresh news). 1994.
Victor and Cía sell their newspaper, *El eco del barrio* (The echo of the neighborhood). Everyone buys it. Everyone reads it. Now they wonder why everyone is so upset with them.
El rockero (The rock star). 1994.
Victor's parents tell him that he has a lot of free time and that he should do some kind of extra-curricular activity. So he starts a rock band and then wonders what's the problem? Sample song lyrics:
Hola ¿puedo ayudar? (Hello, can I help you?)
Un poco de pasta basta (A little bit of pasta is enough)
¡Sálvese que puede! (Save yourself if you can!)
Una boda desmadrada (A mixed-up wedding). 1994.
Victor would have preferred not to go to the wedding but rather to the movies with Cía and the twins. He even has to wear a jacket and tie. But this wedding was unique. There was nothing boring about it, and so much happened he couldn't imagine having missed it.

Silverthorne, E. *Fiesta! Mexico's Great Celebrations*. Brookfield, Conn.: Millbrook Press, 1992. (nonfiction ages 8–14)
An excellent book that not only gives the cultural and historical background for Mexican celebrations, but also provides activity ideas with instructions for making crafts and foods. This book has separate sections on religious, patriotic, and other celebrations.

Silverman, Sarita Chavez. *Good News*! Illus. Melinda Levine. Carmel, Calif.: Hampton-Brown, 1996. (picture book)
Chago writes a letter to his grandmother in the Dominican Republic telling her the news that he has lost his first tooth. A story in rhyme that follows the path of his letter all the way from New York to his grandmother's home.

Sinnott, Susan. *Extraordinary Hispanic Americans*. Children's Press, 1991. (nonfiction ages 8–14)
Short biographies of Latinos from virtually every walk of life beginning with the age of exploration. This book impressively shows the real contributions Latinos have made.

Sisnett, Ana. *Grannie Jus' Come*. Illus. Karen Lusebrink. San Francisco: Children's Book Press, 1997. (picture book)
A Panamanian girl tells the story of preparing for and awaiting a visit from her grandmother. Children can search for animals found on all the pages.

Smith-Ayala, Emilie. *Marisol y el mensajero amarillo* (Marisol and the yellow messenger). Illus. Sami Suomalainen. Trans. Margarita Kénefic. New York: Annick, 1994. (picture book)
Marisol and her family have moved to Canada after the death of her father. Marisol has tender memories of her father, and is able to come to terms with his death with the arrival of a yellow bird in the house that seems to say, "*No tengás miedo, mi pequeña*" (Never fear, my little one).

Solá, Michéle. *Angela Weaves a Dream: The Story of a Young Maya Artist*. Illus. Jeffrey Jay Fox. New York: Hyperion, 1997. (nonfiction ages 7–11)
The story of how Angela practices weaving the seven sacred designs of the Maya is interspersed with Mayan myths regarding these signs. Angela wins first prize in the weaving competition.

Soler, Carola. *El pájaro pinto y otras cosas* (The speckled bird and other things). Madrid: Aguilar, 1963. (anthology ages 7–11)
A collection of stories and poems in a textbook format.

———. *El pájaro de nieve y otras lecturas para niños* (The Snow bird and other texts for children). Madrid: Aguilar, 1967. (anthology ages 7–11)
Collections of stories and poems in textbook format. Useful for storyhours. Includes "*El raton pelado*," a version of "Perez and Martina," and "*Mediogallo y Mediogallina*," a version of "Half-Chicken."

Soto, Gary. *Baseball in April and Other Stories*. San Diego, Calif.: Harcourt Brace, 1990. (short story collection ages 8–14)
Pura Belpré Honor Book for writing, 1996. Includes "No-Guitar Blues," upon which a film was based.

————. *Big Bushy Mustache*. Illus. Joe Capeda. New York: Knopf 1998 (picture book).
Ricky wants to look like his "Papi," who wears a big, bushy mustache. he finds one from a costume at school and wears it home, but he loses it on the way. Papi solves the problem and at the same time shows his love for Ricky when he finds replacement mustache for him.

————. *Boys at Work*. New York: Delacorte, 1995. (chapter fiction ages 7–11)
Rudy and Alex, characters from the novel *Pool Party*, have to raise money when one of them breaks the local neighborhood thug's portable CD player.

————. *Buried Onions*. New York: Harcourt, 1997. (young adult)
Eddie's friends pressure him to seek revenge for the murder of his cousin. A slice-of-life about teenagers living in Fresno, California, Soto's own stomping grounds.

————. *Canto Familiar* (Familiar song). Illus. Annika Nelson: San Diego: Harcourt, 1995. (poetry ages 8–14)
A companion to *Neighborhood Odes*. Twenty-five poems about daily life of Mexican-American children.

————. *The Cat's Meow*. Illus. Joe Cepeda. New York: Scholastic, 1995. (chapter fiction ages 7–11)
Spanish translation: *El maullido de la gata*.
Graciela's cat starts speaking to her in Spanish.

————. *Chato's Kitchen*. Illus. Susan Guevara. New York: Putnam, 1995. (picture book)
Spanish translation: *Chato y su cena*. Pura Belpré Award for Illustration, 1996.
　Chato, a cool, low-riding cat invites the mice who've moved in next door over for dinner. Chato and his friend Novio Boy prepare a feast of tortillas and guacamole to lure the mice, but the mice also bring a surprise with them.

————. *Crazy Weekend*. New York: Scholastic, 1994. (novel ages 8–14)
Hector and Mando and Hector's Uncle Julio are the only witnesses to a robbery.

————. *A Fire in My Hands: A Book of Poems*. Illus. James M. Cardillo. New York: Scholastic, 1991. (poetry ages 8–14)

In addition to the poems, Soto gives advice to young poets and provides anecdotes about the poems. Soto's poetry beautifully celebrates the ordinary and commonplace things in life.

————. *Jesse*. New York: Harcourt, 1994. (young adult)
Jesse leaves home to escape his alcoholic father. Set during the Vietnam war, this story details Jesse's difficulties as he moves in with his brother; takes classes at Fresno City College; becomes involved with César Chavez's farm workers movement; and struggles to communicate with girls and against racial prejudice.

————. *Living Up the Street*. San Francisco: Strawberry Hill Press, 1985. (young adult)
Narrative recollections about growing up in Fresno.

————. *Local News*. New York: Harcourt, 1993. (short story collection ages 8–14)
In this follow-up to *Baseball in April* Soto tells more neighborhood yarns. In "Blackmail" Javier threatens to take a picture he took of Angel in the shower to all the girls at school. "First Job" is a nightmare for Alex when he sets fire to his neighbor's fence. In another, a girl takes what she thinks is her good-natured kitten to school to protect it from another feline back home, only to find it killing a mouse on the playground. Full of humor, the appeal of these stories extends beyond ethnic boundaries.

————. *Neighborhood Odes*. Illus. David Diaz. San Diego: Harcourt, 1992. (poetry ages 8–14)
Twenty-one poems that celebrate *el barrio*.

————. *No Guitar Blues*. New York: Pheonix/BFA, 1991. 27 min.
A video of a story taken from *Baseball in April*. Fausto gets ridden with guilt over the dishonest way he obtains money to buy the guitar he wants. Later he receives a present of a bass *guitarrón* that has been in the family.

————. *Novio Boy: A Play*. San Diego: Harcourt, 1997. (drama ages 8–14)
Rudy doesn't believe it when an older girl (11th grade) accepts a date with him. Now he needs to know what to say, how to behave, and he needs money. And then, everyone shows up at the restaurant during the date itself. Could be presented fully staged or as a reading.

———. *Off and Running*. New York: Delacorte, 1996. (chapter fiction ages 7–11)
This story involves characters from previous Soto books—Miata from *The Skirt*, and Rudy and Alex from *Boys at Work*. They run against each other for class president.

———. *The Old Man and His Door*. Illus. Joe Cepeda. New York: Putnam, 1996. (picture book)
This wise-fool story is about a man who doesn't listen to his wife's instructions, and instead of taking a pig (*puerco*) to a barbecue party, he sets off with a door (*puerta*) on his back. Everything comes out right, however.

———. *Pacific Crossing*. San Diego: Harcourt, 1992. (novel ages 8–14)
Lincoln Mendoza goes to Japan on a summer exchange program. A new look at culture clashes.

———. *The Pool Party*. Illus. Robert Casilla. New York: Delacorte, 1993. (chapter fiction ages 7–11)
Rudy Herrera gets invited to Tiffany Perez's pool party. Tiffany is one of the richest kids in school. His family tries to help him get ready and select a gift.

———. *The Pool Party*. Soto, 1993. 29 min.
A video based on Soto's book. Winner of the Andrew Carnegie Medal for Excellence in Children's Video.

———. *The Skirt*. Illus. Eric Velasquez. New York: Delacorte, 1992. (chapter fiction ages 7–11)
Miata has been preparing to perform with her *folklorico* dance group. A small crisis is precipitated when she leaves her decorative skirt on the school bus. She and her girlfriend have to retrieve it, a process not without complications. This is a very short early reader.

———. *Snapshots from the Wedding*. Illus. Stephanie García. New York: Putnam, 1997. (picture book)
Pura Belpré Award for Illustration. Unique three-dimensional illustrations tell the story of a typical Latino wedding.

———. *A Summer Life*. Hanover, N.H.: University Press of New England, 1990. (young adult)
A collection of 39 essays and short stories. Soto vividly conveys Latino life through a child's eyes.

————. *Summer on Wheels*. New York: Scholastic, 1995. (novel ages 8–14)
This is a sequel to *Crazy Weekend*. Hector and Mando make an eight-day bike ride from L. A. to Santa Monica. They stay with family along the way.

————. *Taking Sides*. San Diego: Harcourt, 1991. (novel ages 8–14)
Lincoln Mendoza deals with prejudice as he moves from the *barrio* into a mostly white neighborhod. Soto shows the kind of stress that racial prejudice puts on children.

————. *Too Many Tamales*. Illus. Ed Martinez. New York: Putnam, 1993. (picture book)
Spanish translation: ¡*Qué montón de tamales*! Illus. Ed Martinez. Trans. Alma Flor Ada and F. Isabel Campos. This delightful story centers around an important cultural tradition—making *tamales* on Christmas Eve. Since *tamales* take so much effort to make, home-made tamales are a special event. Maria tries on the ring her mother has taken off while making the *tamales*. It slips off her finger and into the *masa*. Horrified when she makes the discovery, Maria and her cousins secretly eat all the *tamales* trying to find the missing ring. This is Soto's first picture book, and one of the first picture books to provide an authentic cultural experience.

Spamer, Irene. *El universo* (The Universe). Illus. María Figueroa. Mexico D.F.: Editorial Patria, n.d. (picture book)
Collección Piñata. Series: *El medio ambiente* (The Environment). Citlali and Juan journey through the universe.

Spurr, Elizabeth. *Lupe & Me*. Illus. Enrique O. Sanchez. New York: Gulliver (Harcourt), 1995. (chapter fiction ages 7–11)
Susan forms a friendship with Lupe, the housekeeper, until she disappears with her family, afraid of *La Migra*.

Stanley, Diane. *Elena*. New York: Hyperion, 1996. (chapter fiction ages 7–11)
A story based on tales passed down through her family. Stanley writes in the voice of a young Mexican-American girl who recalls how her mother was forced to take their family to the United States because of the events of the Mexican Revolution.

Stevens, Jan Romero. *Carlos and the Cornfield/ Carlos y la milpa de maiz*. Illus. Jeanne Arnold Trans. Patricia Hinton Davison. Flagstaff, Ariz.: Northland Publishing, 1995. (picture book)
Carlos gets in too much of a hurry to finish planting the cornfield.

Trying to fix his mistake when the corn sprouts he pawns his knife but accidentally buys blue corn. You reap what you sow.

————. *Carlos and the Skunk/Carlos y el zorillo*. Illus. Jeanne Arnold. Trans. Patricia Hinton Davison. Flagstaff, Ariz.: Rising Moon (Northland), 1997. (picture book)
The success of the first book led to this sequel in which Carlos gets sprayed by a skunk. He clears out the church when he forgets to remove the smell from his shoes.
Suárez, Maribel. "Concept Books." Mexico D.F.: Editorial Grijalbo. (picture book)
Series name: *Albores* (Daybreak). These simple concept books are excellent for use with toddlers. The titles in the series are:
Las formas (Shapes) 1988.
Los números (Numbers) 1988.
Los colores (Colors) 1988.
Los contrarios (Opposites) 1988.
Las letras (Letters) 1990.
Mis primeras palabras (My first words) 1992.

Tabor, Nancy María Grande. *Albertina anda arriba: el abecedario Albertina Goes Up: An Alphabet Book*. Watertown, Mass.: Charlesbridge, 1992. (picture book)
An alphabet book that provides an alliterative sentence for each letter of the alphabet, along with questions asking the children to find certain things in the pictures, and asking about elements of the pictures. Cut paper illustrations.

————. *El gusto del mercado mexicano/A Taste of the Mexican Market*. Watertown, Mass.: Charlesbridge, 1996. (picture book)
Shows the food that can be found in a Mexican market. Cut paper illustrations.

Taha, Karen T. *A Gift for Tía Rosa*. Illus. Dee deRosa. New York: Dillon (Macmillan), 1986. (chapter fiction ages 7–11)
Carmela is very close to Tía Rosa. After Tía Rosa dies, she finds a way to express her love when Tía's grandchild is born.

Talbert, Marc. *Heart of a Jaguar*. New York: Simon & Schuster, 1995. (young adult)
A rite-of-passage tale in which a young Mayan boy named Balam participates in the rites of his community, which are designed to bring rain. Enhanced by a bibliography and details of everyday Mayan life.

Tamar, Erica. *Alphabet City Ballet*. New York: HarperCollins, 1996. (chapter fiction ages 7–11)
Marisol is a ten–year-old from Puerto Rico who attends ballet school in New York City. The story provides a realistic portrait of her family's life as it also chronicles her father's efforts to provide for his family, and her brother's struggles as well.

Taylor, Theodore. *Maria: A Christmas Story*. San Diego: Harcourt, 1992. (fiction ages 7–11)
Eleven-year-old Maria Gonzaga and her family enter a float in the Christmas parade in San Lazaro, California.

Temple, Frances. *Grab Hands and Run*. New York: HarperCollins, 1993. (novel ages 8–14)
Felipe, his mother and younger sister make a journey to Canada, trying to leave the political persecution in El Salvador after their father disappears.

Thomas, Jane Resh. *Lights on the River*. Illus. Michael Dooling. New York: Hyperion, 1994. (picture book)
Theresa, the child of migrant workers, keeps memories of her country, Mexico, and her grandmother alive in harsh circumstances.

Torres, Leyla. *Subway Sparrow*. New York: Farrar, Straus and Giroux, 1993. (picture book)
Spanish translation: *Gorrión del metro*.
Two Spanish-speaking young people assist others to help rescue a sparrow trapped in the subway.

———. *Saturday Sancocho*. New York: Farrar, Straus and Giroux, 1995. (picture book)
Spanish translation: *El sancocho del sábado* (Mirasol)
One day there are only eggs in the house. María Lilí and her mother barter in the market for ingredients to make a delicious chicken dish.

Tripp, Valerie. *Meet Josefina*. Middleton, Wis.: Pleasant Company, 1997. (chapter fiction ages 7–11)
The first in the series of six American Girl books about Josefina Montoya who lives in Mexico in 1824. Other titles in this series are
Josefina Learns a Lesson. 1997.
Josefina's Surprise. 1997.
Happy Birthday, Josefina! 1998.
Josefina Saves the Day. 1998.
Changes for Josefina. 1998.

Ulibarrí, Sabine R. *Pupurupú*. Illus. Ivar Da Coll. Boston: Houghton Mifflin, 1987, 1993. (picture book)
A story of roadrunner and Gágara the coyote.

Uribe, Maria de la Luz. *El primer pájaro de piko-niko* (The first piko-niko bird). Illus. Fernando Krahn. Barcelona: Editorial Juventud, 1987. (picture book)
The piko-niko bird is born, but doesn't know his name, or what he's for. He asks a monster in a cave: "Who are you and what am I?" The monster answers: "I am the one who pushes you, and you are the one who falls!" There is a delightful illustration of the piko-niko bird plummeting through space upside-down. He says to himself: "Now I'm going to die, and that's all I know."

Van Laan, Nancy. *La boda: A Mexican Wedding Celebration*. Illus. Andrea Arroyo. Boston: Little Brown, 1996. (picture book)
A bilingual cumulative story. Abuela answers Maria's questions about the wedding of Alfonso and Luisa celebrated in traditional Zapotec Indian style.

Vázquez-Vigo, Carmen. *Caramelos de menta* (Mint candies). Madrid: Ediciones SM, 1981. (chapter fiction ages 7–11)
Pepito and his friends have to raise money to repair the hole they've created in the awning of Don Joaquin's store.

———. *El muñeco de don Bepo* (Don Bepo's dummy). Illus. Arcadio Lobato. Madrid: Ediciones SM, 1984. (novel ages 8–14)
Don Bepo is a ventriliquist. When he retires he goes to the country and puts up his dummy as a scarecrow. A fairy helps the dummy, Ruperto, come alive.

———. *Por arte de magia* (Through the art of magic). Madrid: Ediciones SM, 1986. (novel ages 8–14)
Children discover a magician living in a supposedly abandoned house.

Velasquez, Gloria. *Juanita Fights the School Board*. Houston: Piñata (Arte Publico), 1994. (novel ages 8–14)
Juanita despairs of being able to graduate from high school after she is expelled for fighting with an Anglo girl. This book shows the challenge that Latino children face in trying to go between their two worlds, and also shows the school board being confronted with their racist attitudes.

Viesti, Joe, and Diane Hall. *Celebrate! In Central America*. Illus. Joe Viesti. New York: Lothrop, 1997. (nonfiction ages 7–11)
This useful and welcome book combines beautiful photography with descriptions of how various holidays are celebrated in particular Latin American countries. Holidays covered include the Day of the Dead and the Dance of the Conquistadors in Guatemala; Carnival and Holy Week in El Salvador; the San José Fair in Honduras; the Virgin of Masaya Celebration in Nicaragua; Columbus Day in Costa Rica; and Carnival in Panama.

Villaseñor, Victor. *Walking Stars: Stories of Magic and Power*. Houston: Piñata (Arte Público), 1994. (young adult)
Stories of triumph over difficulty about the author's parents. "Bull-fighting the Train" tells how his father Juan catches up with a train taking his family away by running 100 miles in one day. "Woman's Greatest Power" is the story of Villaseñor's mother and how she helps deliver twins in a primitive settlement.

Volkmer, Jane Anne (retold and illustrated by). *Song of the Chirimia: A Guatemalan Folktale*. Minneapolis: Carolhoda, 1990.
The *chirimia* is an instrument that produces a sound more pure than that of the birds. This folktale relates the origins of this instrument.

Walsh, Maria Elena. *El reino del reves* (The backwards kingdom). Illus. Vilar. Buenos Aires, Argentina: Editorial Sudamericana, 1986. (poetry ages 7–11)
Delightful poems with illustrations reminiscent of Ellen Raskin.

———. *Tutu maramba* (Nonsense rhymes). Illus. Vilar. Buenos Aires, Argentina: Editorial Sudamericana, 1976. (poetry ages 7–11)
Another volume of poetry sure to make children laugh. Walsh's poetry can be used in choral readings to develop oral language skills.

Wheeler, Howard T. *Tales from Jalisco, Mexico*. Philadelphia: American Folk-Lore Society, 1943. (short story collection ages 8–14)
Contains "*El aro de hinojo y el cuero de piojo*," the basis for the story "The Riddle of the Drum," which has been retold by Verna Aardema. A king makes a drum from the skin of an enormous flea. Whoever guesses what the drum is made of will marry the princess, and those who fail will be killed.

Wing, Natasha. *Jalapeño Bagels*. Illus. Robert Casilla. New York: Atheneum, 1996. (picture book)
Pablo can't decide what food to take to school for International Day. His Mexican mother prepares traditional dishes such as *pan*

dulce, but his Jewish father makes bagels. The title reveals what he takes. Multiculturalism at its best.

Winter, Jonah. *Diego*. Illus. by Jeanette Winter. Trans. Amy Prince. New York: Knopf, 1991. (picture book)
A bilingual picture book that discusses the childhood of Diego Rivera and how it influenced his art.

————. *Josefina*. San Diego, Calif.: Harcourt, 1996. (picture book)
Inspired by the Mexican folk artist Josefina Aguilar. It is a kind of counting book, as Josefina makes clay figures in the family tradition. Use in a storytime with *Diego*.

Wojciechowska, Maia. *Shadow of a Bull*. New York: Atheneum, 1964. (novel ages 8–14)
Manolo Olivar is faced with the decision whether to follow in the footsteps of his famous bullfighter father, or to turn his back on that life and be what he really wants to be—a doctor.

Wolf, Bernard. *Beneath the Stone: A Mexican Zapotec Tale*. New York: Orchard, 1994. (nonfiction ages 7–11)
Leo is a Zapotec boy. He and his family weave rugs and wall hangings that are sold throughout Mexico. Illustrated with color photographs, this book tells the story of Leo and his family throughout the year. In doing so it conveys information about the important holidays and culture. It includes a map and a note about the Zapotecs.

Yurchenko, Henrietta. *A Fiesta of Folk Songs from Spain and Latin America*. Illus. Jules Maidoff. New York: Putnam, 1967. (music)
Includes songs in four categories: animals and nature, singing games and dances, songs about people, and Christmas songs. English translations of the lyrics are included. This book is the source for my favorite version of "*Diez perritos*." Includes background information about each of the songs.

Zamorano, Ana. *Let's Eat!* Illus. Julie Vivas. New York: Scholastic, 1996. (picture book)
Antonio's mother is unsuccessful in getting the whole family to sit down and eat at the table together until there is a new arrival in the family.

Zatón, Jesús. *Mi Papá y yo somos piratas* (My father and I are pirates). Illus. Teo Puebla. Madrid: Jucar Infantil (Colección Manzana Mágica), 1987. (picture book)

Premio Nacional de Illustración Infantil. A boy and his father pretend they are pirates until Mom comes to put him to bed. In their game she becomes the *capitana enemiga.* The illustrations on one side of the page show them playing, and those on the other side show what they are imagining themselves to be.

————. *Una excursión al pais de las hadas* (An excursion into the fairy country). Illus. Teo Puebla. Gijon: Ediciones Júcar, 1986. (picture book)
A little girl and her grandmother go through a wardrobe into a fairy country. They battle with ogres and escape a witch. Later they end up as tour guides through this world.

GENERAL INDEX

NAMES INDEX

PROGRAMMING INDEX

ABOUT THE AUTHOR

Tim Wadham has worked for the Dallas Public Library for the past 13 years, working in several different locations with large Latino populations. He has designed and implemented numerous Spanish-language and bilingual programs to serve the Latino community, including storytimes, after-school programs, and special programs for individual groups. He received an $84,000 Library Services and Construction Act Title I grant to provide computer-aided literacy instruction to boost the reading skills of Latino children. Tim was the Dallas Public Library's representative to the International Book Fair in Guadalajara, Mexico, and helped select Spanish-language materials for the library system. He has been active with the Dallas Concilio of Hispanic Service Organizations. Tim is also active in the American Library Association and served on the 1998 Newbery Medal Selection Committee. He lives in a suburb of Dallas with his wife and daughter.